A SHORT COURSE IN READING FRENCH

COLUMBIA UNIVERSITY PRESS *NEW YORK*

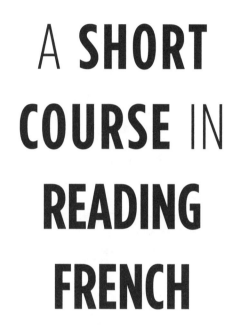

A **SHORT COURSE** IN **READING** **FRENCH**

Celia Brickman

Columbia University Press
Publishers Since 1893
New York   Chichester, West Sussex
cup.columbia.edu
Copyright © 2013 Celia Brickman

Library of Congress Cataloging-in-Publication Data
Brickman, Celia.
 A short course in reading French / Celia Brickman.
      p.   cm.
 Includes bibliographical references and index.
 ISBN 978-0-231-15676-9 (cl : alk. paper) -- ISBN 978-0-231-15677-6 (ppr :
alk. paper) -- ISBN 978-0-231-52745-3 (ebook)
 1. French language--Readers.   2. French language--Textbooks for for-
eign speakers--English. I. Title.

 PC2117.B847 2012
 448.2′421--dc23

                                                          2012029194

Columbia University Press books are printed on permanent and durable
acid-free paper.
This book is printed on paper with recycled content.
Printed in the United States of America

c 10 9 8 7 6 5 4 3 2 1
p 10 9 8 7 6 5 4 3 2

Cover image: (*bottom*) Lynea/Shutterstock Images
Cover design: Lisa Hamm

For My Mother:

Helen Dorothy Friedman Brickman

September 1916–December 2011

CONTENTS

ACKNOWLEDGMENTS

FIRST AND FOREMOST, my thanks go to my many students over the years whose persistent questions have led me to refine my knowledge of French and develop clearer ways of explaining its grammar. I am grateful to an early anonymous reviewer who pointed to the need for sufficient translation practice: this prompted me to envisage an enlarged notion of what could be included for translation, thereby greatly improving the scope of the book. Others, in particular Jean-Michel Robert, were gracious in alerting me to omissions and errors; and several other anonymous readers made useful suggestions for which I am grateful, even if I was not able to incorporate every last one of them into the book. Thanks to Jeannette Darcy for compiling the first draft of the table of contents and to Gregory Freeman for the first round of copy-editing, as well as to Yves Alavo and Sam Shapiro for reading early drafts of the book. Thanks to my editors at Columbia University Press: to Jennifer Crewe and Peggy Garry for their assistance and perseverance, and to Ron Harris for his skillful and meticulous editing. Thanks also to David Tual of Durham University for his unflagging support over the time it took for this book to see the light of day. I am greatly indebted to Alain Epo (Paris), who reviewed all the exercises in the book for spelling, grammar, and syntax; and to Mathieu Jackson (Montreal), who also reviewed the entire text several times and whose etymological insights and overall enthusiasm for grammar were an inspiration and a delight. Both saved me from many errors that would otherwise have remained, as did my students who tirelessly discovered ever more typos as we tried out preliminary versions of the manuscript in my classes. Because of the expert and attentive work of these many readers, it is all the more important for me to offer the customary caveat that any errors that remain here are my own.

INTRODUCTION

THIS BOOK IS a guide to learning French for reading and research and is intended for English speakers who want to learn to translate written French into English. It is a brief but accelerated exposition of the range of basic French grammar, which emerged from a course designed for graduate students learning French for academic research. As such, although it can be used on its own by anyone wanting a clear guide to French grammar, its primary purpose is as a textbook for classroom use. Therefore it assumes the use of a dictionary as well as the assistance of a teacher or tutor.

Unlike many French textbooks, this one will not help you to speak French. If you want to learn to speak French and/or to visit a French-speaking country or area (not only France, but Quebec, the Caribbean, and many parts of Africa and Asia), you should take a separate course in French conversation in addition to completing this one. However, this book will provide a solid introduction to French grammar that can serve as a foundation for reading and speaking French.

The main difficulty in learning any language is in retaining what has been learned. Practice and memorization are key to language retention. Therefore, each element of grammar presented here is followed by an exercise that provides the opportunity to learn and retain it by practicing. Vocabulary lists are not presented; but when it is suggested that something be memorized (e.g., all tense endings), this means that the memorization is essential to build the basic grammatical framework you'll need at all times while translating. Rereading each chapter a few times will also help you retain what you have learned; and doing some French work each day is much more effective for retention than working long hours every once in a while. In addition, after the first few chapters, short translation passages of increasing difficulty have been included so that various elements of grammar can be practiced and the reader can become acquainted with the complexities that reading French presents.

The final chapter consists of extra translation passages. These can be used for more practice throughout the course or at its end. I have not provided an answer key for the exercises and translation passages, because a ready set of "answers" creates an overwhelming temptation to skip the work of figuring out a translation on your own using the explanations of grammar presented in the book. The work of figuring it out on your own will allow you to learn and retain (rather than simply to understand and then forget) the grammar presented here. In classroom use, students' difficulties and errors in assigned translation exercises and passages, which would not show up if an answer key were provided, provide indispensable opportunities for clarifying various grammatical issues and for discussing translation strategies, as well as for assessing where more attention and practice may be needed.

The translation passages have other purposes as well. Although I hope this book will prove useful to a variety of people who want to learn French, its primary audience—graduate students and academics in the social sciences and humanities—will simultaneously be studying the scholarship written in French that is pertinent to their own fields. Therefore, the translation passages have been selected from a variety of prominent French theoretical, historical, and literary sources, classical and contemporary, in order to encourage students to develop the confidence that they too can translate such works. In addition, translation passages from distinguished francophone authors from around the world are included, so that this book may serve as an introduction to French as the global language it actually is rather than solely the national language of France, as has so often been presumed. I have included short notes of introduction for authors who may not be well known to the majority of anglophone students, but, for the sake of brevity, have not provided notes for authors familiar to most readers.

This book is based on a course I've been teaching over many years, during most of which time I used Edward Stack's *Reading French in the Arts and Sciences* (Houghton Mifflin, 1987, 4th edition) as the main textbook. A few years ago, Stack's book went out of print, which provided me with the incentive to write this one. Because I used his book for the first part of my course for many years, its influence can be seen throughout the book I have written. Thus I owe a great debt of gratitude to Mr. Stack for some of the ways in which the grammar is presented here, and for the patterns of some of my exercises.

Some study tips:

1. Take your time. One of the most common obstacles in this course is the urge to get through the exercises as quickly as possible. The importance of doing even the simplest exercise slowly and deliberately cannot be stressed enough. Write out all translation

exercises according to instructions, even if some phrases or sentences seem easy enough to gloss over: writing them will help you retain what you've learned.

Each exercise refers directly to the section or sections that precede it. Do each exercise with constant reference to these preceding sections, determining the exact grammatical issue at play in each sentence by tracking down its explanation in order to translate the phrase or sentence correctly, and looking up each unknown word in the dictionary (even if it looks like an English cognate, it may not be one). Taking your time to get each detail right will pay off as time goes on: by the latter part of the course you will have mastered many small details simply by having translated them correctly earlier in the course.

2. Verb conjugations together with all their appropriate translations should be written out as assignments for every class as an aid to memorization of tenses, and as a way to become introduced to the wide range of irregularities in French verbs. By the end of chapter 2, *avoir, être, aller, faire,* and *finir,* along with a sprinkling of regular *-er* verbs should be written out in the present tense (even if these are assigned over two or more classes). As new tenses are learned, the first four of the previously mentioned verbs should be conjugated in the new tense, and three or four new verbs should be written out in the new tense as well as in all the tenses learned up to that point. All verbs mentioned in chapters 2 and 10 should be conjugated in written form over the course of using this book, as should at least one verb from each family in chapter 24.

3. Memorization is best accomplished by reciting out loud repeatedly over several days. The more senses that are activated (visual, aural, kinesthetic) while you learn, the more solid your learning will be. Be sure to memorize all verb tense endings; *avoir* and *être* in every tense, as the tenses are learned; and all other grammatical issues wherever memorization is suggested.

4. Never guess. When you come across what seems to be a cognate, you have no way of really knowing whether it is a cognate or a false friend (see section B in this introduction). Guessing will probably accustom you to the wrong meaning. Looking words up in the dictionary, however tedious it may seem at times, will help you retain their meaning. Similarly, if the gender of a noun is not clear from its related adjectives, look it up in the dictionary.

5. As mentioned earlier, some French work daily is much more effective than a lot of work every once in a while. Try and spread out each homework assignment as evenly as possible over the days in which you have to do it.

6. Many students will eventually face the requirement of an exam with a strict time limit. This means that both speed and accuracy in translating must be developed. What might seem like the obvious solution—pushing yourself to translate faster—does not work: the inevitable result is a loss in accuracy. The following approach has proven to be the most useful and dependable: once most of the grammar in the book has been covered (which should occur at or before approximately one month prior to the exam), about half a page of French should be translated each day for one week. This should be done as slowly as necessary to look up in the dictionary every word that is unclear; to figure out the meaning of the sentence; and finally, to work out a way of expressing it that makes sense in English. The second week, an entire page should be translated daily, in the same manner, making sure to take your time and not to worry about how long it may take. The third week, two entire pages should be translated daily in the same fashion (no rushing, looking everything up in the dictionary, and so on). By following this method, your translation time will speed up *of its own accord* and without any loss of accuracy in translation, by sheer dint of practice. Only during the final week before the exam should you begin to work with a clock, trying to fit your translating time into the time that will be allotted for the exam, and assessing when it is time to give up on a particularly difficult sentence in order to move on to the next. If, by the very last week, your time is still far from where it should be, double the amount of translating that you do each day (i.e., four pages a day instead of two); after several days, the desired results will have been achieved.

A. GUIDE TO PRONUNCIATION

Although this book gives no guidelines to conversation, it is a good idea to get a rough sense of how French is pronounced. North American scholars abroad have a reputation for acting as though they know a language when they can barely express themselves in it, often with an accent that is significantly off-base. This course, sadly enough, contributes to this very problem by treating only written French and neglecting spoken French entirely. As a small but inadequate contribution to addressing this issue, a brief outline of basic French pronunciation follows. Students and teachers may choose to use, skim, or skip this section according to their needs. It is placed here instead of in a chapter of its own to indicate that it is a resource that can be referred to as needed, rather than a critical element of grammar that must be mastered for written translation proficiency.

Although both French and English share the same alphabet and even share many of the same words, students of the French language should be aware that letters, letter combinations, and even words that look the same in both languages can be pronounced entirely differently in French than they are in English. Pronunciation of

French is presented here using the phonetic signs of the International Phonetic Alphabet (IPA). The IPA consonants are fairly close to what we would expect in English, with the exception of

ʒ	as in *joue* (cheek), *aubergine* (eggplant)	in English, sounds like the *s* in mea**s**ure
ɲ	as in *agneaux* (sheep)	in English, sounds like the *ny* in ca**ny**on

The IPA vowel signs for French vowels are as follows:

a	as in p*a*tte (paw),	in English, sounds like the *a* in p**a**t
ɑ	as in p*â*te, (paste, pasta)	in English, sounds like the *a* straw
e	as in cl*é* (key);	in English, sounds like the *a* in cl**ay**
ɛ	as in f*ai*te, (done);	in English, sounds like the *e* in f**e**stival
ə	as in *je* (I)	in English, sounds like the *e* in Stud**e**baker
i	as in s*i* (if)	in English, sounds like the *ee* in s**ee**
œ	as in s*œu*r (sister)	in English, sounds like *i* in b**i**rd
ø	c*eu*x (those)	in English, sounds like the *oo* in g**oo**d
o	s*o*t (foolish)	in English, sounds like the *o* in h**o**le
ɔ	s*o*rt (fate)	in English, sounds like the *o* in s**o**rt
u	s*ou*s (under)	in English, sounds like the *oo* in z**oo**
y	t*u* (you)	in English, combines the *y* and *u* sound, sounds similar to the *u* in c**u**te

A tilde (~) above any of these vowel signs indicates that the vowel is nasalized.[1]

A.1. Whereas in English, one syllable—usually the first syllable—of any two- or multisyllable word is stressed, in French, syllables are generally stressed more or less equally.

English: probably   pro' bab ly   French: *probablement*   *pro bab le ment'*

A.2. Unlike in English, most final consonants in French are usually not pronounced. Thus, the final consonant is silent in such words as:

depuis	də pwi	(since)
maintenant	mɛ̃t nã	(now)
profond	pro fɔ̃	(deep)

---

1. For more information about the use of this alphabet for French pronunciation, used in French-English dictionaries, see http://en.wikipedia.org/wiki/Wikipedia:IPA_for_French#cite_note-3 , from which these signs have been taken.

début	de by	(beginning)
nous	nu	(we)
vous	vu	(you)
ils	il	(they)
étudiant	ety dyã	(student)

However, when a word that ends with a silent consonant is followed by a word beginning with a vowel, the vowel beginning the new word retroactively causes the final
consonant of the first word to be sounded:

ils	il	(they)
ils ont	ilz‿ɔ̃	(they have)

Here the final, silent *s* in *ils* is awakened by the vowel *o* that follows it, and therefore
is sounded, connecting the two words together. This is called a *liaison*.

A.3. Some words end in syllables with specific pronunciations very different from
those in English. The final syllables *-er*, and *-ez* are all pronounced like a shorter,
sharper version of the "long a" in English, as in "say," represented by IPA as *e*:

parler	par le	(to speak)
Allez!	a le	(Go!)

whereas the final syllable *-et* is pronounced like the softer "short e" in English, as in
"bed," represented by IPA as ɛ:

billet	bi jɛ	(ticket)
valet	va lɛ	(valet)

A.4. The letter *e* without an accent in the middle of a word is sometimes pronounced
like the vowel sound of the word *good*, represented by the IPA as ə:

renaissance	genou	tenir	demi
(rebirth)	(knee)	(to hold)	(half)

and at other times like the soft *e* in English, as in the word *bed*, represented by the
IPA as ɛ:

br*e*f	commerce	gestion	appel	t*e*l
(in brief)	(commerce)	(management)	(call)	(such)

The letter *e* at the very end of a word is barely pronounced, if at all (just enough to make sure the preceding consonant is clearly enunciated):

table   centre   théâtre   livre   détente

A.5. The consonants *g* and *c* are pronounced "hard" or "soft" as in English: "hard" when followed by an *a, o,* or *u* as in *go, gum, gather,* and *cake, cook, cucumber,* and "soft" when followed by an *i* or an *e* as in *gender, gin,* and *centipede, cinder:*

il mange	gérant	gestion	gant	gâteau
il mãʒ	ʒeʀã	ʒɛstjõ	gã	gɑto
(he eats)	(manager)	(management)	(glove)	(cake)

cadeau	couleur	cuisine	ceinture	cinéma
kado	kulœʀ	kɥizin	sẽtyʀ	sinema
(gift)	(color)	(kitchen)	(belt)	(movies)

However, if a *g* is to be followed by an *i* or an *e* but is to be pronounced "hard" none-theless, the letter *u* is placed after the *g.* The *u* is not pronounced, as in the English word *tongue,* where it has the same function. If the letter *u* after a *g is* to be pro-nounced, a *tréma* (two dots) is placed above the *u,* as in the feminine adjective *aigüe* (see more about *trémas* in section A.9.5).

langue	meringue	amuse-gueule	aigüe	ambigüe
lãg	məʀẽg	amyzgœl	egy	ãbigy
(language)	(meringue)	(appetizer)	(sharp)	(ambiguous)

A.6. Although most final consonants are not pronounced, there are some exceptions: when the following letters end a word, they tend to be pronounced: *c, r, f,* or *l* (a mne-monic device to remember these letters is: *careful*)

parc	sur	chef	animal
(park)	(on)	(chef)	(animal)

A.7. An important class of exceptions to the rule that final consonants are not pro-nounced consists of words or syllables that end with a vowel followed by a final *n,* or a final -*nt,* -*nts,* -*nce,* and so on. The *n* following the vowel is not fully pronounced, but it causes the preceding vowel to be pronounced nasally; that is, through the nose. The nasalization of a vowel or vowel combination is represented in the IPA by the vowel sound capped by a tilde (~):

-an, -ans, -ant (IPA: ã) *-en, -ens, -ent* (IPA: ã) *-in, -ins, -int* (IPA: ɛ̃) *-on, -ons, -ont* (IPA: õ)

le Tali*ban*	*en*	prince	*on*
Jacques Lacan	évé*nement*	*intervenir*	nous a*vons*
comman*dant*	*tendance*	mince	le p*ont*
maint*enant*	*lendemain*	*intelligence*	ils s*ont*

The vowel combination of *ai* followed by a consonant is pronounced like the English short *e* as in *bed* (IPA: ɛ):

mais	frais	lait	fontaine	fait
(but)	(fresh)	(milk)	(fountain)	(fact)

When *ai* is followed by an *n*, it is pronounced nasally and sounds slightly more open than *–in* (IPA: ɛ̃):

pain	main	train	maintenant
(bread)	(hand)	(train)	(now)

A.8. Other vowel combinations:

ai	IPA: e	"long a" in English: sounds like: say	e.g., *j'ai* (I have)
au, eau	IPA: o	"long o" in English: sounds like: go	e.g., *eau de cologne*
aux, eaux	same as above, since the final consonant *x* is not pronounced		e.g., *faux* (false)
eu, eux	IPA: ø:	the vowel sound of "curling"	e.g., *jeu, jeux* (game/s)
eil	IPA: ej	"long a" in English: sounds like: say	e.g., *soleil* (sun)
ail	IPA: aj	sounds like "aye" in (old) English	e.g., *travail* (work)
-lle	IPA: j	"y" in English: sounds like: **y**es,	e.g., *fille* (girl)
-lle		but sometimes pronounced as a full "double *ll*" in English	e.g., *belle* (beautiful); *ville* (city)

A.9. Some vowels in French—mostly, but not exclusively, the vowel *e*—are accompanied by accents, also called diacritical marks.

A.9.1. *Accent aigu.* The addition of the *accent aigu* (acute accent) to the letter *e* to form *é* changes the sound of the letter to a sound slightly shorter and sharper than the long *a* in English as in *say*, represented by the IPA as *e*:

équipe	éliminer	écrire	séance
(team)	(to eliminate)	(to write)	(séance)

A.9.2. *Accent grave.* The addition of the *accent grave* to the letter *e* to form *è* changes the sound of the letter to the broad, soft sound of the short *e* in English as in *bed* or *spread*, represented by the IPA as ɛ:

mère	père	frère	élève	interprète
(mother)	(father)	(brother)	(student)	(interpreter)

The *accent grave* is also occasionally found on the letters *a* (as in *à*) and *u* (as in *où*), where it is used to indicate that words with these letters have different meanings, depending on whether they have the accent or not; but the accent does not change the pronunciation.

A.9.3. Circumflex/*circonflexe* The letter *e* and occasionally other vowels sometimes have a circumflex: *ê, î, û.* This accent keeps the *e* sounding like the English short *e* as in *bed.* The pronunciation of *â* (IPA: ɑ as in the French *théâtre*) is like the English *calm*, in comparison to an *a* without the circumflex (IPA: a as in the French *patte*), which rhymes with the English word *hat.* The pronunciation of *ô,* (IPA: o as in *le vôtre*) sounds like what we call in English a *long o* as in *whole;* whereas the *o* in the French *votre*, without the circumflex (IPA: ɔ), sounds like the *o* in the English *sort.* The circumflex does not alter the sound of the vowel *i.*

The circumflex is an etymological sign: it indicates that earlier on in the development of the language, an *s* used to be present in the word. Over the centuries the *s* has dropped out, leaving the circumflex as its trace. Some words in English have preserved the *s* that has dropped out in French:

hôpital	forêt	fête	île	hâte
(hospital)	(forest)	(festival, celebration)	(isle)	(haste)

A.9.4. *Cédille.* If a *c* is followed by an *a, o,* or *u* but is to be pronounced "soft" nonetheless, a *cédille,* or cedilla, is placed underneath the *c* to render it soft:

français	aperçu	garçon	ça	leçon
(French)	(insight)	(boy)	(that)	(lesson)

A.9.5. *Tréma.* When two vowels are placed together, the *tréma*—two dots placed above an *e, i,* or *u* and occasionally above a *y*—serves to indicate that they both are pronounced separately (rather than pronounced as a single, blended sound):

naïf / naïve	maïs	archaïque	astéroïde	païen
(naive)	(corn)	(archaic)	(asteroid)	(pagan)

A *tréma* is also placed over a *u* following a *g* when that *u* is to be pronounced (rather than serving solely to render the preceding *g* "hard" as in section A.5):

argüer	aigüe	ambigüe
(to argue)	(sharp)	(ambiguous)

A.10. When a word begins with *h*, the *h* is generally silent (not aspirated); the word is treated as though it begins with the following vowel:

homme	honnête	hirondelle	habitude	humeur	hâte
(man)	(honest)	(swallow)	(habit)	(mood)	(haste)

A.11. The consonant combination *ch* in French in pronounced like the *sh* in English:

chic	choquant	choix	chou-fleur	douche
(chic)	(shocking)	(choice)	(cauliflower)	(shower)

B. COGNATES

French and English share almost all the letters of the alphabet and a lot of vocabulary. This is because both English and French trace many of their roots back to Latin and some shared Germanic languages. In addition, over the centuries they have been influenced by the political interactions between the countries in which they each originated, France and England. (The reader may remember the Norman conquest of England in 1066, which replaced the English ruling class with a French-speaking monarchy and aristocracy.) Those words in both languages that come down to us from the same root tend to be the same, or similar, in both languages (except, of course, that they are pronounced differently). Thus the English speaker who knows no French at all is already familiar with some French vocabulary:

train	table	force	scène	ministre
théâtre	centre	restaurant	province	science
excellent	minéral	membre	article	alliance
résumé	impact	commerce	impossible	nation

Some words are not exactly the same in both languages, but they are still close enough for the French to be recognizable to speakers of English:

victoire	horreur	danse	musique
système	progrès	romantique	compromis

choquant	urbain	majeur	anonyme
gigantesque	significatif	coloniale	ambitieux

Most words ending in -ion are cognates and share the same meaning in both French and English:

satisfaction	condition	publication	introduction
révolution	production	solution	discussion
consultation	réalisation	modernisation	interprétation
région	administration	position	civilisation

Many words that end in *y* in English have cognates in French that end in *ie* or *é*:

priorité	sécurité	unanimité	société
beauté	identité	qualité	unité
sociologie	géographie	industrie	stratégie

Many words that end in *ic*, *ics*, or *ical* in English have cognates in French that end in *ique*:

politique	écologique	atlantique	électrique
dynamique	chronique	linguistique	disque
typique	magnifique	technique	fantastique

However, there are also many words that look exactly, or almost exactly, the same in both English and French, and yet are completely unrelated to each other. The French call these words *les faux amis*, meaning *false friends*. For example:

actuel	current
ancien	former
but	aim, goal
court	short
davantage	more
destitution	removal, dismissal (from office)
éditeur	publisher
essence	gasoline
journée	day
librairie	bookstore
lien	link, bond

médecin	doctor
physicien	physicist
sensibilité	sensitivity

False friends will trick you into thinking that you know what they mean. Therefore, regardless of how familiar a word may look, the novice translator always has to look it up in the dictionary. By doing so, one can be certain of having the right meaning and can begin to get a feeling for which words are truly cognates and which ones are not.

A SHORT COURSE IN READING FRENCH

NOUNS, ARTICLES, AND PREPOSITIONS, AND THE PRINCIPLE OF AGREEMENT

1.1. NOUNS, GENDER, AND THE PRINCIPLE OF AGREEMENT

All nouns in French are gendered. As in all Romance languages—that is, all languages derived from Latin—all nouns are either masculine or feminine. (In English our nouns have no grammatical gender.) The gender of nouns is a grammatical quality that in most instances has no relationship to the meaning of the word. Occasionally, some noun endings indicate the gender of the noun: Those that end in *-ion* or *-ie* are usually feminine, whereas those that end in *-ment*, *-eur*, and *-ien* tend to be masculine.

All words in French that modify nouns—all adjectives—agree in number and gender with the nouns that they modify. This is called the principle of agreement. (As we will see later on, in some tenses, certain verb forms agree with nouns as well.) This means that any adjective that modifies a masculine noun must be masculine in form, and any adjective that modifies a feminine noun must be feminine in form. If a noun is plural, the adjective must be plural in form, as well as masculine or feminine, according to the noun it modifies.

1.2. ARTICLES

1.2.1. DEFINITE ARTICLES

Articles, both definite and indefinite, are a subgroup of adjectives and therefore agree in number and gender with the nouns they modify. In English, we have only one definite article: *the*. In French, however, the definite article varies according to the grammatical gender of the noun (masculine or feminine) and according to its number (singular or plural):

masculine singular definite article: *le*

feminine singular definite article: *la*

alternative singular definite article: *l'*

masculine and/or feminine plural definite article: *les*

Definite articles always precede the noun they modify:

le livre	the book	*les livres*	the books
la pomme	the apple	*les pommes*	the apples
le garçon	the boy	*les garçons*	the boys
la fille	the girl	*les filles*	the girls

1.2.2. THE GLOTTAL STOP AND THE ALTERNATIVE SINGULAR DEFINITE ARTICLE

In speaking, we usually can hear where one word ends and the other begins by the enunciation of the consonant that ends the first word, or of the consonant that begins the second word. When one word ends with a vowel and the next word begins with a vowel, we are forced to indicate where one word ends and the other begins by closing the *glottis,* the space the between the vocal cords in the throat, ever so slightly (try to say "zoo owner" or "bee eater"). This action is called a *glottal stop.* The French language dislikes the glottal stop, and goes to great lengths to avoid it. Therefore, when a definite article—*le* or *la*—is followed by a noun that begins with a vowel, an alteration of the article has been devised in order to avoid the glottal stop that would otherwise occur. This altered, alternative definite article is the letter *l* followed by an apostrophe, which replaces the *le* or *la* when the following word begins with a vowel: Therefore,

RATHER THAN	THERE IS ONLY	
le arbre	*l'arbre*	the tree
la occasion	*l'occasion*	the occasion
le animal	*l'animal*	the animal
la expérience	*l'expérience*	the experiment; the experience

Since the *h* in French is silent (i.e., it is not aspirated) when it begins a word, a word beginning with *h* sounds as though, and is treated as though, it begins with its second letter, the vowel following the *h*. The abbreviated article *l'* will be used as the definite article for these words as well. Therefore,

RATHER THAN	THERE IS ONLY	
le homme	*l'homme*	the man
la histoire	*l'histoire*	the history; the story
le héritage	*l'héritage*	the heritage; the inheritance
la heure	*l'heure*	the time; the hour

However, as with almost all grammatical rules in French, there are exceptions. (In this case the exceptions are generally words with a Germanic, rather than a Latin, origin.)

le haricot	the bean

In French, nouns are almost always preceded by a definite or indefinite article, even when in English we might not use one. French uses the definite article both for the specific and the general case, whereas in English we tend to use the definite article for the specific case only. For example, in English, *the apples* refers to a particular set of apples. But when we speak in generalities in English, we don't use the definite article: we speak of *apples* in general.

In French, the definite article denotes both the general and the particular. *The apples* (a particular set of apples) would be expressed in French as *les pommes,* as in: *Les pommes dans le jardin sont mûres.* (The apples in the garden are ripe.) But the word for *apples* in general, without the definite article in English, still takes the definite article in French: *I like apples* is found in French as *J'aime les pommes.*

As another example: We speak of *science* in English, without any definite article; only when speaking or writing of a particular form of science (e.g., *the human sciences*) do we introduce the definite article. French would use the definite article in both cases: *la science* for *science, les sciences humaines* for *the human sciences.*

Because French at times uses the definite article where it would not be used in English, only the context of a given sentence and the translator's ear for the idiom of English will indicate whether it sounds better to keep the definite article or to drop it. However, it is a good rule of thumb to start out by translating the article first and seeing how it sounds in the sentence before deciding whether it should be translated or dropped. Since the following exercises in this chapter are intended to help you memorize the precise meaning of French articles (whether you end up using them or not), translate each and every article in each example given.

Translation Exercise A

Translate the following, being sure to translate the definite article as well as the noun. Then give the gender (masculine or feminine) and number (singular or plural) of the noun (e.g.: m. s., f. s., m. pl., f. pl.)

1.	la famille	16.	le restaurant
2.	le propriétaire	17.	la cuisine
3.	la majorité	18.	le climat
4.	les projets	19.	le sommet
5.	le technicien	20.	le président
6.	le cirque	21.	l'architecture
7.	la télévision	22.	l'immigration
8.	la scène	23.	la pollution
9.	le public	24.	l'accord
10.	la permission	25.	la visite
11.	le moment	26.	l'importance
12.	l'histoire	27.	le centre
13.	la condition	28.	la victoire
14.	la nation	29.	l'occasion
15.	le théâtre	30.	le village

1.2.3. INDEFINITE ARTICLES

Indefinite articles in English are *a, an* for the singular, and *some* for the plural. (Note how English too avoids the glottal stop through its use of the indefinite article *an*.) French indefinite articles, like French definite articles, are adjectives that are placed before the noun they modify. Like all adjectives, they must agree with the nouns they modify in gender and number:

masculine singular indefinite article:	*un*	a, an
feminine singular indefinite article:	*une*	a, an
masculine and/or feminine plural indefinite article:	*des*	some

Although *une,* the feminine singular indefinite article, ends with a vowel, this vowel is barely if at all pronounced; therefore, *une* may be followed, without any alteration, by a noun that begins with a vowel:

une armée	an army
une attraction	an attraction
une opération	an operation
une hypothèse	a hypothesis

Articles, both definite and indefinite, are one of the principal ways that the gender of nouns can be determined. As you will discover, determining the gender of all parts of speech is an important tool for parsing complex sentences.

As with definite articles, indefinite articles are sometimes translated into English and sometimes not, because in French, almost all nouns must be preceded by an article, whereas in English, we use articles only under certain specific conditions. Again, the context and your ear for the idiom of English will guide you as to whether to translate the indefinite article or to drop it. And again, it is a good idea to translate the article first and see how it sounds in the sentence before deciding whether to translate it. Continue to translate each definite or indefinite article in the rest of the exercises in this chapter.

1.3. GENDERED NOUNS

Most of the time the gender of the noun is a purely grammatical affair with no particular reference to the noun's intrinsic meaning. However, some nouns referring to people have always had both masculine and feminine forms (e.g., *voisin, voisine,* neighbor), whereas in other cases, certain social roles, occupations, and professions that have historically been considered masculine in French are now recognized as applying to women as well. In these cases, to varying degrees in different countries, French has begun to challenge the presumed gender neutrality of the masculine noun by providing a feminine form. Sometimes this is done simply by changing the gender of the article that modifies the noun:

un/une architecte	an architect
un/une astronaute	an astronaut
un/une collègue	a colleague
un/une commissaire	a commissioner
un/une dentiste	a dentist
un/une journaliste	a journalist
un/une juge	a judge

un/une maire	a mayor
un/une philosophe	a philosopher
un/une pianiste	a pianist
un/une témoin	a witness
un/une touriste	a tourist

In other cases, this is done by changing the ending of the noun from a typically masculine ending (e.g., *-eur, -en*) to a typically feminine ending (e.g., *-euse, -ice,-enne*); or by simply adding the feminine ending *-e* to the previously masculine noun. Thus while *le citoyen*, for example, had traditionally been presumed to refer to any citizen, the female form, *la citoyenne*, has recently come into use when referring to female citizens in particular, or to citizens in general (as in *les citoyens et les citoyennes* for *the citizens*). Similarly, one finds the inclusive *les élus et les élues* for *the elected officials*; and in some places one might come across *une docteure, une femme médecin*, or *une femme docteur* when the doctor in question is a woman.

MASCULINE NOUN	FEMININE NOUN	ENGLISH TRANSLATION
un acteur	*une actrice*	an actor/actress
un ami	*une amie*	a friend
un avocat	*une avocate*	a lawyer
un chanteur	*une chanteuse*	a singer
un citoyen	*une citoyenne*	a citizen
un écrivain	*une écrivaine*	a writer
un étudiant	*une étudiante*	a student
un Parisien	*une Parisienne*	a Parisian
un pharmacien	*une pharmacienne*	a pharmacist
un travailleur	*une travailleuse*	worker
un serveur	*une serveuse*	waiter/waitress
un voisin	*une voisine*	neighbor

Nonetheless, it is important to keep in mind that in most French usage, aside from words denoting occupations, professions, and social roles, the gender of a word has no inherent relationship to its meaning: *la personne* means *the person*, whether the person in question is masculine or feminine.

1.4. THE PLURAL OF NOUNS

1.4.1. THE GENERAL RULE

As in English, the most common way to form the plural of a noun in French is to add an *s* to the end of the noun:

la robe	the dress	*les robes*	the dresses
une attraction	an attraction	*des attractions*	some attractions
le livre	the book	*les livres*	the books
un débat	a debate	*des débats*	some debates

Notice that when the noun becomes plural, the definite article or indefinite article that precedes it must become plural as well.

1.4.2. EXCEPTIONS TO THE GENERAL RULE

There are exceptions to the rule of adding an *s* to make a noun plural (as there are occasionally in English: we say *one sheep, many sheep; one foot, two feet; one mouse, two mice; one knife, several knives*).

Some nouns—especially those that end in *-eu* or *-au*—form their plural by adding an *x* rather than an *s* at the end:

l'oiseau	the bird	*les oiseaux*	the birds
le feu	the fire	*les feux*	the fires
un jeu	a game	*des jeux*	some games

Nouns that already end in *s, x,* or *z* in the singular form do not add an extra *s* to form the plural; they remain the same in the plural as they are in the singular:

un cas	a case	*des cas*	some cases
un choix	a choice	*des choix*	some choices
le fils	the son	*les fils*	the sons
le nez	the nose	*les nez*	the noses

In these cases, the only way that we can know whether the noun is singular or plural is by looking at the definite or indefinite article (or other adjective) that accompanies it. If the article, definite or indefinite, is encountered in the plural form, the noun it accompanies is a plural noun.

Nouns that end in -*al* or -*ail* tend to be masculine nouns that change the -*al* or -*ail* to -*aux* when they become plural:

l'animal	the animal	*les animaux*	the animals
un journal	a newspaper	*des journaux*	some newspapers
le minéral	the mineral	*les minéraux*	the minerals
l'hôpital	the hospital	*les hôpitaux*	the hospitals
le travail	the work	*les travaux*	the works (e.g., the public works)

Because all nouns are listed in dictionaries in their singular form, when you encounter one of these nouns in the plural (ending in -*aux*) you'll be expected to be able to trace it back to its singular form ending in –*al* or –*ail* in order to locate its meaning in the dictionary.

The exceptional exception:

l'œil	the eye	*les yeux*	the eyes

Translation Exercise B

Translate the following, making sure to translate the indefinite or definite article as well as the noun. Then give the gender (masculine or feminine) and the number (singular or plural) of the noun. For this exercise only, false friends—words that look like, but are not, English cognates—are accompanied by footnotes giving the correct translation.

1.   un animal
2.   des animaux
3.   le choix
4.   une solution
5.   un débat
6.   la crise
7.   un membre
8.   des trains
9.   les consultations
10.   des actions
11.   l'interprétation
12.   le fils
13.   la sociologie
14.   les discussions
15.   une ville
16.   une armée
17.   l'armée
18.   des armées
19.   les armées
20.   une heure
21.   la danse
22.   une librairie[1]

---

1.   *librairie:* bookstore

23. des médecins[2]   27. des journaux[5]

24. des cas   28. une forêt

25. des frontières[3]   29. la table

26. un journal[4]   30. des hôpitaux

1.5. PREPOSITIONS

The following is a (not exhaustive) list of common prepositions that you will encounter when reading French. This is a good list to become familiar with, or even to memorize.

à	to, at	*en*	in
à côté de	beside	*entre*	between, among
après	after	*en face de*	in front of, across from
avant	before	*face à*	facing, in front of, faced with
avec	with	*par*	by
chez	at the home/place of	*parmi*	among
contre	against	*pour*	for, to, in order to
dans	in (contained within)	*sans*	without
de (d')	of, from	*sous*	under
derrière	behind	*sur*	on
devant	in front of, before	*vers*	towards

Exercise C

Translate the following preposition/noun phrases with reference to the preceding chart of prepositions. Translate each article, definite or indefinite, and give the gender and number of each noun:

1. dans l'environnement
2. contre les décisions
3. à l'auteur[6]
4. sans patience[7]
5. à côté de la montagne

6. pour l'indépendance
7. face à la coalition
8. sous les arbres[8]
9. avec la permission
10. en France

---

2. *médecins:* doctors
3. *frontières:* borders
4. *journal:* newspaper
5. *journaux:* newpapers
6. *auteur:* author
7. The preposition *sans* (without) is always used without any article accompanying the noun it governs.
8. *arbres:* trees

11. avant la saison

12. sur la table

13. en face de l'ambassade[9]

14. derrière les édifices[10]

15. le président de l'association

16. sur la route

17. sous la chaise

18. après l'introduction

19. par l'administration

20. devant les combattants

21. vers le magasin[11]

22. contre le gouvernement

23. chez elle

24. à la question

25. en cas d'urgence

26. sous le titre

27. avant la révolution

28. à la condition

29. en vue de

30. le centre de la ville

1.6. CONTRACTION OF PREPOSITIONS WITH DEFINITE ARTICLES

When the prepositions *à* and *de* are followed by the masculine or the plural definite article (*le* or *les*), they combine with these definite articles to form the following contractions:

à + *le* =	*au*	to the, at the
à + *les* =	*aux*	to the, at the
de + *le* =	*du*	of the, from the
de + *les* =	*des*	of the, from the

These contractions include the meaning of both the preposition and the definite article, so always remember to translate the definite article when translating a contraction.

When the preposition *à* or *de* is followed by the feminine singular article *la,* there is no contraction, as in:

à la mode   *Walter de la Mare*

1.7. THE PARTITIVE AND NEGATIVE USES OF *DE*

Although the general meaning of the preposition *de* is *of* or *from, de* can also be used in a partitive sense to mean *part of*, or *some of*, something. Sometimes the partitive is

---

9. *ambassade:* embassy

10. *édifices:* buildings

11. *magasin:* store

translated as such into English, and sometimes it is implied but not translated, according to English usage. Therefore *du* or *de la* can also be translated simply as *some,* or not translated at all. Remember, when followed by the masculine definite article *le*, the *de* will contract with the *le* to form *du*. For example:

Je veux du *café.*	I want some coffee.
Il boit du *lait.*	He drinks some milk.
Elle mange du *pain.*	She eats some bread.
Il a du *courage.*	He has courage.
Elle prend de la *crème dans son thé.*	She takes cream in her tea.
Elle écrit de la *prose.*	She writes prose.

In negative sentences, *de* is used to mean (not) *any*:

Il n'a pas de *sœurs.*	He doesn't have any sisters.
Je n'ai pas d'*argent.*	I don't have any money.
Elle ne veut pas de *sucre.*	She doesn't want any sugar.

1.8. THE MULTIPLE MEANINGS OF *DES*

The contraction of *de* + *les* to make *des* poses a translation problem: When is *des* translated as *of the* or *from the,* and when is it translated as the indefinite plural article, *some*? Similarly, how can we know when *du* is to be translated as *of the,* or *from the,* or the partitive *some*? And when is *au* translated as *to the* or *at the*? As you will see in the following examples, the context of the sentence generally obliges you to make the right choice, because only one of the possible meanings will make sense in any particular context.

Translation Exercise D

Give the full meaning of the sentence, including the precise translation of prepositions and contractions as well as the number and gender of the words in parentheses.

1. He saw [*des animaux*] at the zoo.
2. We will go [*au théâtre*] this evening.
3. She saw him [*au restaurant*].
4. They don't have [*d'enfants*].
5. He lives [*au Canada*].

6. I want to eat [*du gâteau*] for dessert.

7. The union [*des employés*] went on strike.

8. They signed [*des contrats*] that were favorable to them.

9. We picked the flowers [*des jardins*] behind the buildings.

10. She returned [*du cimetière*] in tears.

11. The tale [*du soldat*] was put to music by Stravinsky.

12. He drinks [*du café*] every morning.

13. The two countries had [*des désaccords*] over the years, but remained friendly.

14. The diplomatic actions [*du nouveau président*] have taken place on several levels.

15. Erosion is affecting more than a quarter [*du littoral français*].

16. The zoo, situated to the west [*de la ville*], is very popular with small children.

17. On Tuesday, 2.6 million voters went [*aux urnes*] to elect a new mayor.

18. The former minister [*des affaires étrangères*] stated that he supported the new recommendations.

19. The return [*des oiseaux*] marks the beginning of spring.

20. He removed the software [*des ordinateurs*].

21. She played the beautiful Symphonie Espagnole [*du Français Édouard Lalo*].

22. A group of lawyers were at the head [*du mouvement*] to investigate the conduct of the army.

23. The president was under pressure [*des États-Unis*] to reinforce his country's borders.

24. The government draws its strength [*de la participation et du consentement du peuple et du respect du règne de la loi*].

VERBS, SUBJECT PRONOUNS, AND THE PRESENT TENSE/*PRÉSENT DE L'INDICATIF*

2.1. INFINITIVES AND VERB FAMILIES

The infinitive in English is indicated by the word *to* before the main verb form (e.g., *to write, to walk, to sing*). French has no separate word corresponding to the English *to*; the infinitive in French is denoted by the verb form's final two letters, known as the *infinitive ending.* There are three major infinitive endings in French: *-er, -re,* and *–ir*; and a subset of the latter that end in *-oir.* Although French verbs, like those in any other language, are more various than any categorization can fully account for, a useful arrangement begins by dividing all verbs into three major families according to the infinitive endings they display: the family of *-er* verbs, the family of *-re* verbs, and the family of *-ir* verbs. The *-oir* subset of *-ir* verbs encompasses so many variations that it will be presented separately later on, in chapters 10 and 24.

2.2. SUBJECT PRONOUNS

To learn how a verb is used in French, we learn how it is conjugated—that is, how its form changes according to what tense is being used (e.g., present, future, past) and according to who or what the subject is. Subjects, grammatically speaking, are the people or things that perform the action of the verb, represented by subject nouns or pronouns. In French, the subject may occur in any one of six *persons*, or grammatical positions. There is a different *subject pronoun* for each of the six persons:

PERSON	CORRESPONDING SUBJECT PRONOUN	ENGLISH TRANSLATION
1st person singular	*je*	I
2nd person singular	*tu*	you (for intimate or friendly use, or for use with a child)
3rd person singular	*il*	he / it
	elle	she / it
	on	one (often used in place of *we* or *they*)
1st person plural	*nous*	we
2nd person plural	*vous*	you (grammatically plural; may be used to mean either *you* in the plural or *you* in the singular, to denote respect)
3rd person plural	*ils*	they (masculine)
	elles	they (feminine)

In French, the subject or subject pronoun is not implied by the verb form alone, as it is in some other languages. A separate subject or subject pronoun is always required, unless the verb is being used in the imperative form (see chapter 13). Therefore, when conjugating verbs in any tense in French, the subject pronoun has to be included.

Note that because all nouns in French are gendered, there is no nongendered word for the English word *it. It* always refers to a noun that is either masculine or feminine in French, so the third-person singular subject pronouns *il* and *elle* may refer either to *he* or *she,* or to a masculine or feminine *it.*

The French third person singular subject pronoun *on* is not at all related to the English *it. On* is cognate with the English *one,* as in, "One cannot enter the building in the evening." This usage in English is rather pedantic and not often used. *On,* however, is used ubiquitously in French to refer to the unspecified general case: *On* is used not only where we in English might say *one,* but more often where we would say *they* (when the speaker is not part of the group referred to) or where we would use *we* (when the speaker is part of the group referred to). Additionally, sentences in French using the subject *on* are often translated into the passive voice in English. In tense conjugations throughout this book *on* will be translated as *one* for the sake of brevity; but the various alternative translations of *on* should always be kept in mind, as they are actually the more common translations. These alternative possibilities are given in more detail in chapter 14, section 14.3.

On is sometimes represented as *l'on* when it is preceded by a vowel. This *l'* has no meaning or grammatical function, and serves only to separate the sound of a preceding vowel from the sound of *on.*

2.3. THE PRESENT TENSE/*PRÉSENT DE L'INDICATIF* OF *-ER* VERBS

The form of any verb in the present tense varies according to which grammatical *person* (e.g., first person singular, second person plural) the subject is found in. Within each family of verbs, each grammatical person has its own, specific present tense ending. These endings differ, however, from one verb family to another. The *-er* verbs are considered to be the regular verbs, because almost all *-er* verbs follow the exact same pattern:

To conjugate an *-ER* verb in the present tense, the infinitive ending (*-er*) is removed. What is left is the *stem* of the verb. To this stem are added the following tense endings, each of which corresponds to a specific person or subject position:

PERSON	SUBJECT PRONOUN	PRESENT TENSE ENDING
1st person singular	*je*	*- e*
2nd person singular	*tu*	*- es*
3rd person singular	*il/elle/on*	*- e*
1st person plural	*nous*	*- ons*
2nd person plural	*vous*	*- ez*
3rd person plural	*ils/elles*	*- ent*

Memorize these endings now. They are part of what you will need to keep at your fingertips as you move forward in your ability to translate French.

For example: To conjugate the verb *donner* (to give) in the present tense, the *-er* is removed, leaving the stem, *donn-*. This stem is placed right after the subject pronoun (subject pronouns are always listed in the order shown here), and the present tense endings are added to the stem, according to the subject to which they correspond:

1st person singular	je donn*e*
2nd person singular	tu donn*es*
3rd person singular	il/elle/on donn*e*
1st person plural	nous donn*ons*
2nd person plural	vous donn*ez*
3rd person plural	ils/elles donn*ent**

---

*The *-ent* ending of the third person plural in the present tense is always silent.

Keep in mind that any verb is found in the dictionary only in its infinitive form. You will need to be able to recognize all tense endings at sight in order to know what tense the verb is in, and from there, to be able to figure out what infinitive form to look up in the dictionary. For example: If you come across *parlent* in the text you are reading, you will need to recognize that the ending *–ent* is the third person plural of the present tense. Once you take off this ending, you'll be left with the stem, *parl—*. You'll then add back to the stem the infinitive ending *-er* to arrive at the infinitive form of the word, *parler*, which is the word you will finally look up in the dictionary.

2.4. TRANSLATION OF THE PRESENT TENSE/*PRÉSENT DE L'INDICATIF*

In English, we have two forms of the present tense: the simple present (a simple tense is made up of only one word)—as in *I write, I read, I walk*—and the continuous, or progressive, present, as in *I am writing, I am reading, I am walking*. (We also have the form *I do give*, which is used only occasionally for emphasis; this form provides the basis for the negative form of the present tense: *I do not give*, which contracts to *I don't give*.) French has only one form of the present tense, the simple present, so it has to do double duty: It is translated into English *either* as the simple present *or* as the continuous present, according to the context and to the translator's ear for the idiom of English. When translating French verbs, both possibilities must be considered, and when conjugating and translating French verbs for practice, both possible translations must be given. The simple present is the more common translation, so it is given first:

je donne	I give, I am giving
tu donnes	you give, you are giving
il/elle/on donne	he/she/it/one gives, is giving
nous donnons	we give, we are giving
vous donnez	you give, you are giving
ils/elles donnent	they give, they are giving

2.5. THE NEGATIVE FORM OF THE PRESENT TENSE

The most common negative form of the present tense, and of all other tenses, requires two words: *ne*, placed directly before the verb, and *pas*, placed right after the verb. Like the affirmative form of the present tense, there are generally two possible translations for any verb in the negative form of the present tense: the simple present negative and the continuous, or progressive, present negative:

je ne donne pas	I do not give, I am not giving
tu ne donnes pas	you do not give, you are not giving
il/elle/on ne donne pas	he/she/one does not give, he is not giving
nous ne donnons pas	we do not give, we are not giving
vous ne donnez pas	you do not give, you are not giving
ils/elles ne donnent pas	they do not give, they are not giving

2.6. TWO IMPORTANT IRREGULAR VERBS: *AVOIR*, TO HAVE, AND *ÊTRE*, TO BE

Avoir and *être* are two of the most important commonly used verbs in the French language, and they are essential components of the many compound tenses that exist in French that will be taught later on in this book. Both verbs have idiosyncratic conjugations in the present tense. In addition, the translations into English of *avoir* and of *être* are irregular: Whereas most French verbs in the present tense have two possible translations in English, *avoir* and *être* always have only one possible translation: the simple present. These two verbs and their translations in the present tense must be learned and memorized at the very outset. They are key elements of French grammar.

With the conjugation of *avoir* in the present tense, the problem of the glottal stop arises again. The first person singular of *avoir* would seem to be *je ai*. But this would give us a word ending in a vowel (*je*), followed by a word beginning with a vowel (*ai*)—a glottal-stop situation to be avoided! Therefore, the *e* of *je* is removed and is replaced with an apostrophe, so that *je ai* becomes the much smoother-sounding *j'ai*. In the negative form, the *je* is followed by *ne*, so there is no need to alter the *je*. However, now it is the *e* of the *ne* that is followed by a vowel: *je ne ai pas*. So here the *e* of the *ne* is removed and replaced by an apostrophe: *je n'ai pas*. Notice, however, that *tu* does not pose this problem, and its *u* remains as is, even though it is followed by another vowel. *U* is a "hard" vowel, whereas in general, it is only "soft" vowels—*e* and *i*—that pose the problem of the glottal stop and that are replaced by apostrophes when followed by another vowel.

AVOIR, TO HAVE

j'ai	I have	*je n'ai pas*	I do not have
tu as	you have	*tu n'as pas*	you do not have
il/elle/on a	he/she/one has	*il/elle/on n'a pas*	he/she/one does not have
nous avons	we have	*nous n'avons pas*	we do not have
vous avez	you have	*vous n'avez pas*	you do not have
ils/elles ont	they have	*ils/elles n'ont pas*	they do not have

ÊTRE, TO BE

je suis	I am	*je ne suis pas*	I am not
tu es	you are	*tu n'es pas*	you are not
il/elle/on est	he/she/one is	*il/elle/on n'est pas*	he/she/one is not
nous sommes	we are	*nous ne sommes pas*	we are not
vous êtes	you are	*vous n'êtes pas*	you are not
ils/elles sont	they are	*ils/elles ne sont pas*	they are not

2.7. A THIRD IRREGULAR VERB: *ALLER*, TO GO

Not quite as crucial as the previous two verbs, *aller* is nonetheless very important and very commonly used. Its conjugations, too, are irregular (because it is derived from the combination of three different Latin verbs with related meanings: *vadere, ire,* and *ambulare*). Its present tense needs to be memorized now as well because, as with *être,* the first letter of several of its present tense forms differs from the first letter of the infinitive, making some of the conjugated forms impossible to locate in the dictionary on their own. Although *aller* is irregular in its conjugation of the present tense, its translation into English (unlike those of *avoir* and *être*) is regular: Like most verbs in the present tense, it has two possible translations in English, the simple present and the continuous present.

ALLER, TO GO

je vais	I go, I am going	*je ne vais pas*	I do not go, I am not going
tu vas	you go, you are going	*tu ne vas pas*	you do not go, aren't going
il/elle/on va	he/she/one goes, is going	*il/elle/on ne va pas*	he/she/one does not go, is not going

nous allons	we go, are going	*nous n'allons pas*	we do not go, are not going
vous allez	you go, are going	*vous n'allez pas*	you do not go, are not going
ils/elles vont	they go, are going	*ils/elles ne vont pas*	they do not go, are not going

These irregular verbs (along with a few others) are presented for reference in tables at the back of this book, in all tenses, in the appendix. Memorize these three verbs in the present tense now so that you'll always have them at your fingertips.

Translation Exercise A

Translate the following simple sentences.

1.	ils vont	17.	je vais
2.	elle parle	18.	vous allez
3.	nous avons	19.	nous regardons
4.	il est	20.	elles sont
5.	je ne suis pas	21.	nous allons
6.	vous êtes	22.	il a
7.	elles ont	23.	je n'ai pas
8.	j'ai	24.	tu ne vas pas
9.	tu es	25.	vous n'avez pas
10.	il ferme	26.	nous ne sommes pas
11.	elle va	27.	elles ferment
12.	tu parles	28.	on est
13.	ils sont	29.	vous parlez
14.	vous ne donnez pas	30.	ils n'ont pas
15.	on a	31.	elles ne sont pas
16.	il cherche	32.	En Haïti, on parle français.

2.8. FORMATION OF SIMPLE QUESTIONS

To form simple questions, the subject–verb order of simple statements is inverted. The inverted verb–subject unit is then linked together with a hyphen and is followed by a question mark. In this way, the statement *Il est* (He is) becomes the question *Est-il?* (Is he?). When the subject-verb order is inverted to form a question, sometimes a word ending in a vowel is followed by another word that begins with a vowel. To avoid the glottal stop that would arise in these cases, a *t* is added between these two words, to separate the two vowel sounds. This letter *t* has no meaning and no grammatical function; it simply exists to separate two different vowels. To form a question from the statement *Il a* (He has), therefore, we get *A-t-il?* (Has he? or, Does he have?).

Translation Exercise B

Translate the following simple questions.

1.	êtes-vous?	17.	vont-elles?
2.	avez-vous?	18.	Aimez-vous Brahms?
3.	va-t-elle?	19.	ont-ils?
4.	a-t-il?	20.	Où allez-vous?
5.	as-tu?	21.	Ferme-t-elle la porte?
6.	donne-t-il?	22.	Parlez-vous français?
7.	cherchent-elles?	23.	Regardent-ils la télévision?
8.	allons-nous?	24.	Sont-ils là?[2]
9.	sont-elles?	25.	avons-nous?
10.	parle-t-il?	26.	Allons-nous à New York?
11.	Aime-t-il la classe?	27.	Vont-ils au cinéma?
12.	Allez-vous à l'université?	28.	Donne-t-il des leçons de piano?
13.	Regarde-t-elle l'édifice?	29.	As-tu une cigarette?
14.	Aiment-elles?	30.	Cherche-t-il le train?
15.	Où[1] sommes-nous?	31.	ont-ils?
16.	est-il?	32.	Sont-elles ici?[3]

2.9. PRESENT TENSE/*PRÉSENT DE L'INDICATIF* OF *−RE* AND *−IR* VERBS

These two families of verbs are less regular than the *-er* verbs. This means that several patterns exist that these verbs may follow in their present tense conjugations. Even among these models, other irregularities may appear. The verb tense charts in the appendix give some of the most common regular and irregular models, in all tenses.

---

1. *où:* where
2. *là:* there
3. *ici:* here

2.9.1. THE PRESENT TENSE/*PRÉSENT DE L'INDICATIF* OF -*RE* VERBS

To conjugate an -*RE* verb in the present tense, the infinitive ending is removed, and the following tense endings are added to the stem:

PERSON	SUBJECT PRONOUN	PRESENT TENSE ENDING
1st person singular	*je*	- s
2nd person singular	*tu*	- s
3rd person singular	*il/elle/on*	- __
1st person plural	*nous*	- ons
2nd person plural	*vous*	- ez
3rd person plural	*ils/elles*	- ent

Memorize these endings now.

Some examples:

VENDRE, TO SELL			
je vends	*I sell, am selling*	je ne vends pas	*I don't sell, I am not selling*
tu vends	*you sell, are selling*	tu ne vends pas	*you don't sell, are not selling*
il/elle/on vend	*he/she/one sells, is selling*	il/elle/on ne vend pas	*he/she/one doesn't sell, isn't selling*
nous vendons	*we sell, are selling*	nous ne vendons pas	*we do not sell, are not selling*
vous vendez	*you sell, are selling*	vous ne vendez pas	*you do not sell, are not selling*
ils/elles vendent	*they sell, are selling*	ils/elles ne vendent pas	*they do not sell, are not selling*

One of the most common irregularities that occurs in -*re* verbs (and in –*ir* verbs as well) is that the consonant that precedes the -*re* is dropped *in addition* to the infinitive ending, for the first three persons singular (*je, tu, il/elle/on*). However, this dropped consonant is added back in to the stem for the three plural persons (*nous, vous, ils*). For example:

METTRE, TO PUT, TO PLACE

je mets	*I put, I am putting*	je ne mets pas	*I don't put, am not putting*
tu mets	*you put, you are putting*	tu ne mets pas	*you don't put, are not putting*
il/elle/on met	*he/she/one puts, is putting*	il/elle/on ne met pas	*he/she/one does not put, is not putting*
nous mettons	*we put, are putting*	nous ne mettons pas	*we do not put, are not putting*
vous mettez	*you put, are putting*	vous ne mettez pas	*you do not put, are not putting*
ils/elles mettent	*they put, are putting*	ils/elles ne mettent pas	*they do not put, are not putting*

An even more irregular yet common –RE verb:

PRENDRE, TO TAKE

je prends	*I take, I am taking*	je ne prends pas	*I don't take, am not taking*
tu prends	*you take, you are taking*	tu ne prends pas	*you don't take, are not taking*
il/elle/on prend	*he/she/one takes, is taking*	il ne prend pas	*he/she/one doesn't take, is not taking*
nous prenons	*we take, are taking*	nous ne prenons pas	*we don't take, are not taking*
vous prenez	*you take, are taking*	vous ne prenez pas	*you don't take, are not taking*
ils/elles prennent	*they take, are taking*	ils/elles ne prennent pas	*they don't take, are not taking*

2.9.2. THE PRESENT TENSE/*PRÉSENT DE L'INDICATIF* OF *-IR* VERBS

To conjugate an *-IR* verb in the present tense, the infinitive ending is removed, and to the stem are added the following tense endings:

PERSON	SUBJECT PRONOUN	PRESENT TENSE ENDING
1st person singular	*je*	- s
2nd person singular	*tu*	- s
3rd person singluar	*il/elle/on*	- t

1st person plural	*nous*	- ons
2nd person plural	*vous*	- ez
3rd person plural	*ils/elles*	- ent

Notice that the endings for -*RE* and -*IR* verbs are identical except for the third person singular ending, where -*RE* verbs add nothing, while -*ir* verbs add the letter –*t*. Memorize these endings now, as well. As with -*RE* verbs, quite often the consonant preceding the -*IR* is dropped in the first three persons singular, then added back in for the last three persons plural, as in *dormir*:

COURIR, TO RUN		**DORMIR**, TO SLEEP	
je cours	*I run, I am running*	je dors	*I sleep, am sleeping*
tu cours	*you run, are running*	tu dors	*you sleep, are sleeping*
il/elle/on court	*he/she/one runs, is running*	il/elle/on dort	*he/she/one sleeps, is sleeping*
nous courons	*we run, are running*	nous dormons	*we sleep, are sleeping*
vous courez	*you run, are running*	vous dormez	*you sleep, are sleeping*
ils/elles courent	*they run, are running*	Ils/elles dorment	*they sleep, are sleeping*

A small subgroup of -*RE* and -*IR* verbs adds an additional –*ss*- prior to the endings for the last three persons (the plural persons):

FINIR, to finish (as with *BÂTIR*, to build; *CHOISIR*, to choose; *CONNAÎTRE*, to know someone)

FINIR, TO FINISH			
je finis	*I finish, I am finishing*	je connais	*I know (someone)**
tu finis	*you finish, are finishing*	tu connais	*you know*
il/elle/on finit	*he/she/one finishes, is finishing*	il/elle/on connaît	*he/she/one knows*
nous fini-ss-ons	*we finish, are finishing*	nous connai-ss-ons	*we know*
vous fini-ss-ez	*you finish, are finishing*	vous connai-ss-ez	*you know*
ils/elles fini-ss-ent	*they finish, are finishing*	ils/elles connai-ss-ent	*they know*

---

* Some verbs, such as *to know*, or *to love*, sound awkward in the continuous present in English, and thus are translated only in the simple present.

There are often other irregularities in -RE and -IR verbs as well. It is not possible to know simply from looking at a verb whether it is irregular or not; and if it is irregular, it is not possible to know at sight in what way or to what extent it is irregular. For this reason, nothing can replace the use of a good irregular verb index, which can generally be found in any French–English dictionary, and which must be checked before conjugating any -RE or -IR verb. If you make sure to memorize all tense endings as we go along, almost any irregular verb that cannot be easily identified with a straightforward use of the dictionary can be tracked down by discerning the tense ending (e.g., third person plural of the present tense), and then searching the irregular verb index in the column in which your verb's tense is given (e.g., the present tense column) for verbs beginning with the same letter(s) as your verb. There is only a handful of irregular verbs beginning with any given letter, so once you've found the right tense column, you should find your verb easily.

2.10. ANOTHER IMPORTANT IRREGULAR VERB: *FAIRE*, TO DO, TO MAKE

FAIRE, TO DO, TO MAKE	
je fais	*I do, I make; I am doing, I am making*
tu fais	*you do, you make; you are doing, you are making*
il/elle/on fait	*he/she/one does, makes; he/she/one is doing, is making*
nous faisons	*we do, we make; we are doing, we are making*
vous faites	*you do, you make; you are doing, you are making*
ils/elles font	*they do, they make; they are doing, they are making*

This verb is so ubiquitous and yet so irregular that it too should be memorized, along with *avoir, être,* and *aller.* Having the present tense of these four verbs soundly memorized is an important part of the foundation on which your future translation ability will rest.

2.11. THE HISTORIC PRESENT IN FRENCH

The historic present is the use of the present tense to convey events that took place in the past, lending a sense of immediacy and vividness to the passage. This usage is more common in French than it is in English. The context of the present tense must be taken into account, along with the translator's ear for the idiom of English, to know whether it would be better to translate such a sentence or passage into the past tense (because that is the actual temporality implied) or into the present tense (because that is the literal meaning, and better conveys the sense of immediacy of the event). For students preparing for a basic language exam, examiners are generally more interested in seeing that you can recognize each tense for what it is (i.e., that you can translate the present tense in French into the present tense in English), than in the finer nuances of narrative style (i.e., translating the historic present in French into the past tense in English). For the purposes of this chapter and this book in general, the present tense will be used to indicate the present tense only.

Translation Exercise C

Write out the translations of the following sentences by first underlining the verbs, identifying the person (1st person singular, 3rd person plural, etc.) and the family of verbs to which each verb belongs, then using the dictionary to look up the verb and all other vocabulary. All translation exercises from here on should be written out: even if you think you can translate the exercises at sight, writing will help you retain what has just been learned.

1. Ils vendent la maison.
2. Nous allons au cinéma.
3. Tu fais un repas pour la famille.
4. Il sort du théâtre.
5. Ils finissent les devoirs.
6. Ces conditions créent des difficultés pour les élèves.
7. Je prends le parapluie.
8. Tu ne manges pas de chocolat.
9. Le petit garçon dort dans le lit.
10. L'article décrit une crise actuelle.
11. Elle court vers l'hôtel.
12. Cendrillon met la chaussure à son pied.
13. Ils font souvent des fautes.
14. L'université donne un prix au professeur.
15. Je mets le livre sur la table.
16. Il ne finit pas le travail.
17. Le projet ne réussit pas.
18. Elle prend le train aujourd'hui.
19. Nous mettons les bagages dans l'auto.
20. Vous avez beaucoup à faire.
21. Ils connaissent des touristes américains.
22. Nous partons en vacances.
23. Elle rougit quand il parle.
24. Je mange de la salade.
25. Il rend le livre à la bibliothèque.
26. Nous descendons de l'autobus.
27. L'argent ne fait pas le bonheur.
28. Vous faites beaucoup de progrès.

ADJECTIVES AND ADVERBS

3.1. ADJECTIVES

3.1.1. THE GENERAL RULE FOR PLACEMENT OF ADJECTIVES

All adjectives modify nouns. Most, but not all, adjectives in French are placed *after* the noun, rather than before the noun as they would be in English.

la table ronde	the round table
le choix difficile	the difficult choice
la famille moderne	the modern family

3.1.2. THE GENERAL RULE FOR AGREEMENT OF ADJECTIVES

As mentioned earlier, all adjectives agree in number and gender with the nouns they modify. The basic form of any adjective—the form under which it is listed in the dictionary—is the masculine singular form. The feminine singular form is made by adding a final *e* to the end of the masculine singular form. The masculine plural form is made by adding a final *s* to the masculine singular form. The feminine plural form is made by adding a final *es* to the masculine singular form. This results in four basic forms for most adjectives:

	MASC. SINGULAR	FEM. SINGULAR	MASC. PLURAL	FEM. PLURAL	ENGLISH
Endings:		*-e*	*-s*	*-es*	
Examples:	*petit*	*petite*	*petits*	*petites*	small, little
	vert	*verte*	*verts*	*vertes*	green

The ending of the adjective—the presence or absence of an *e* or an *s*—can often be helpful in determining the gender and/or number of a noun:

des choix intéressants (m. pl.)	some interesting choices
l'parbre vert (m. s.)	the green tree
l'armée américaine (f. s.)	the American army

Remember, it is almost always the endings of adjectives, and not the endings of nouns, that can tell us about gender. Make sure to memorize the basic adjectival endings according to gender (*masculine or feminine*) and number (*singular or plural*).

3.1.3. EXCEPTIONS TO THE GENERAL RULE FOR AGREEMENT OF ADJECTIVES

A. Some adjectives already end in an *-e* in their masculine singular form:

rouge	*utile*	*magnifique*	*historique*	*contradictoire*
red	useful	magnificent	historic	contradictory

A second *e* cannot be added to an adjective that already ends in an *e*, so if an adjective ends in *e* in its masculine singular form, it will not change for the feminine singular form. Therefore, the presence of an *e* at the end of an adjective does not necessarily mean that it is feminine. However, the *absence* of an *e* at the end of an adjective does mean, necessarily, that it is masculine.

le livre rouge (m. s.)	the red book
la table rouge (f. s.)	the red table
un projet historique (m. s.)	a historic project
une fête magnifique (f. s.)	a magnificent celebration
des plans contradictoires (m. pl.)	some contradictory plans
des idées contradictoires (f. pl.)	some contradictory ideas

B. Some adjectives already end in an *s* or an *x* in their masculine singular forms. A second *s* cannot be added to an adjective that already ends in an *s* or an *x*, so in these cases, the masculine plural form remains the same as the masculine singular form.

heureux (m. s., m. pl.)	happy
sérieux (m. s., m. pl.)	serious
mauvais (m. s., m. pl.)	bad
haineux (m. s., m. pl.)	hateful

These adjectives do add an *e* to make the feminine form; and an *es* to make the feminine plural form. However, the *x* that ends the masculine singular form must change

to an *s* before the feminine *-e* ending can be added to form the feminine singular
form or before an *-es* ending can be added to form the feminine plural form:

MASCULINE SINGULAR	FEMININE SINGULAR	MASCULINE PLURAL	FEMININE PLURAL	ENGLISH
heureux	*heureuse*	*heureux*	*heureuses*	happy
sérieux	*sérieuse*	*sérieux*	*sérieuses*	serious
mauvais	*mauvaise*	*mauvais*	*mauvaises*	bad
haineux	*haineuse*	*haineux*	*haineuses*	hateful

C. Other irregularities may occur in the masculine singular form and/or in the formation of the feminine and plural forms. For example: when an adjective ends with a
final consonant preceded by an *e*, we get such masculine endings as *-el, -et, -er,* or *–en.*
To produce the feminine form from these masculine endings, the final consonant is
doubled, and only then a final *e* is added: *naturel* becomes *naturelle; ancien* becomes
ancienne. In the dictionary, adjectives will be listed in their masculine singular form,
followed by *–e* if only an *e* is added for the feminine form, or by *-te* or *-ne,* etc., if the final consonant is doubled before the feminine *e* is added. If the final syllable is changed
completely in the feminine form, the entire feminine form will be given right after
the masculine form in the dictionary entry. The following is a list of irregularities that
can occur as an adjective changes from its masculine to feminine form:

MASCULINE SINGULAR	FEMININE SINGULAR	MASCULINE PLURAL	FEMININE PLURAL	ENGLISH
actif	*active*	*actifs*	*actives*	active
ancien	*ancienne*	*anciens*	*anciennes*	former
bon	*bonne*	*bons*	*bonnes*	good
blanc	*blanche*	*blancs*	*blanches*	white
doux	*douce*	*doux*	*douces*	soft, sweet
faux	*fausse*	*faux*	*fausses*	false
fondamental	*fondamentale*	*fondamentaux*	*fondamentales*	fundamental
fou	*folle*	*fous*	*folles*	crazy
frais	*fraîche*	*frais*	*fraîches*	fresh
gentil	*gentille*	*gentils*	*gentilles*	kind
loyal	*loyale*	*loyaux*	*loyales*	loyal
national	*nationale*	*nationaux*	*nationales*	national
premier	*première*	*premiers*	*premières*	first
sec	*sèche*	*secs*	*sèches*	dry

Translation Exercise A

Write out the translations of the following noun/adjective phrases, giving the number and gender of each. Be sure to distinguish the noun from the adjective, remembering that it is the ending of the adjective, and not the ending of the noun, that indicates gender. For *du, des, au,* and *aux,* give all possible translations.

1.   la situation financière
2.   du choix difficile
3.   une histoire contradictoire
4.   l'animal brun
5.   des débats sérieux
6.   une fille heureuse
7.   les cas intéressants
8.   la famille européenne
9.   la maison blanche
10. un garçon actif
11. des fruits frais
12. la musique folklorique
13. des théories économiques
14. la protection de l'environnement
15. des offres exclusives
16. les sciences humaines
17. après la campagne présidentielle
18. dans une terre inhospitalière
19. derrière la scène politique
20. par des exploits militaires
21. avec une manière douce
22. le lait enrichi
23. des tendances actuelles
24. le directeur général
25. à la planète entière
26. les langues étrangères
27. contre la pauvreté extrême
28. dans l'économie globalisée
29. la révolution technologique
30. les écrivains français
31. avec les découvertes littéraires
32. des difficultés énormes

3.1.4. ADJECTIVES THAT PRECEDE THE NOUN

3.1.4.1. Preceding Adjectives, General

Although most adjectives follow the noun they modify, some precede the noun. The translator must look both before and after any given noun to find all the adjectives. The following is a (nonexhaustive) list of adjectives that precede the noun:

autre	other
bon, -ne	good
bref, brève	brief
haut, haute	high
jeune	young
joli, -e	pretty

long, -ue	long
mauvais, -e	bad
petit, -e	small
vaste	vast

3.1.4.2. Preceding Adjectives That Have an Alternative Masculine Form

There are four adjectives which precede nouns that use an extra, alternative masculine form when the regular masculine adjective ends in a vowel and the noun that follows it begins with a vowel. To avoid the glottal stop that would otherwise ensue, the alternative masculine form, which is made by taking the feminine form of the adjective and dropping its feminine ending, is used:

PRIMARY MASC. FORM	ALTERNATIVE MASC. FORM	FEM. SING	M. PLURAL	FEM. PLURAL	TRANSLATION
ce	*cet*	*cette*	*ces*	*ces*	this, these
beau	*bel*	*belle*	*beaux*	*belles*	beautiful, handsome
nouveau	*nouvel*	*nouvelle*	*nouveaux*	*nouvelles*	new
vieux	*vieil*	*vieille*	*vieux*	*vieilles*	old

When the letter *h* begins a word, it is not pronounced, so the alternative masculine adjective is also used when these preceding adjectives are followed by nouns that begin with *h*.

Some examples of these four preceding adjectives with their alternative masculine forms:

m. s.	*ce livre*	this book	*un beau cheval*	a beautiful horse
f. s.	*cette chaise*	this chair	*la belle ville*	the beautiful city
alt. m. s.	*cet ordinateur*	this computer	*le bel arbre*	the beautiful tree
m. s.	*le nouveau projet*	the new project	*le vieux bateau*	the old boat
f. s.	*la nouvelle maison*	the new house	*la vieille dame*	the old lady
alt. m. s.	*le nouvel appartement*	the new apartment	*le vieil homme*	the old man

3.1.4.3. Adjectives Whose Meaning Changes, Depending on Whether They Precede or Follow the Noun

Some adjectives can be placed either before or after the noun they modify, but the meaning may change, depending on the placement of the adjective:

l'ancien président	the former president	*la ville ancienne*	the ancient city
mon cher ami	my dear friend	*un veston cher*	an expensive jacket
son propre nom	his own name	*un plancher propre*	a clean floor
la même chose	the same thing	*le livre même*	the book itself

3.1.4.4. Possessive Adjectives

Possessive adjectives in French always precede the noun they modify. As adjectives, they agree in number and gender with the noun. Therefore, unlike in English, there is more than one form for each possessive adjective: masculine singular, feminine singular, and one plural form for the first three persons singular; one singular and one plural form for the second three persons plural. The English speaker has to keep in mind that the gender of the possessive adjective agrees with the gender *of the noun that is being modified* rather than with the gender of the person who possesses that noun:

my	*mon*	*ma*	*mes*
your	*ton*	*ta*	*tes*
his/her/one's/its*	*son*	*sa*	*ses*
our	*notre*		*nos*
your	*votre*		*vos*
their	*leur*		*leurs*

*Remember, *son* is masculine because the noun that follows it is masculine, and *not* because it means *his*. *Son* means either *his, her, one's,* or *its,* depending on the antecedent to which it refers.

However, whenever the feminine singular possessive pronouns—*ma, ta, sa*—are followed by nouns that begin with a vowel or the letter *h,* the feminine possessive pronouns are replaced by the corresponding masculine possessive pronouns, in order to avoid the glottal stop that would otherwise occur:

mon âme (*f. s.*)	my soul
ton école (*f. s.*)	your school
son histoire (*f. s.*)	his/her/one's story

Memorize all the possessive adjectives, since you will encounter them frequently.

Translation Exercise B

Write out the translations for the following phrases, giving number and gender for each, and giving multiple translations for contractions whenever appropriate:

1. ces beaux arbres
2. cette jolie jeune fille
3. le vieil homme
4. notre bel avenir
5. une bonne idée
6. son origine ethnique
7. une longue maladie
8. des conditions idéales
9. ses belles cartes postales
10. le nouvel an
11. des vieilles photos
12. leur nouvelle histoire
13. la grande entreprise pharmaceutique mondiale
14. un autre village
15. l'ancien ministre
16. son accident
17. la date même
18. une nouvelle saison
19. la belle ville
20. leurs vieux animaux
21. la même rue
22. les nouveaux documents officiels
23. votre situation difficile
24. ta grande famille
25. leur vieux projet
26. ses théories importantes
27. mes petits enfants
28. la grande maison rouge
29. un nouvel ordinateur
30. un bel arbre
31. la troisième année consécutive

3.1.4.5. Adjectives Expressing Quantity

Adjectives expressing quantity precede the nouns or noun structures they modify:

assez de	enough (of)
autant de	as many
beaucoup de	a lot, many (of)
bien des	many (of)
chaque	each
la majorité	the majority
la plupart de	most (of)
moins de	less (of), fewer
peu de	little (of)
plus de	more than
plusieurs	several

| *quelques* | some, a few |
| *trop de* | too much (of), too many (of) |

3.1.4.6. Numbers

Numbers are adjectives too, and in French, they are adjectives that always precede the nouns they modify. Only the number *one* (*un, une*) has a masculine and a feminine form; all the others have only one form for both genders. Notice that the number one is the same as the indefinite article. Only the context and your ear for the idiom of English will tell you when to translate *un* or *une* as *a(n)* or as *one*.

In English, we form our ordinal numbers—after the first three (first, second, third)—by adding *-th* to the cardinal number. In French, except for the first two ordinal numbers (*premier, première; second, seconde*), the suffix *-ième* is added to the cardinal to form the ordinal.

It's a good idea to memorize the cardinal numbers one through twenty:

Cardinals		Ordinals			
1	*un, une*	1st	*premier, première*	1er/^{ière}	1^e
2	*deux*	2nd	*second,-e; deuxième*	2ème	2^e
3	*trois*	3rd	*troisième*	3ème	3^e
4	*quatre*	4th	*quatrième*	4ème	4^e
5	*cinq*	5th	*cinquième*	5ème	5^e
6	*six*	6th	*sixième*	6ème	6^e
7	*sept*	7th	*septième*	7ème	7^e
8	*huit*	8th	*huitième*	8ème	8^e
9	*neuf*	9th	*neuvième*	9ème	9^e
10	*dix*	10th	*dixième*	10ème	10^e
11	*onze*	11th	*onzième*	11ème	11^e
12	*douze*	12th	*douzième*	12ème	12^e
13	*treize*	13th	*treizième*	13ème	13^e
14	*quatorze*	14th	*quatorzième*	14ème	14^e
15	*quinze*	15th	*quinzième*	15ème	15^e
16	*seize*	16th	*seizième*	16ème	16^e
17	*dix-sept*	17th	*dix-septième*	17ème	17^e
18	*dix-huit*	18th	*dix-huitième*	18ème	18^e
19	*dix-neuf*	19th	*dix-neuvième*	19ème	19^e
20	*vingt*	20th	*vingtième*	20ème	20^e

From twenty through sixty, numbers are formed the same way as in English, with one small alteration: instead of the equivalent of *twenty-one,* the French say *vingt et un* (twenty and one), *trente et un* for thirty-one, and so forth. But the rest of the numbers between twenty-one and thirty, between thirty-one and forty, and so on, follow the same pattern as in English:

21	*vingt-et-un*	31	*trente-et-un*	41	*quarante-et-un*
22	*vingt-deux*	32	*trente-deux*	42	*quarante-deux*
23	*vingt-trois*	33	*trente-trois*	. . .	*etc.*
24	*vingt-quatre*	34	*trente-quatre*	50	*cinquante*
25	*vingt-cinq*	35	*trente-cinq*	51	*cinquante-et-un*
26	*vingt-six*	36	*trente-six*	52	*cinquante-deux*
27	*vingt-sept*	37	*trente-sept*	. . .	*etc.*
28	*vingt-huit*	38	*trente-huit*	60	*soixante*
29	*vingt-neuf*	39	*trente-neuf*	61	*soixante-et-un*
30	*trente*	40	*quarante*	62	*soixante-deux*

However, something unusual happens once we reach seventy. *Seventy* is represented by *soixante dix,* in other words, sixty (plus) ten; the following numbers up to seventy-nine are represented by sixty plus the numbers between eleven and nineteen. *Eighty* is represented by *quatre-vingts,* that is, four twenties ($4 \times 20 = 80$), to which the first nine numbers are added to form the numbers in the eighties. *Ninety* is represented by *quatre-vingt-dix,* or four twenties plus ten ($4 \times 20 = 80 + 10 = 90$); the rest of the nineties are represented by adding the numbers between 11 and 19 to *quatre-vingt.*

70	*soixante-dix*	80	*quatre-vingts*	90	*quatre-vingt-dix*
71	*soixante-et-onze*	81	*quatre-vingt-un*	91	*quatre-vingt-onze*
72	*soixante-douze*	82	*quatre-vingt-deux*	92	*quatre-vingt-douze*
73	*soixante-treize*	83	*quatre-vingt-trois*	93	*quatre-vingt-treize*
74	*soixante-quatorze*	84	*quatre-vingt-quatre*	94	*quatre-vingt-quatorze*
75	*soixante-quinze*	85	*quatre-vingt-cinq*	95	*quatre-vingt-quinze*
76	*soixante-seize*	86	*quatre-vingt-six*	96	*quatre-vingt-seize*
77	*soixante-dix-sept*	87	*quatre-vingt-sept*	97	*quatre-vingt-dix-sept*
78	*soixante-dix-huit*	88	*quatre-vingt-huit*	98	*quatre-vingt-dix-huit*
79	*soixante-dix-neuf*	89	*quatre-vingt-neuf*	99	*quatre-vingt-dix-neuf*

100	*cent*	1,000	*mille*	1,000,000	*un million*
1,000,000,000		*un milliard*			

If an author wishes to talk about something that happened in *the nineties,* for example, he or she will write *les années quatre-vingt-dix.*

| the sixties | *les années soixante* | the seventies | *les années soixante-dix* |
| the eighties | *les années quatre-vingts* | the nineties | *les années quatre-vingt-dix* |

Translation Exercise C

1.	beaucoup d'édifices	14.	quelque chose
2.	assez de travail difficile	15.	la première année
3.	la deuxième lettre	16.	plusieurs nouvelles chansons
4.	plusieurs idées intéressantes	17.	de plus en plus
5.	trop de responsabilités	18.	la plupart des producteurs
6.	quelques nouvelles théories	19.	depuis plusieurs années
7.	un peu d'argent	20.	soixante-dix enfants
8.	quelques bons amis	21.	quatre-vingts élèves
9.	la plupart d'entre nous	22.	les années quatre-vingt-dix
10.	le troisième discours	23.	sept petits animaux
11.	moins de choix	24.	le premier ministre
12.	bien des problèmes	25.	plus de cent personnes
13.	dans plusieurs pays		

3.1.5. MORE THAN ONE ADJECTIVE MODIFYING THE SAME NOUN

A noun can, of course, be modified by more than one adjective. All the adjectives may follow the noun, all of them may precede the noun, or some may precede and some may follow:

leur vieux projet abandonné	their old abandoned project
une autre idée merveilleuse	another marvelous idea
la grande maison rouge et blanche	the large red and white house
cette jolie jeune fille	this pretty young girl

Sometimes a list of adjectives following a noun is joined together by the conjunction *et* (and) or *mais* (but). Be sure to recognize when a conjunction is holding a list of adjectives together, rather than thinking that a conjunction can serve only to join two separate clauses together:

une idée choquante et controversée
a controversial and contentious idea

les collectivités politiques, sociales et religieuses de notre temps
the political, social, and religious groups of our times

un objectif secondaire mais non négligeable
a secondary but not negligible objective

3.1.6. ADJECTIVES FOLLOWED BY PREPOSITIONAL PHRASES

In general, adjectives that follow the noun in French are placed before the noun in English. However, if the adjective that follows the noun is, in turn, followed by a prepositional phrase that modifies the adjective, then the adjective will be placed *after* the noun in English, so that it can stay together with the prepositional phrase that modifies it. This is an issue that may easily trip you up later on as you translate more complex passages in French, so take the time to learn it well now:

un gouvernement élu	an elected government
un gouvernement élu au suffrage universel	a government elected by universal suffrage
des réalités vécues	(some) lived realities
des réalités vécues par la majorité des citoyens	realities lived through by the majority of the citizens
un projet menacé	a threatened project
un projet menacé par l'économie	a project threatened by the economy
des officiers condamnés	some condemned officers
des officiers condamnés pour des crimes	some officers condemned for some crimes

3.1.7. ADJECTIVES MADE FROM NOUNS AND VERBS

In English, we are able to take a noun and use it as an adjective. For example, *fire* is a noun. But in the phrase *fire engine,* the word *fire* has become an adjective modifying the noun *engine.* This is not as easily done in French. To convert a noun into an adjective in French, the main noun has to be linked to the noun-that-has-become-an-adjective with the prepositions *à* or *de,* which are in this usage not translated. Sometimes the *à* becomes *au* or *aux.* For example:

une maison à deux étages	a two-storey house
un bateau à vapeur	a steamboat
un camion d'incendie	a fire engine
une ceinture de sécurité	a seat-belt
la salle de conférence	the conference room
coq au vin	wine (stewed) chicken
la petite fille aux cheveux rouges	the little red-haired girl
la dame aux camélias	the camellia lady (the lady of the camellias)

Sometimes when the noun-that-becomes-an-adjective is the material out of which the noun is made, it is connected to the main noun by *de* or *en*:

une dent en or	a gold tooth (a tooth of gold)
une maison en briques	a brick house (a house of brick)
un bonhomme de neige	a snowman

In some cases, a verb can become an adjective in the same way—the noun it modifies is followed by *à* or *de,* which is then followed by the infinitive form of the verb, translated as an adjective:

la salle à manger	the dining-room
une machine à coudre	a sewing machine
une machine à calculer	a calculator (a calculating machine)

Translation Exercise D

Translate, referring to sections 5, 6, and 7, above:

1. un gâteau au chocolat
2. un gouvernement d'union nationale
3. la bande de Gaza
4. des instruments de musique
5. des décisions d'affaires[1]
6. une symphonie à quatre mouvements
7. Cette symphonie a quatre mouvements.
8. l'homme au chapeau noir
9. les instituts de sondage
10. une centaine de personnes
11. une dent en or
12. une robe de soie
13. la conférence de presse
14. un agent de police
15. plusieurs albums à succès
16. la tarte aux pommes
17. trois églises byzantines étonnantes
18. des gaz à effet de serre
19. un pont aérien humanitaire

---

1. *affaires:* business

20. la maison d'édition
21. une meilleure utilisation des
équipements informatiques
22. l'agence fédérale américaine
de l'environnement
23. de² magnifiques paysages fleuris
24. l'article caché
25. l'article caché à la dixième
page du journal
26. une région déstabilisée
27. une région déstabilisée par des
tremblements de terre
28. l'espace organisé par les
techniques de la production
29. les gens inégaux sur le plan social
30. une impureté incompatible
avec les normes

3.2. ADVERBS

Adverbs modify verbs, or they modify adjectives. Adverbs don't agree with anything. In English, adverbs are often (but not always) formed by adding an –ly to the adjective: *quick, quickly; slow, slowly.* Similarly, in French, adverbs are often (but not always) formed by adding –*ment* to the adjective. This ending is added to the masculine form of the adjective if the masculine adjective already ends in *e;* otherwise, it is added to the feminine form of the adjective:

ADJECTIVE		CORRESPONDING ADVERB	
lent	slow	*lentement*	slowly
facile	easy	*facilement*	easily
parfait	perfect	*parfaitement*	perfectly
naturel	natural	*naturellement*	naturally
heureux	happy	*heureusement*	happily

Some exceptions:

bon	good	*bien*	well
mauvais	bad	*mal*	badly
gentil	kind	*gentiment*	kindly
courant	fluent	*couramment*	fluently
énorme	enormous	*énormément*	enormously
précis	precise	*précisément*	precisely
vite	quick	*vite*	quickly

2. When *des* precedes a preceding adjective, it is often replaced by *de*, which is not translated as a separate word.

The following are very common adverbs that you will come across frequently. It is a good idea to become familiar with them. Notice how many of them are similar to adjectival expressions of quantity:

à peu près	more or less, approximately
assez	rather
beaucoup	very much
bien	well, very much, very, really
moins	less
plus	more
si	so
tant	so, so much
très	very
trop	too much (modifying a verb); too (modifying an adjective)

Translation Exercise E

1. Elle rentre lentement chez elle.
2. Vous lisez facilement le français.
3. Après le dîner, je suis bien fatiguée.
4. Je vais très bien, merci.
5. J'aime beaucoup ce livre.
6. Je veux[3] bien aller au cinéma.
7. Elle est extrêmement heureuse.
8. Cet enfant mange trop de chocolat.
9. Ils demeurent dans la très grande maison au coin de la rue.
10. Il préside actuellement l'union européenne.
11. Trois biologistes travaillent indépendamment sur le même projet.
12. Elle marche légèrement sur la glace.
13. Il ne mange pas suffisamment quand il est malade.
14. Les étudiants font leurs devoirs résolument.
15. Le physicien répond aux questions poliment.
16. Les enfants parlent l'anglais couramment.
17. Elle joue tranquillement avec ses amies.
18. Les membres discutent de leurs problèmes franchement.
19. L'enquête concerne les immigrants nouvellement arrivés.
20. une entreprise structurellement déficitaire

---

3. *Je veux:* I want

3.3. COMPARATIVE AND SUPERLATIVE FORMS OF ADJECTIVES AND ADVERBS

3.3.1. COMPARATIVES

In English, we have two ways of forming the comparative and superlative forms of adjectives and adverbs. With some, we simply add the comparative and superlative suffixes -er and -est to the adjective: *fast, faster, fastest; quick, quicker, quickest; pretty, prettier, prettiest*. With others, we have to resort to the words *more, most; less, least;* or *as* to indicate a comparison of equality: *She is as quick as he is*. In French, there is no comparative or superlative suffix. All comparative adjectives place the comparative word—*plus* for *more, moins* for *less, aussi* for *as*—before the adjective or adverb, and when necessary, its companion *que*, meaning *than* (more *than*, less *than*) or *as* (as . . . as, as . . . as), right after the adjective or adverb.

une situation compliquée	a complicated situation
une situation plus compliquée	a more complicated situation
une situation moins compliquée	a less complicated situation
une situation aussi compliquée	a situation as complicated (*as something else*)

Used with the comparative companion-word *que* (*than*, or *as*), there are the following possibilities, used for adjectives and adverbs alike:

plus . . . que	more . . . than
moins . . . que	less . . . than
aussi . . . que	as . . . as
ne . . . pas aussi . . . que	not as . . . as

For example, for an adjective:

Elle est plus jolie que *sa sœur.*	She is *prettier than* her sister.
Elle est moins jolie que *sa sœur.*	She is *less pretty than* her sister.
Elle est aussi jolie que *sa sœur.*	She is *as pretty as* her sister.
Elle n'est pas aussi jolie que *sa sœur.*	She is *not as pretty as* her sister.

For an adverb:

Il écrit plus lentement que *moi.*	He writes *more slowly than* I do (than me).
Il écrit moins lentement que *moi.*	He writes *less slowly than* I do.
Il écrit aussi lentement que *moi.*	He writes *as slowly as* I do.
Il n'écrit pas aussi lentement que *moi.*	He doesn't write *as slowly as* I do.

When comparing two quantities, the following expressions:

plus de . . . *que*	more of . . . than
moins de . . . *que*	less of . . . than
autant de . . . *que*	as much . . . as / as many . . . as

are used:

Jean lit plus de *romans* que *Marie.*	John reads *more* novels *than* Marie.
Elle fait moins de *fautes* que *moi.*	She makes *fewer* mistakes *than* I do.
Georges écrit autant de *lettres* que *Jacques.*	George writes *as many* letters *as* Jack.

3.3.2. SUPERLATIVES

As mentioned earlier, French does not have an equivalent of our English suffix *-est*, to form the superlative (*big, bigger, biggest*). In order to form the superlative, French takes the definite article together with the noun (*la maison*, the house) and follows it by a *repetition* of the same definite article, followed by the comparative, *plus*. *Plus* means *more*; *plus . . . que* means more than; but *le plus, la plus,* or *les plus* means *the most*. *Moins* means *less*, *moins . . . que* means *less than*; and *le moins, la moins, or les moins,* means *the least*. For example:

la robe la plus belle	the most beautiful dress
le livre le plus intéressant	the most interesting book
l'examen le plus difficile	the most difficult exam
les familles les moins riches	the least wealthy families
les discussions les moins intéressantes	the least interesting discussions

For adverbs:

l'homme qui court le plus vite	the man who runs the fastest

As in English, the comparative and superlative forms of the adjectives *bon* (good) and *mauvais* (bad) are irregular:

bon, bonne, bons, bonnes	good
meilleur, meilleure, meilleurs, meilleures (que)	better (than)
le meilleur, la meilleure, les meilleur(e)s	the best
mauvais, mauvaise	bad
pire, pires (que)	worse (than)
le pire, la pire, les pires	the worst

The comparative and superlative forms of the adverbs *bien* (well) and *mal* (badly) are also irregular:

bien	well	*mal*	badly
mieux	better	*pire, pis (no longer very common)*	worse
le mieux	the best	*le pire*	the worst

Translation Exercise F

1. Jean est plus intelligent que son ami.
2. Elle fait autant de devoirs que moi.
3. La bibliothèque publique a moins de livres que la bibliothèque universitaire.
4. Il a la voiture la plus rapide du quartier.
5. Le journal est le plus distribué de la ville.
6. Cette forêt a plus d'arbres que l'autre.
7. Il est moins sportif que son frère.
8. Le vingt et un juin est le jour le plus long de l'année.
9. Ses idées ne sont pas aussi compliquées que d'habitude.
10. La situation politique est plus grave cette année.
11. Il arrive à l'école le plus tard possible.
12. Elle lit le journal le plus récent.
13. Il veut[4] continuer à travailler cinq ans de plus.
14. La réforme fiscale permet une plus grande égalité sociale.
15. Les ballets de cette chorégraphe sont les plus émouvants.

---

4. *il veut:* he wants

3.4. TRANSLATION PASSAGE

LE CORBEAU ET LE RENARD[5]

Un corbeau est perché[6] sur un bel arbre. Dans son bec, il a un grand morceau de fromage. Un renard passe sous l'arbre et sent l'odeur du fromage. Le renard dit, « M. Corbeau, vous êtes très joli! Vous êtes l'oiseau le plus beau de toute la forêt! Sans doute, votre voix est aussi très belle lorsque vous chantez ». Le corbeau, très heureux d'entendre ces mots flatteurs, ouvre la bouche pour montrer sa belle voix—et le fromage tombe par terre.[7] Le renard prend le fromage et court vite chez lui. Le corbeau apprend ainsi, trop tard, les effets de la flatterie.

5. Very freely adapted from the rhymed tale composed by Jean de La Fontaine (1621–1695), whose fables hold a place in French literature similar to that held by Aesop's fables in English (from which La Fontaine often borrowed). For the original, see http://poesie.webnet.fr/lesgrandsclassiques/poemes/jean_de_la_fontaine/le_corbeau_et_le_renard.html, retrieved November 26, 2011.

6. *perché:* perched

7. *par terre:* on the ground

REFLEXIVE VERBS

4.1. REFLEXIVE PRONOUNS AND THE FORMATION OF REFLEXIVE VERBS

Reflexive verbs are verbs in which the subject (I, you, he, she, etc.) is the same person as the object (me, you, him, her, etc.). For example, in a reflexive verb a subject in the first person singular must be accompanied by an object in the first person singular; a subject in the third person plural must be accompanied by an object in the third person plural. In English we often express reflexive verbs by adding the suffix *-self* to the object pronoun. (*I love him*: not a reflexive verb, since the object is a different person than the subject. *I love myself*: a reflexive verb, since the object is the same person as the subject.) In French there is no reflexive suffix corresponding to the English *-self*: instead, reflexive verbs are represented by the use of the *reflexive pronoun*, which is placed right after the subject pronoun and right before the verb. To learn and recognize reflexive verbs, first learn and memorize the reflexive pronouns:

PERSON	SUBJECT PRONOUNS	CORRESPONDING REFLEXIVE PRONOUNS	*SE LAVER* IN THE PRESENT TENSE	ENGLISH TRANSLATION OF *SE LAVER* IN THE PRESENT TENSE
1st person sing.	je	*me*	*je me lave*	I wash myself
2nd person sing.	tu	*te*	*tu te laves*	you wash yourself
3rd person sing.	il/elle/on	*se*	*il/elle/on lave*	he/she/one washes oneself
1st person pl.	nous	*nous*	*nous nous lavons*	we wash ourselves

2nd person pl.	vous	*vous*	*vous* vous *lavez*	you wash yourself/ selves
3rd person pl.	ils/elles	*se*	*ils/elles* se *lavent*	they wash themselves

Note that the reflexive pronouns cannot be mixed and matched with the subject pronouns. Only the reflexive pronoun that corresponds to the subject pronoun in question can be used to form a reflexive verb: the subject pronoun and the reflexive pronoun must refer to the same grammatical person.

The infinitive of a reflexive verb is represented by placing the third person singular reflexive pronoun, *se*, right before the main verb: *laver* means *to wash,* but *se laver* means *to wash oneself.* Reflexive verbs are listed in the dictionary under the main verb, rather than under *se.* To look up a reflexive verb in the dictionary, first look up the main verb, then follow along the paragraph that follows the definition until coming to the reflexive form, which will be indicated by *se* preceding the infinitive and printed in boldface. When conjugating a reflexive verb such as *se laver,* remember that the *se* refers only to the infinitive form and will be replaced by the appropriate reflexive pronouns corresponding to each subject pronoun.

4.2. THE NEGATIVE FORM OF REFLEXIVE VERBS

In the negative, the *ne* precedes the reflexive pronoun, whereas the *pas* follows the verb:

je ne *me lave* pas	I don't wash myself
tu ne *te laves* pas	you don't wash yourself
il/elle/on ne *se lave* pas	he/she/one doesn't wash oneself
nous ne *nous lavons* pas	we don't wash ourselves
vous ne *vous lavez* pas	you don't wash yourself/selves
ils/elles ne *se lavent* pas	they don't wash themselves

4.3. VARIOUS WAYS IN WHICH TO TRANSLATE REFLEXIVE VERBS

In French, reflexive verbs are considered part of a larger family of verbs called *les verbes pronominaux.* These verbs all use reflexive pronouns, but their meanings are not always reflexive. The various ways in which verbs with reflexive pronouns can be translated into English reflect the more comprehensive category of *les verbes pronominaux.*

4.3.1. As in English, many reflexive verbs in French are simply reflexive uses of verbs that are also commonly used nonreflexively. In English *I wash the car* is not reflexive, but *I wash myself* is reflexive. In French *Je lave la voiture* is not reflexive, because the subject is not the same person (or thing) as the object. The verb becomes reflexive when the object is the same person (or thing) as the subject, which is done in French by adding the reflexive pronoun: *Je me lave,* I wash myself.

Regular (nonreflexive) use of *laver*	*Je lave la voiture.*	I wash the car.
Regular (nonreflexive) use of *regarder*	*Il regarde la télévision.*	He is watching television.
Reflexive use of *laver*	*Je me lave.*	I wash myself
Reflexive use of *regarder*	*Il se regarde.*	He is looking at himself.

4.3.2. Reflexive verbs are used in French for actions performed for oneself and/or on one's body. In English we speak of *washing my hands* or *brushing my teeth,* using the possessive adjective (e.g., *my*) to indicate that it is one's own body that one is washing. In French the possessive pronoun is not used in this instance; the reflexive pronoun is used instead. Because the reflexive pronoun indicates that the action is performed for or on oneself, the use of the possessive adjective would be redundant, and the definite article is used instead.

Je me lave les mains.	I wash my hands.
Il se brosse les dents.	He brushes his teeth.
Il se coupe le doigt.	He cuts his finger.
Elle se serre la ceinture.	She tightens her belt.

4.3.3. Some verbs exist only or mainly in reflexive form in French, but the idea of reflexivity is embedded in the verb itself. In these cases the reflexive pronoun itself is not translated into English.

Il se dépêche.	He hurries.
Je me lève.	I get up.
Ils se souviennent.	They remember.
Elle se promène.	She takes a walk.

4.3.4. Sometimes the addition of a reflexive pronoun changes the meaning of a verb. For instance, *attendre* means to wait; but *s'attendre à* means to expect something. This makes it particularly necessary to look up the definition of a reflexive verb even if its nonreflexive form is familiar to you:

Elle attend l'autobus.	She is waiting for the bus.
Elle s'attend à recevoir des fleurs.	She is expecting to receive some flowers.
Il tire le rideau.	He draws the curtain (closes the curtain).
Il se tire de ses difficultés.	He extricates himself from his difficulties.

4.3.5. In the plural forms, the reflexive form of a verb can be reciprocal rather than strictly reflexive in meaning:

Ils s'embrassent.	They kiss each other.
Ils se connaissent.	They know each other.
Ils se rencontrent cet après-midi.	They are meeting each other this afternoon.

4.3.6. Finally, a most important use of the reflexive form is to express the passive voice. Although this is not intuitive to the English speaker, reflexive verbs are very commonly used to express the passive voice, which is therefore often the best translation for them. See chapter 14, section 14.2 for a fuller discussion of the use of reflexive verbs to construct the passive voice in French.

Il s'appelle Jean.
He is called John (His name is John).

Il s'intéresse aux sciences politiques.
He is interested in political science.

La controverse ne se limite pas à un débat entre spécialistes.
The controversy is not limited to a debate among specialists.

La bibliothèque se trouve[1] près du parc.
The library is (found) near the park.

For an example of the conjugation of reflexive verbs in all tenses, see Appendix A at the end of the book.

Translation Exercise A

Translate these sentences with reflexive verbs, considering which of the various translations mentioned in sections 4.3.1–4.3.6 is the most appropriate in each case.

1. Il se lève très tôt le matin.
2. Je me couche à minuit.
3. Elle se brosse les cheveux.
4. L'université se trouve dans le quartier sud.
5. Les enfants s'amusent[2] bien au cirque.
6. Les journalistes s'intéressent aux conflits nationaux.

---

1. *se trouver,* literally, to find oneself = to be found. But it is commonly used as a locative form of *to be,* stating *where* something *is.*
2. *s'amuser:* to enjoy oneself (rather than "to amuse oneself").

7. Le ministre s'adresse directement aux citoyens.

8. Les amis s'offrent des cadeaux à Noël.

9. Comme[3] il est en retard[4] à son cours, il se dépêche.

10. Le rapport se limite à l'examen des différents sites convenables pour un grand théâtre.

11. La division du travail se produit au sein des sociétés complexes.

12. Elle se souvient des jeux olympiques de l'année passée.

13. Les échanges culturels se font sous la forme de cadeaux.

14. Je m'attends à recevoir vos commentaires.

15. Au sujet d'un musée de l'histoire, les chercheurs universitaires et les conservateurs du musée s'opposent.

---

3. *comme:* as
4. *en retard:* late

THE IMPERFECT/*L'IMPARFAIT*

5.1. EXPLANATION OF THE TENSE

The imperfect tense, or *l'imparfait,* is a past tense named in contradistinction to the concept of a perfect tense. A perfect tense is a tense in which the action has been completed. The simple past is a perfect tense in which action took place and was completed: *I came, I saw, I conquered.* By contrast, the imperfect tense, or *l'imparfait,* describes continuous or repetitive action that began in the past and has continued over time. It corresponds most closely to the English usage of *I was doing something.* In English the imperfect tense is also referred to as the past continuous or the past progressive.

5.2. FORMATION OF THE *IMPARFAIT*

The *imparfait* is formed by taking the first person plural form (the *nous* form) of the present tense, dropping the *-ons* ending, and to the stem that remains, adding the following endings, which should be memorized now:

PERSON	CORRESPONDING ENDING
je	*-ais*
tu	*-ais*
il/elle/on	*-ait*
nous	*-ions*
vous	*-iez*
ils/elles	*-aient*

The formation of the *imparfait* is one of the very few foolproof rules of grammar in the entire French language. Your dictionary knows this, and therefore its irregular verb index will not provide an entry for the *imparfait*: It expects you to be able to construct the *imparfait* from the present tense on your own, or, conversely, to deduce the present tense and then the infinitive by working backward from the *imparfait*. Even very irregular verbs such as *avoir* follow this rule for the formation of the *imparfait*. The single exception is the verb *être*, for the simple reason that its first person plural form *nous sommes* does not end in *–ons*. For *être*, the syllable *ét-* takes the role of the *imparfait* stem; all the *imparfait* endings remain the same.

For many regular verbs, the *imparfait* stem—the *nous* form of the present tense minus the *-ons* ending—is exactly the same as the stem for the present tense: the infinitive minus the infinitive ending:

donner	minus *-er*	= *donn-*	*je donn-*	+ *ais*	= *je donnais*
donnons	minus *-ons*	= *donn-*	*tu donn-*	+ *ais*	= *tu donnais*
			il donn-	+ *ait*	= *il donnait*
			nous donn-	+ *ions*	= *nous donnions*
			vous donn-	+ *iez*	= *vous donniez*
			ils donn-	+ *aient*	= *ils donnaient*

This can make it seem superfluous to insist that the *imparfait* stem is anything other than the same stem that is used in the present tense. However, for some verbs, the *nous* form of the present tense minus the *-ons* is significantly different from the infinitive minus the infinitive ending. Note the critical difference between using a stem formed by the infinitive minus the infinitive ending and one formed by using the first person plural minus the *–ons*, in *finir*:

finir	minus *-ir*	= *fin-*	*je fin-* (not used)		
finissons	minus *-ons*	= *finiss*	*je finiss-*	+ *ais*	= *je finissais*
				+ *ais*	= *tu finissais*
				+ *ait*	= *il finissait*
				+ *ions*	= *nous finissions*
				+ *iez*	= *vous finissiez*
				+ *aient*	= *ils finissaient*

Hence the importance of memorizing the specific form of the *imparfait* stem as the *nous* form of the present tense minus the *-ons*.

Looking back at the list of *imparfait* endings, notice how the first and second person plural endings of the *imparfait*—the *nous* and *vous* forms—differ from the present tense endings for these persons by only one letter: *-ons* and *-ez* are the present tense endings, whereas *-ions* and *-iez* are the *imparfait* endings. This makes it important to consider not only what seems to be the ending of a verb form, but also what precedes that ending, every time you come across a verb that ends in *-ons* or *-ez*. What at first glance might seem to be the first or second person plural ending of the present tense may on further inspection turn out to be the first or second person plural of the *imparfait* (if the present tense ending is preceded by the letter *i*). The correct translation of any given sentence can depend on your recognition of the presence or absence of that one vowel.

5.3. TRANSLATIONS OF THE *IMPARFAIT*

By expressing action that began in the past and continued over time, the *imparfait* implies incomplete, continuous, repetitive, and/or habitual action. Because of this range of implications, there are three or even four possible translations for the *imparfait*. In other words, whereas continuous action begun in the past is expressed in French with the *imparfait,* in English it can be expressed in a variety of ways. The most common translation into English of the *imparfait* is the *I was doing* form (i.e., the continuous past); so we often translate the *imparfait* into English as *I was [writing, speaking, eating, etc.].* Because the *imparfait* is often used in sentences that include other kinds of past tenses in order to bring out the difference between an ongoing action and a completed action, it is necessary always to consider this translation first, even though much of the time it will have to be rejected in favor of one of the other possible translations.

For some verbs, translating the *imparfait* into the *I was doing* form in English can sound awkward. With verbs such as *to think* or *to live* (and many others), we are more likely to say *I thought* or *I lived*—that is, we are more likely to use the simple past— even when referring to action over time. For instance, we would generally say *I lived there for ten years* or *I loved him all my life*, even though these sentences clearly refer to action begun in the past and continued over a significant amount of time. Therefore, a second possible translation of the *imparfait* is the simple past (e.g., *I lived,* as in *I lived there for ten years*).

In addition, the *imparfait* can refer to action over time that took place long before the time of narration; for example, when describing how people *used to live* during the seventeenth century in France. So the third possible translation of the *imparfait* is the *I used to live* form.

Finally, the repetitive implications of this tense can sometimes best be translated with the word *would*, as in, *Every morning he would walk to his favorite café and read the newspaper*. Although in this example the implication of repetitive action in the past is quite clear, this use of *would* to translate the *imparfait* could, for the novice translator, easily be confused with *would* as the translation for the conditional tense (discussed in chapter 12, section 12.4). Therefore, for now it is suggested that this possible translation be left for a later stage of learning French. At this stage, three possible forms of translation must be considered whenever the *imparfait* is encountered, of which the *was doing* form must always be considered first of all. The importance of considering this form first is explained in more detail in chapter 7, section 7.7.

When conjugating verbs in the *imparfait*, then, three translations must be given, in the following order (indicating the order in which you have to consider them):

je parlais	I was speaking	I spoke	I used to speak
tu parlais	you were speaking	you spoke	you used to speak
il/elle/on parlait	he/she/one was speaking	he/she/one spoke	he/she/one used to speak
nous parlions	we were speaking	we spoke	we used to speak
vous parliez	you were speaking	you spoke	you used to speak
ils/elles parlaient	they were speaking	they spoke	they used to speak

5.4. *AVOIR* AND *ÊTRE* IN THE *IMPARFAIT*

The translations of *avoir* and *être* in the *imparfait* are exceptions to the rule governing the translation of this tense. Contrary to other verbs, the translations of these two verbs should be memorized and translated *only* in the simple past (which, in the case of these two verbs, is able to convey action over time in English).

The conjugations of *avoir* and *être* should be memorized in the *imparfait* as in every simple (i.e., one-word) tense. This is because they are very common yet irregular; and because they function as part of compound tenses. For both these reasons you'll need to be able to recognize them at sight. Learn and memorize *avoir* and *être* in the *imparfait* now:

j'avais	I had	*j'étais*	I was
tu avais	you had	*tu étais*	you were
il/elle/on avait	he/she/one had	*il/elle/on était*	he/she/one was
nous avions	we had	*nous étions*	we were
vous aviez	you had	*vous étiez*	you were
ils/elles avaient	they had	*ils/elles étaient*	they were

5.5. THE NEGATIVE FORM OF THE *IMPARFAIT*

The negative form of the *imparfait* follows the same pattern as the negative form of the present tense:

je ne donnais pas	I was not giving	I didn't give	I didn't used to give
tu ne donnais pas	you were not giving	you didn't give	you didn't used to give
il/elle/on ne donnait pas	he/she/one was not giving	he/she/one didn't give	he/she/one didn't used to give
nous ne donnions pas	we were not giving	we didn't give	we didn't used to give
vous ne donniez pas	you were not giving	you didn't give	you didn't used to give
ils/elles ne donnaient pas	they were not giving	they didn't give	they didn't used to give

5.6. REFLEXIVE VERBS IN THE *IMPARFAIT*

Reflexive verbs, like any other verbs, may be expressed in the *imparfait* as well:

je me lavais	I was washing myself	I washed myself	I used to wash myself
il se dépêchait	he was hurrying	he hurried	he used to hurry
elle se levait	she was getting up	she got up	she used to get up
il s'intéressait au cinéma	he was interested in the movies	he used to be interested in the movies.	

Translation Exercise A

1. Il était le vice-président d'une corporation mondiale.
2. Cette décision changeait la fonction de la capitale.
3. Elle déjeunait en compagnie d'une journaliste.
4. Nous parlions de toutes sortes de choses.
5. Ils savaient de moins en moins d'où ils venaient et où ils allaient.

6. Le petit garçon jouait avec ses amis et travaillait bien à l'école.

7. Sa blouse avait des trous, et il n'avait pas de chaussures à ses pieds.

8. Le chien allait et venait chaque fois que[1] son maître ouvrait la porte.

9. Les gens arrivaient au théâtre l'un après l'autre à partir de[2] l'après-midi.

10. Le livre avait pour objectif de donner une image positive de cette époque.

11. Les partisans rappelaient leur existence face à l'indifférence gouvernementale.

12. Les chercheurs du Moyen-Âge consacraient leur vie à la découverte de la pierre philosophale.

13. L'économie et le réchauffement climatique préoccupaient les citoyens et les citoyennes pendant les élections.

14. Le traité de Methuen de 1703 favorisait l'importation sur le marché anglais des vins de Madère et de Porto.

5.7. TRANSLATION PASSAGE

Parse the first two paragraphs of this passage: above each word, write what part of speech it is. If it is a noun or adjective, give number and gender. If it is a verb, give person and tense. Then, having identified all these parts of speech, translate the entire passage:

LA CHARTE DE MÉDECINS SANS FRONTIÈRES[3]

Médecins Sans Frontières est une association privée à vocation internationale. L'association rassemble majoritairement des médecins et des membres des corps de santé et est ouverte aux autres professions utiles à sa mission. Tous souscrivent sur l'honneur aux principes suivants:

Les Médecins Sans Frontières apportent leur secours aux populations en détresse, aux victimes de catastrophes d'origine naturelle ou humaine, de situations de guerre, sans aucune discrimination de race, de religion, de philosophie ou de politique.

Œuvrant[4] dans la neutralité et l'impartialité, les Médecins Sans Frontières re-

---

1. *que:* that
2. *à partir de:* from...on.
3. Adapted from http://www.msf.ch/a-propos-de-msf/la-charte-de-msf/ and http://www.msf.ca/fr/themes/haiti-six-mois-apres/ . Retrieved September 25, 2010.
4. *œuvrant:* working

vendiquent,[5] au nom de l'éthique médicale universelle et du droit à l'assistance humanitaire, la liberté pleine et entière de l'exercice de leur fonction.

Ils s'engagent à respecter les principes déontologiques[6] de leur profession et à maintenir une totale indépendance à l'égard de tout pouvoir,[7] ainsi que[8] de toute force politique, économique ou religieuse.

Le chef de mission MSF était présent à Port-au-Prince au moment du séisme catastrophique à Haïti en 2010. Des centaines de milliers de personnes étaient tuées ou blessées.[9] Deux mois après le tremblement de terre, MSF comptait plus de 350 collaborateurs internationaux sur le terrain. Les manifestations et émeutes continuaient en Haïti malgré les appels au calme.

---

5. from *revendiquer:* to claim
6. *déontologiques:* ethical
7. *le pouvoir:* power
8. *ainsi qui:* as well as
9. *tués ou blessés:* killed or wounded

PAST PARTICIPLES/*LES PARTICIPES PASSÉS*

6.1. FORMATION OF PAST PARTICIPLES

Past participles are forms of verbs that state that something has been done. *Done, given, written, finished,* and *eaten* are all examples of past participles in English. In French, each family of verbs has its own way of forming the past participle. Each family of verbs removes the final infinitive ending (*-er, -re, -ir,* or *-oir*) and then adds a specific past participle ending: *é* for *-ER* verbs; *-u* for *-RE* verbs; *-i* for *-IR* verbs; *-u* for *-OIR* verbs.

	-ER VERBS	*-RE* VERBS	*-IR* VERBS	*-OIR* VERBS
past participle ending:	-*É*	-*U*	-*I*	-*U*
infinitive:	*donner*	*vendre*	*finir*	*vouloir*
	to give	to sell	to finish	to want
past participle:	*donné*	*vendu*	*fini*	*voulu*
	given	sold	finished	wanted

Memorize -*é,* -*u,* and -*i* now, as the most common past participle endings.

The following are some irregular verbs that take the endings *-is,-it,* or *-ert* for their past participles:

INFINITIVE		PAST PARTICIPLE	
mettre	to put, to place	*mis*	put
prendre	to take	*pris*	taken
dire	to say	*dit*	said
écrire	to write	*écrit*	written

faire	to do, to make	*fait*	done, made
ouvrir	to open	*ouvert*	opened

Many other verbs have irregular past participles but always end in one of the previously mentioned endings.

Note that the past participle for *faire* is *fait* (done, made). This is potentially confusing, because it is the same word as the third person singular of the present tense (*il/elle/on fait*), and spelled exactly like the related noun (*le fait*, the fact). Sort out this potential confusion by memorizing the past participle of *faire* now.

Also, be sure to find out exactly where past participles are located in the irregular verb index of your dictionary. They are often listed, along with present participles, in a column or section for participles. Remember to be careful to distinguish past participles from present participles (presented in chapter 13); they are different parts of speech and cannot be used interchangeably.

6.2. PAST PARTICIPLES AS ADJECTIVES

Past participles can be used as regular adjectives (e.g., the *written* word, the *parked* car, the *graven* image, a *carved* pumpkin, a *drunken* fool). When past participles are used as adjectives, they must act like all adjectives in French: They must agree in number and gender with the noun they modify. Thus, the same endings that are added to any adjective in order to form the feminine singular, masculine plural, or feminine plural forms are added to past participles when used as adjectives:

INFINITIVE	MASC. SINGULAR	FEM. SINGULAR	MASC. PLURAL	FEM. PLURAL	ENGLISH TRANSLATION
donner	donné	donnée	donnés	données	given
vendre	vendu	vendue	vendus	vendues	sold
finir	fini	finie	finis	finies	finished
mettre	mis	mise	mis	mises	put
dire	dit	dite	dits	dites	said
ouvrir	ouvert	ouverte	ouverts	ouvertes	opened

The following are some examples of past participles used as adjectives:

le saumon fumé (m. s.) *l'œuvre finie* (f. s.) *les représentants élus* (m. pl.) *les lettres écrites* (f. pl.)
smoked salmon   the finished work   the elected representatives   the written letters

Although we saw earlier that in order to form the feminine adjective, the letter *e* cannot be added to an adjective that already ends in the letter *e* in its masculine singular form, the letter *e* can and must be added to the final *é* of the masculine singular form of the past participles of –ER verbs. This is because the letter *é* (with the acute accent) is considered to be a different letter than the letter *e* (without any accent). Thus, *mangé* is the masculine singular past participle of *manger*, and *mangée* is the feminine singular form. (We see this in certain words that English has borrowed from French: The *fiancé* is the guy, and the *fiancée* is the girl.)

Now memorize the past participle endings along with their feminine and plural endings, so that when you encounter a verb that ends in

-é	*-ée*	*-és*	*-ées*
-u	*-ue*	*-us*	*-ues*
-i	*-ie*	*-is*	*-ies*

or in any of the irregular past participle endings such as

-is	*-ise*	*-is*	*-ises*
-it	*-ite*	*-its*	*-ites*
-ert	*-erte*	*-erts*	*-ertes*

you will recognize that you are probably in the presence of a past participle.

6.3. PAST PARTICIPLES AS PREDICATE ADJECTIVES

Past participles are often used as predicate adjectives. A predicate of a sentence or clause is the part that contains the verb. A predicate adjective is an adjective that accompanies the verb rather than accompanying the noun, although it continues to modify the noun (and therefore, in French, it continues to agree with the noun). For example, in the English sentence, "The grass is green," *The grass* is the subject, and *is green* is the predicate, constituted by the verb *is* and the adjective *green*, which modifies the subject, *grass*. The use of the past participle as a predicate adjective is one of the central ways that the passive voice is constructed in French (along with reflexive verbs and the nonspecific pronoun *on*: For more on the passive voice, see chapter 14, especially section 14.1). In the following examples, note how past participles used as predicate adjectives, in spite of their placement after the verb, still agree in number and gender with the nouns they modify:

Le gâteau est mangé.	The cake is eaten.
La pomme est mangée.	The apple is eaten.
La guerre est finie.	The war is over.

Les livres sont trouvés.	The books are found.
Les portes sont fermées.	The doors are closed.
Les maisons sont vendues.	The houses are sold.

Translation Exercise A

Underline the past participle, determine its number and gender from its ending, and then write out the translation of the phrase or sentence:

1. La maison est vendue.
2. L'ordinateur est réparé.
3. L'enfant paraît fatigué.
4. La porte est ouverte.
5. Les amis sont réunis.
6. Les gâteaux sont mangés.
7. La construction est finie.
8. Les fleurs sont cueillies.
9. à un moment donné
10. une cause négligée
11. les forces armées
12. l'économie globalisée
13. des théories compliquées
14. des espèces menacées d'extinction
15. La désertification reste une «urgence oubliée».
16. Le dissident est condamné à un long exil.
17. une image fondée sur des faits réels
18. Le journal est lu par tout le monde.[1]
19. La chanson est chantée par les enfants.
20. Le ministre est désigné par le président.
21. la conservation des données[2] privées
22. Le livre est maintenant publié.
23. L'élection du nouveau gouvernement est annoncée à la radio.
24. Ces liquides ne sont pas destinés à être bus.
25. Tout le monde est préoccupé par la situation au Moyen-Orient.
26. La conférence de presse est tenue en face de la mairie.

---

1. *tout le monde:* everyone
2. *données:* data

LE PASSÉ COMPOSÉ/THE COMPOUND PAST

7.1. EXPLANATION OF THE TENSE

While a *simple* tense is made up of only one word, a *compound* tense is made up of two words. The *passé composé* is the past tense in French that is made up of two component parts, an auxiliary verb and a past participle. It is one of the most common ways of expressing the past tense in speech and in writing. The *passé composé* expresses action that began and ended prior to the present. The rules for the formation of the *passé composé* are especially important because they are the same rules that are followed to form all the other many compound tenses in the language (see chapter 17, More Compound Tenses). It is therefore critical to learn and memorize the following rules governing the formation of the *passé composé*:

7.2. RULES GOVERNING THE FORMATION AND TRANSLATION OF THE *PASSÉ COMPOSÉ*

The following rules govern the formation and translation of the *passé composé*:

1. The *passé composé* is formed with an auxiliary verb in the present tense plus a past participle.
2. The two auxiliary verbs are *avoir* and *être*. Most verbs take *avoir* as their auxiliary verb.
3. When *avoir* is the auxiliary verb, the past participle does not agree with the subject in number and gender.

4. The verbs that take *être* as their auxiliary verb are the following: the family of twenty intransitive verbs listed below and *all* reflexive verbs.

5. When a verb takes *être* as its auxiliary verb, the past participle must agree with the subject in number and gender.

6. Although the *passé composé* is structurally identical to the compound past in English, it is generally used in French where English would use the simple past. Therefore the most common translation in English for the *passé composé* is the simple past.

7. With verbs that take *avoir*, when the direct object precedes the verb, the past participle agrees with the direct object in number and gender. (This rule will be discussed in the next chapter.)

• Formation of the *Passé Composé.*

The *passé composé* is formed with an auxiliary verb in the present tense plus a past participle. The two auxiliary verbs are *avoir* and *être.* You have already learned and memorized *avoir* and *être* in the present tense, so you already know the auxiliary verbs for the *passé composé.* You have also already learned about past participles in the previous chapter, so you are familiar with both components of the *passé composé.* Because most verbs use *avoir* as their auxiliary verb in the *passé composé, avoir* in the present tense + a past participle is the most common pattern for forming this tense:

AVOIR IN PRESENT TENSE	PAST PARTICIPLE	ENGLISH TRANSLATION
j'ai	*parlé*	I spoke, I have spoken
tu as	*vu*	you saw, you have seen
il/elle/on a	*fini*	he/she/one finished, he/she/one has finished
nous avons	*écrit*	we wrote, we have written
vous avez	*pris*	you took, you have taken
ils/elles ont	*ouvert*	they opened, they have opened

• *Avoir* as the Auxiliary Verb.

When *avoir* is the auxiliary verb, the past participle does not agree with the subject in number and gender. This is different from the use of the past participle as an adjective, as in the previous chapter. When used as an adjective, the past participle agrees with the noun it modifies, but when it is used as an auxiliary verb with *avoir,* it does not agree with the subject (noun or pronoun) of the verb. Note how the plural subjects in the preceding list are followed by past participles that do not have plural endings.

• *Être* as the Auxiliary Verb.

Twenty intransitive verbs and all reflexive verbs take *être* as their auxiliary verb in the *passé composé. Transitive* verbs are verbs that have a direct object, whereas *intransitive* verbs are verbs that do not have a direct object. (There will be a fuller discussion of direct objects and direct object pronouns in the next chapter.) Here is the family of twenty intransitive verbs that use *être* as an auxiliary verb, together with their past participles:

INFINITIVE	PAST PARTICIPLE	INFINITIVE	PAST PARTICIPLE
aller (to go)	*allé(e)(s)*	*parvenir* (to attain, to reach)	*parvenu(e)(s)*
arriver (to arrive; to happen)	*arrivé(e)(s)*	*repartir* (to leave again)	*reparti(e)(s)*
descendre (to go down)	*descendu(e)(s)*	*rentrer* (to come back)	*rentré(e)(s)*
décéder (to die, to decease)	*décédé(e)(s)*	*rester* (to remain, to stay)	*resté(e)(s)*
devenir (to become)	*devenu(e)(s)*	*retourner* (to return)	*retourné(e)(s)*
entrer (to enter)	*entré(e)(s)*	*revenir* (to come back)	*revenu(e)(s)*
monter (to go up)	*monté(e)(s)*	*sortir* (to go out)	*sorti(e)(s)*
mourir (to die)	*mort(e)(s)*	*survenir* (to arise)	*survenu(e)(s)*
naître (to be born)	*né(e)(s)*	*tomber* (to fall)	*tombé(e)(s)*
partir (to leave)	*parti(e)(s)*	*venir* (to come)	*venu(e)(s)*

• Agreement with Verbs that Take *Être.*

When a verb takes *être* as its auxiliary verb, unlike verbs that take *avoir,* the past participle *must* agree with the subject in number and gender. As with adjectives, the letter -*e* is added to the past participle for agreement with a feminine subject; the letter -*s,* for agreement with a masculine plural subject; and the letters -*es,* for agreement with a feminine plural subject. The second person plural (*vous*) is grammatically plural in all simple tenses (i.e., all one-word tenses), whether it refers to a single person or to several people. In compound tenses, however, when referring to a single person (to be more formal or polite), the past participle remains single; when it refers to more than one person, the past participle becomes plural. When conjugating verbs with *être* in the *passé composé, possible* endings of the past participles are given in parentheses; *necessary* endings are given without parentheses. In any given sentence, of course, the past participle will appear only with the ending that agrees with the particular subject of the verb in that sentence.

ÊTRE IN PRESENT TENSE	PAST PARTICIPLES WITH AGREEMENT	ENGLISH TRANSLATION
je suis	*venu(e)*	I came, I have come
tu es	*allé(e)*	you went, you have gone

il/elle/on/est	*descendu(e)*	he/she/one went down, has gone down
nous sommes	*sorti(e)s*	we went out, we have gone out
vous êtes	*resté(e)(s)*	you remained, you have remained
ils/elles sont	*tombé(e)s*	they fell, they have fallen

• **Verbs that Take *Avoir* or *Être*.**

Some of the twenty verbs that take *être* are sometimes used in a transitive sense (i.e., they may take a direct object). In these cases, such verbs take *être* as their auxiliary verb when used in an intransitive sense but take *avoir* when they are used in a transitive sense:

Elle est montée les escaliers.	She went up the stairs.
Il est sorti de la pièce.	He went out of the room.
Il est rentré chez lui.	He returned home.

But:

Elle a monté les valises.	She took the luggage upstairs.
Il a sorti la voiture du garage.	He took the car out of the garage.
Il a rentré le chien.	He brought the dog in.

However, the most important thing at this stage is to learn to recognize which verbs take *être* and which take *avoir* as their auxiliary verbs. You may want to continue to refer to the table on page 62 throughout this course.

• **The *Passé Composé* with Reflexive Verbs.**

All reflexive verbs take *être* as their auxiliary verb, and in the *passé composé* they are subject to the same range of possible translations as described in chapter 4, section 4.3. Reflexive verbs in the *passé composé* are formed with the subject pronoun, its corresponding reflexive pronoun, *être* in the present tense, and the past participle, which agrees with the subject.

However, there is an exception to this general rule: If the reflexive verb is used with a direct object in addition to the reflexive pronoun, as in *elle s'est lavé les mains,* the past participle does not agree with the subject (nor with the reflexive pronoun). This is because the past participle agrees with the subject and reflexive pronoun only when the reflexive pronoun is truly the direct object of the action. In the preceding sentence, although the verb uses the reflexive pronoun, the actual direct object of the action is *les mains,* which follows the verb; so the past participle does not agree with the subject and the reflexive pronoun. If *les mains* were to be dropped from the sentence, then the reflexive pronoun would regain its function as the object of the sentence, and the past participle would agree with the subject and the reflexive pronoun: *elle s'est lavée.*

SUBJECT PRONOUN	REFLEXIVE PRONOUN	*ÊTRE* IN THE PRESENT TENSE	PAST PARTICIPLE WITH AGREEMENT	ENGLISH TRANSLATION
je	*me*	*suis*	*lavé(e)*	I washed myself
tu	*t'*	*es*	*regardé(e)*	you looked at yourself
il/elle/on	*s'*	*est*	*levé(e)*	he/she /one got up
nous	*nous*	*sommes*	*dépêché(e)s*	we hurried
vous	*vous*	*êtes*	*amusé(e)(s)*	you enjoyed yourself/yourselves,
ils/elles	*se*	*sont*	*rencontré(e)s*	they met each other

- **Translation of the *Passé Composé*.**

Although the *passé composé* in French is structurally identical to the compound past in English (e.g., *il a mangé* follows the exact same word pattern as *he has eaten*), the *passé composé* is used in French where in English we would commonly use the simple past (*he ate*). Therefore, the most common translation of the *passé composé* in French is the simple past tense in English. For example, *j'ai donné* is most commonly translated as *I gave.* Occasionally it may sound better to use the compound past in English, but only the context in which the verb is used, together with your ear for the idiom of English, can tell you which translation—simple past or compound past, *I gave* or *I have given*—will sound better.

This applies to verbs that take *avoir* as well as to those that take *être*. However, in those cases where the context suggests that a verb that takes *être* would best be translated by the compound past in English, *être must be translated as though it were avoir,* because English has only one auxiliary verb—*to have*—for all verbs in any compound tense. For example, *Je suis venu* is most often translated as *I came.* But should we want to translate it into the compound past in English, it would never be translated literally as *I am come,* but only as *I have come.*

When conjugating verbs in the *passé composé*, both English translations—the simple past and the compound past—are given. The simple past is given first, indicating that it is the more common of the two possible translations:

j'ai parlé	I spoke, I have spoken
elle est tombée	she fell, she has fallen

Examples of the *passé composé* (and all other tenses) of some regular, irregular, and reflexive verbs are given in the appendix at the end of the book.

7.3. THE *PASSÉ COMPOSÉ* IN THE NEGATIVE FORM

In the negative form, the *ne* precedes the auxiliary verb, or in the case of reflexive verbs, the *ne* precedes the reflexive pronoun. The *pas* (or other complement to the *ne*, as will be seen in chapter 9) follows immediately after the auxiliary verb:

je n'ai pas parlé	I didn't speak, I have not spoken
tu n'as pas vu	you didn't see, you have not seen
il/elle/on n'est pas descendu(e)	he/she/one didn't go down, has not gone down
nous ne sommes pas sorti(e)s	we didn't go out, we have not gone out
vous ne vous êtes pas amusé(e)(s)	you didn't enjoy yourself/selves, you haven't enjoyed yourself/selves
ils/elles ne se sont pas souvenu(e)s	they didn't remember, they haven't remembered

7.4. *AVOIR* AND *ÊTRE* IN THE *PASSÉ COMPOSÉ*

Avoir and *être* are surprisingly regular in their formation of the *passé composé*. All that is irregular about them is their past participles, which should be learned and memorized now:

INFINITIVE	PAST PARTICIPLE	ENGLISH TRANSLATION
avoir	*eu*	had
être	*été*	been

Both verbs take *avoir* as their auxiliary verb:

j'ai eu	I had, I have had	*j'ai été*	I was, I have been
tu as eu	you had, you have had	*tu as été*	you were, you have been
il/elle/on a eu	he/she/one had, has had	*il/elle/on a été*	he/she/one was, has been
nous avons eu	we had, we have had	*nous avons été*	we were, we have been
vous avez eu	you had, you have had	*vous avez été*	you were, you have been
ils/elles ont eu	they had, they have had	*ils/elles ont été*	they were, they have been

Be careful not to confuse *have* and *had* as auxiliary verbs in English—they are not at all interchangeable. Whenever the *passé composé* is to be translated as the compound past in English and the auxiliary is to be translated as a separate word (rather than the more common translation of the *passé composé* as the simple past in English), the auxiliary verb can only be translated as *have* or *has,* but *never* as *had.*

j'ai trouvé	I found, I *have* found
il a eu	he had, he *has* had

In both of the preceding cases, *have* or *has* is the auxiliary verb. In the case of *il a eu* = *he has had, had* is the past participle, not the auxiliary verb. (For the use of *had* as an auxiliary verb in the pluperfect tense, see chapter 17, section 17.1.)

7.5. THE *PASSÉ COMPOSÉ* USED TOGETHER WITH THE *IMPARFAIT*

In sentences that combine the *passé composé* with the *imparfait,* the importance of always trying the *I was doing* form first when translating the *imparfait* becomes clear. Consider the following sentence: *Quand Marie est arrivée, Jean finissait son travail.* If we use the translation rules laid out in chapter 5. section 5.3 and begin by translating the *imparfait* as the continuous past in English, we get the following translation: *When Marie arrived, John was finishing his work,* which indicates that John was in the midst of working when Marie arrived, and may even have continued working once she arrived. This gives a distinctly different temporal significance than if we were to translate the *imparfait* as the second option given in chapter 5 (i.e., the simple past): *When Marie arrived, John finished his work,* which erroneously indicates that upon Marie's arrival, John closed up shop and finished his work there and then.

The problem is that both of the preceding translations are viable sentences in English, even though the second one does not capture the intent of the French. Because the second translation is perfectly good English, the novice translator has no way of knowing that it is nonetheless an incorrect translation. Hence the necessity of memorizing the rules governing the translation of the *imparfait* in chapter 5, section 5.3.: Always first consider the *I was doing* translation. Only if and when this option clearly does not work in English can the translator move on to consider the other options.

7.6. THE *PASSÉ COMPOSÉ* WITH ADVERBS

When an adverb is used to modify the verb in the *passé composé*, it is often placed *in between* the auxiliary verb and the past participle:

Ils ont beaucoup aimé la nouvelle voiture.   They really liked the new car. (They liked the new car a lot.)

Translation Exercise A

1. J'ai cherché son livre dans la bibliothèque.
2. Ils ont regardé le film à la télévision.
3. Les enfants sont arrivés à l'heure.[1]
4. Elle n'est pas entrée dans la chambre.
5. Il est né le 5 décembre 1965.
6. Il a perdu son stylo.
7. Nous ne sommes pas allés au cinéma.
8. Avez-vous vu[2] mon frère?
9. J'ai écrit trois lettres cet après-midi.
10. Je me suis levée à six heures du matin.
11. Il est sorti de la voiture.
12. Il a sorti la voiture du garage.
13. Elle n'a pas fini son travail.
14. Les enfants se sont lavé les mains.
15. Le pilote a volé partout dans le monde.
16. Je suis monté sur le pont pour regarder le fleuve en bas.
17. Nous avons beaucoup lu pendant le cours.
18. Ils ont pris le train pour aller en ville.
19. Il s'est brossé les dents.
20. Nous sommes descendus de l'autobus.
21. Elle est partie après le dîner.
22. Nous mangions quand mon père est entré.
23. Après de nombreux échecs, l'écrivain a reçu un prix.
24. Il a eu l'air très surpris.

---

1. *à l'heure:* on time
2. *vu:* past participle of *voir*, to see.

25. Les grands événements ont eu des suites incalculables.

26. Ils sont venus de très loin.

27. Le marchand a installé une chaise devant sa porte et il s'est assis à côté de moi.

28. Vous avez fait beaucoup de progrès.

7.7. PAST PARTICIPLES USED AS PREDICATE ADJECTIVES IN THE PRESENT TENSE COMPARED WITH PAST PARTICIPLES USED IN THE *PASSÉ COMPOSÉ* TO FORM THE PAST TENSE

Verbs in the *passé composé* that take *être* can easily be confused with the past participle used as a predicate adjective with *être* in the present tense, as described in the previous chapter. It's best to confront this potential confusion head on, because it tends to crop up again and again. When you come across *être* in the present tense followed by a past participle, how can you know whether this is the *passé composé* with *être* as the auxiliary verb or whether it is part of a predicate adjectival structure? In the first case, the correct translation is the past tense, whereas in the second case, the correct translation is the present tense.

The only way to distinguish between these two possibilities is to determine whether the past participle in question belongs to one of the two groups of verbs that take *être* as their auxiliary verb in the *passé composé*: Is it one of the twenty intransitive verbs that take *être* in the *passé composé*, or is it a reflexive verb? If the verb is indeed one of the twenty verbs that take *être* as their auxiliary, or is reflexive, then the entire verb—*être* in the present tense + the past participle—*is translated in the past tense*: *il est venu* = he came, he has come; *il s'est levé* = he got up.

If, however, the past participle that follows *être* is *not* a reflexive verb and is *not* one of the twenty intransitive verbs that take *être* in the *passé composé*, then it is being used as a predicate adjective with *être*, and *être* must be *translated in the present tense*: *le livre est publié* = the book is published.

This can be seen in the following two sentences that are structurally identical but that represent two different tenses:

> *L'autobus est arrivé. Arriver* is one of the twenty intransitive verbs that always take *être* as their auxiliary verb, so this is the *passé composé* (past tense). The bus ARRIVED *or* The bus HAS ARRIVED..
>
> *Le gâteau est mangé. Manger* is not one of the twenty verbs that take *être*, nor is it reflexive: *Mangé* is being used as a predicate adjective, so this is the *present tense*. The cake IS eaten.

Translation Exercise B

Translate these sentences, distinguishing between the past participle used as part of the *passé composé*, on the one hand, and the past participle as predicate adjective, on the other:

1. Les étudiants sont déjà partis en vacances.
2. Toutes les portes et les fenêtres sont fermées.
3. Les utilisateurs de Wikipédia sont invités à écrire des articles eux-mêmes.[3]
4. Après le concert, les musiciens sont rentrés à l'hôtel.
5. Ils sont convaincus que[4] leur candidat est le meilleur.
6. Les fruits destinés à faire la confiture remplissent des camions.
7. Les nouveaux cosmétiques sont faits à base d'huile d'olive.
8. Les deux politiciens se sont rencontrés en privé.
9. Le camion est venu remorquer la voiture.
10. Les enfants sont arrivés à l'école en retard.
11. Il est né en France mais il a vécu au Canada.
12. Beaucoup de romans intéressants sont publiés chaque année.
13. Les réfugiés sont confrontés à des problèmes d'immigration.
14. Cuba est devenu le nouveau sujet de conversation des candidats à la Maison Blanche.
15. L'exploitation optimale des nouvelles opportunités multimédia est restée un enjeu majeur pour les entreprises de presse.

7.8. TRANSLATION PASSAGE

LE PETIT CHAPERON ROUGE

Il était une fois une jeune fille qui s'appelait Le Petit Chaperon rouge. Un beau matin, sa mère lui[5] a dit de prendre un gâteau et une bouteille de vin et d'aller chez sa grand-mère, qui était malade. Sa grand-mère habitait à une demie-heure de marche du village, de l'autre côté de la forêt. Alors le Petit Chaperon rouge est sortie de sa maison avec le gâteau et le vin, et elle est entrée dans la forêt. Dans la forêt, elle a rencontré un loup, mais elle n'était pas effrayée, car elle ignorait qu'il était une bête méchante et cruelle.

---

3. *eux-mêmes:* themselves
4. *que:* that. See chapter 11, section 11.6, and chapter 14, section 14.1.2.
5. *lui:* to her

—Bonjour, Petit Chaperon rouge, a dit le loup. Où[6] vas-tu donc de si bonne heure[7]?

—Je vais chez ma grand-mère, qui est malade, a répondu le Petit Chaperon rouge.

—Et où habite-t-elle? a demandé le loup.

—Plus loin dans la forêt, a répondu le Petit Chaperon rouge.

Cette fille et sa grand-mère feront[8] un repas délicieux, s'est dit le loup.

Et pendant que le Petit Chaperon rouge cueillait des fleurs pour offrir un bouquet à sa grand-mère, le loup a vite couru chez la grand-mère.

Une fois arrivé[9] chez la grand-mère, le loup a frappé à la porte.

—Qui est là? a crié la grand-mère.

—C'est moi, Petit Chaperon rouge, a crié le loup d'une voix aigüe.

—Ouvre[10] la porte toi-même[11], ma chère enfant, je suis trop faible pour me lever.

Le loup a ouvert la porte, il a sauté sur la grand-mère et il l'a avalée.[12] Ensuite, il a mis la chemise et le bonnet de nuit de la vieille dame, il a fermé les rideaux et il s'est couché dans le lit.

Quand le Petit Chaperon rouge est arrivée devant la maison de sa grand-mère, elle était surprise de trouver la porte ouverte et la pièce plongée dans l'obscurité.

—Bonjour, grand-mère, a-t-elle dit.

Mais il n'y avait pas[13] de réponse.

Alors elle s'est avancée vers le lit. Sa grand-mère était là, mais elle avait un air bien étrange.

—Oh, grand-mère! a crié le Petit Chaperon rouge, comme tu as de grandes oreilles!

---

6. *où:* where
7. *de si bonne heure:* so early
8. *feront:* will make
9. *Une fois arrivé:* Once having arrived
10. *Ouvre:* Open
11. *toi-même:* yourself
12. *il l'a avalée:* he swallowed her
13. *il n'y avait pas:* there wasn't

DIRECT AND INDIRECT OBJECT PRONOUNS

8.1. RECOGNIZING OBJECTS IN TRANSITIVE SENTENCES

To understand the use and placement of direct and indirect object pronouns in French, it's a good idea to reflect for a moment on the use of direct and indirect objects in general:

Direct objects occur in transitive sentences. Transitive sentences are sentences in which the subject performs an action that is transferred to another person or thing, the *object*. In the sentence "He washes the table," *He* is the subject, *washes* is the transitive verb that transfers the action performed by the subject to *the table,* which is the *direct object*. The subject performs the action, the verb expresses the action, and the direct object receives the action expressed by the verb. This same pattern of transitive sentences is found in French as well:

SUBJECT	VERB	DEFINITE ARTICLE	DIRECT OBJECT
Il	lave	la	table.

8.2. DIRECT OBJECT PRONOUNS: MEANING AND PLACEMENT

Sometimes the direct object is replaced by a pronoun: the *direct object pronoun*. In English, the direct object pronoun is put in the same place in the sentence as the direct object that it replaces:

He washes the table.   She loves her son.
He washes *it*.   She loves *him*.

In French, however, unlike in English, once a direct object is replaced by a direct object pronoun, its position in the sentence is changed. Direct objects that are nouns are placed after the verb; but all direct object *pronouns* *precede* the verb:

Il lave la table.	He washes the table.
Il la *lave.*	He washes it.
Il lavait la table.	He was washing the table.
Il la *lavait.*	He was washing it.

In French, each grammatical *person* (first, second, and third persons singular and plural) has its own, specific direct object pronoun, which should be learned and memorized now:

	SUBJECT PRONOUN	CORRESPONDING DIRECT OBJECT PRONOUN	ENGLISH TRANSLATION
1st person sing.	*je*	*me*	me
2nd person sing.	*tu*	*te*	you
3rd person sing.	*il, elle, on*	*le, la*	him, her, it
1st person pl.	*nous*	*nous*	us
2nd person pl.	*vous*	*vous*	you
3rd person pl.	*ils, elles*	*les*	them

Note that the direct object pronouns for the first and second persons singular and plural are the same as the reflexive pronouns for these persons. Indeed, *me, te, nous,* and *vous* are all reflexive pronouns when the subject pronoun is, respectively, *je, tu, nous,* or *vous* (i.e., they are reflexive pronouns when the subject is the same *person* or *thing* as the object), but they are object pronouns when the subject is a different *person* or *thing* than the object.

Je me regarde dans le miroir.	I look at myself in the mirror.
Nous nous dépêchons.	We hurry up.

The French *me* in the first sentence and the second *nous* in the second sentence are both reflexive pronouns: They each refer to the same person as the subject of their sentences.

L'homme me regarde.	The man looks at me.

Here the French *me* is a direct object pronoun and not a reflexive pronoun because it refers to a different person from the subject: The subject is the third person singular (the man), whereas the object is first person singular (me). Similarly, in the sentence

L'homme nous regardait dans la rue.   The man was looking at us in the street.

nous is the direct object pronoun, because the subject, *L'homme,* is the third person singular, that is, a different person than *nous,* the first person plural.

8.3. *LE, LA,* AND *LES* AS DIRECT OBJECT PRONOUNS

Looking back at the chart of direct object pronouns, note that the third person singular direct object pronouns are *le* and *la,* and the third person plural direct object pronoun is *les.* These words are, of course, the very same as the definite articles. How will you know in any given sentence whether *le, la,* or *les* is to be translated as a definite article or as a direct object pronoun?

Definite articles always precede the *noun* they modify, or else they precede another adjective that already precedes the noun in question. But direct object pronouns always precede the *verb.* Therefore, *le, la,* and *les* will be translated as direct object pronouns when they are followed by a verb, but they will be translated as definite articles if they are followed by a noun, or by a preceding adjective followed by a noun:

Où est le *livre?*	Where is the book?	*le* = definite article	(the)
Je le *lis maintenant.*	I am reading it now.	*le* = direct object pronoun	(it)
Aime-t-il les *pommes?*	Does he like apples?	*les* = definite article	(the)
Oui, il les *aime beaucoup.*	Yes, he likes them a lot.	*les* = direct object pronoun	(them)

8.4. DIRECT OBJECT PRONOUNS IN THE *PASSÉ COMPOSÉ*: PLACEMENT AND AGREEMENT

The direct object pronoun is always placed before the verb. When the verb is in the *passé composé,* the direct object pronoun is placed before the *auxiliary* verb.

J'ai lu le livre.	I read the book.
Je l'ai lu.	I read it.

This leads us back to the seventh and last rule for the formation of the *passé composé,* as given in chapter 7, section 7.2. In the *passé composé* with verbs that take *avoir,* when the direct object precedes the verb (as it always does when the direct object is a pronoun), the past participle must agree in number and gender with the *direct object:*

J'ai mangé les pommes.	I ate the apples.	(direct object follows the verb)
Je les ai mangées.	I ate them.	(direct object pronoun precedes the verb)

Note the ending *-es* appended to *mangé* in the last example, making the past participle agree with the direct object pronoun *les,* which precedes the verb and which refers to *les pommes,* which is feminine plural. Since direct object *pronouns* always precede the verb, whenever there is a direct object pronoun in a sentence with the *passé composé,* the past participle will agree in number and gender with the direct object pronoun. In these cases, the ending of the past participle is often the best guide to the gender of the direct object:

Je l'ai vu hier.	I saw him (or it) yesterday.
Je l'ai vue hier.	I saw her (or it) yesterday.

In both cases, even if the direct object pronoun refers to a thing (it), we know the gender of the word to which it refers.

8.5. INDIRECT OBJECT PRONOUNS: MEANING AND PLACEMENT

An indirect object is the person (or thing) *to* or *for* which (or whom) the action of the verb is occurring:

I was reading *the book.*	*the book* is the direct object.
I was reading the book *to him.*	*to him* is the indirect object.

French has a specific indirect object pronoun for each of the six grammatical persons, which should be learned and memorized now:

	SUBJECT PRONOUN	DIRECT OBJECT PRONOUN	INDIRECT OBJECT PRONOUN	ENGLISH TRANSLATION OF INDIRECT OBJ. PRONOUN
1st person sing.	*je*	*me*	*me*	to me, for me
2nd person sing.	*tu*	*te*	*te*	to you, for you
3rd person sing.	*il, elle, on*	*le, la*	*lui*	to/for him, her, it

1st person pl.	*nous*	*nous*	*nous*	to us, for us
2nd person pl.	*vous*	*vous*	*vous*	to you, for you
3rd person pl.	*ils, elles*	*les*	*leur*	to them, for them

Indirect objects, too, are always placed before the verb. But past participles never agree with indirect objects.

J'ai lu le livre.	I read the book.
Je lui ai donné le livre.	I gave the book to her/him.
Je le lui ai donné.	I gave it to him.

Again, the first and second person singular and plural indirect object pronouns (*me, te, nous,* and *vous*) are the same words as those used for the first and second person singular direct object pronouns, as well as for the reflexive pronouns. It seems as though it would be difficult to tell when to translate the French words *me, te, nous,* or *vous* as direct object pronouns and when to translate them as indirect object pronouns, because they are the same words in both cases. However, as with the multiple translations for *des,* the sentence itself will almost always clue you in. The presence of another object pronoun that is incontrovertibly a direct object pronoun will let you know that the ambiguous pronoun (the pronoun that can be translated in more than one way) is an indirect object pronoun, and vice versa:

Il me regarde.	He looks at me.
Il me le donne.	He gives it to me.

In the first sentence, *me* is the direct object. In the second sentence, *le* precedes the verb, so it is a direct object pronoun; therefore the *me* in this case has to be the indirect pronoun: *to me.*

Another possible source of confusion is the indirect object pronoun *leur,* meaning *to them* or *for them.* This is the same word as the third person plural possessive adjective, *leur,* meaning *their.* The difference between the two can be seen by recognizing that, like definite articles, possessive adjectives always precede nouns, whereas indirect objects always precede verbs.

Je leur *donne mes livres.*	*leur* = indirect object	I give my books to them.
Ils me donnent leur *piano.*	*leur* = possessive adjective	They give me their piano.
Ils me donnent leurs *livres.*	*leurs* = possessive adjective	They give me their books.

Translation Exercise A

1. Je l'ai cherché partout.
2. Elle le regarde toujours.
3. Je lui ai donné le livre.
4. Il le mangeait avec plaisir.
5. L'enfant leur obéit.
6. Elle les a donnés à Marie.
7. Il se brosse les dents.
8. Elle leur donne un cadeau.
9. J'étais très content de vous voir.
10. Il ne m'a pas parlé.
11. Je lui ai parlé de ma sœur.
12. Ils m'ont donné leurs livres.
13. Ils me les ont donnés.
14. Je lui ai écrit deux lettres.
15. Je les ai écrites hier.
16. Nous lisons ce livre. Nous le trouvons difficile.
17. Je ne lisais pas quand tu es venu.
18. Le journaliste décrit la situation aux lecteurs. Il la leur décrit en détail.
19. L'écrivain m'a expliqué le sens des mots latins dans le texte.
20. J'ai pensé à cette histoire pendant quelques instants, puis je l'ai oubliée.
21. Sa conviction l'a soutenu dans ce travail long et ardu.
22. Les magistrats ont estimé qu'il est dans l'intérêt de l'enfant d'avoir des liens juridiques avec les adultes qui l'ont désiré et élevé depuis sa naissance.

8.6. THE PARTITIVE PRONOUN *EN*

Review the partitive use of *de la, du,* and *des,* discussed earlier in chapter 1, sections 1.7 and 1.8. The direct object pronouns *le, la,* and *les* replace nouns that have been preceded by a definite article (*le, la,* or *les*). But when a direct object preceded by the partitive *de la, du,* or *des* is replaced by a pronoun, the pronoun it is replaced by is the partitive pronoun *en.* The partitive pronoun *en* therefore stands for *part of* or *some of* the noun to which it refers. *En* can be translated by any of the meanings of *de* plus a pronoun referring to the noun indicated. Thus *en* can mean: *of it, of them; from it; from them; some; some of it; some of them; not any* (in the negative); and occasionally, *from there.*

Because this word is so small, novice translators tend to overlook it. Be sure always to account for the meaning of *en* in your translations!

Il m'a envoyé l'argent.	He sent *the* money to me.
Il me l'a envoyé.	He sent *it* to me.

Il m'a envoyé de l'argent.	He sent *some* money to me.
Il m'en a envoyé.	He sent *some* to me.

Jean a beaucoup d'amis.	John has a lot *of* friends.
Il en a beaucoup.	He has a lot *of them.*

Que pensez-vous de ce livre?	What do you think *of this* book?
Qu'en pensez-vous?	What do you think *of it?*

Je n'ai pas de cigarettes.	I don't have *any* cigarettes.
Je n'en ai pas.	I don't have *any.*

8.7. THE PRONOUN *Y*

The pronoun *y* has two distinct, unrelated meanings. *Y* refers to a place. It means *there,* as in the answer to the question *where? Y* can also be used as an indirect object pronoun when the indirect object pronoun refers to a thing rather than to a person:

Est-il à la maison? Oui, il y est.	Is he at the house? Yes, he is *there.*
Le livre est sur la table. Le livre y est.	The book is on the table. The book is *there.*
Avez-vous répondu à sa lettre? Oui, j'y ai répondu.	Have you replied to his letter? Yes, I have replied *to it.*
Il pense à sa leçon. Il y pense.	He is thinking about his lesson. He is thinking *about it.*

8.8. THE ORDER OF OBJECT PRONOUNS WHEN THERE ARE MORE THAN ONE OF THEM

me	precedes							
te	"	*le*	precede	*lui*				
nous	"	*la*	"	*leur*	precede	*y*	precedes	*en*
vous	"	*les*						

Notice that this order does not follow grammatical function; that is, one cannot say that direct object pronouns precede indirect object pronouns or vice versa. *Me, te, nous,* and *vous* will precede any other pronouns, whatever their grammatical function:

Il me le donne.	He gives it to me.	*me* is the indirect object, preceding *le*, the direct object: here the indirect object precedes the direct object
Il le lui donne.	He gives it to him.	*le* is the direct object, preceding *lui*, the indirect object: here the direct object precedes the indirect object

Translation Exercise B

1. Avez-vous une auto? Oui, j'en ai une.
2. Voulez-vous[1] encore du café? Non, merci, j'en ai bu assez.
3. A-t-il donné de l'argent à Paul? Oui, il lui en a donné.
4. Vend-on des ordinateurs à l'université? Oui, on en vend de très bons.
5. Quelle[2] belle robe! J'en aime surtout la couleur.
6. Il a acheté cette maison parce qu'[3] il en aime le style.
7. La grandeur des malfaisances économiques crée un orgueil secret à ceux[4] qui en profitent.
8. La nouvelle traduction lui en a donné une vision incomparable.
9. Il n'a pas mentionné cette question dans son livre parce qu'il voulait en faire une étude spécifique.
10. Au lieu de[5] revenir chez lui trois jours plus tard, il y est retourné le lendemain.
11. Une approche simpliste risque d'être contre-productive: plusieurs exemples en témoignent.
12. Quand on étudie l'histoire du passé, on y voit le développement des institutions sociales.

---

1. *Voulez-vous?* Do you want? From *vouloir,* to want. See chapter 10, section 10.2.
2. *Quelle:* What! Feminine form of exclamatory adjective *quel.* See chapter 16, section 16.2.
3. *parce qu'* (short for *parce que*): because
4. *ceux:* those. See chapter 11, section 11.3.
5. *au lieu de:* instead of

8.9. TRANSLATION PASSAGE

LA BELLE AU BOIS DORMANT[6]

Il était une fois un Roi et une Reine qui ont donné naissance à une petite fille. Ils ont invité au baptême toutes les fées du pays. Chaque fée lui a fait un don, et par ce moyen la petite princesse avait toutes les perfections imaginables. Mais tout d'un coup,[7] une vieille fée est arrivée, qui n'avait pas été[8] invitée au baptême. La vieille fée croyait que tout le monde la méprisait. Elle aussi voulait donner un don à la princesse. Mais elle a dit: « La princesse se percera la main et elle en mourra ».[9]

Toute la compagnie avait peur pour la petite princesse. Mais une jeune fée est venue et a dit: « La princesse n'en mourra pas. Elle se percera la main; mais au lieu d'en mourir, elle va tomber dans un profond sommeil qui va durer cent ans. À ce moment-là le fils d'un roi viendra[10] la réveiller ».

Seize ans plus tard, la jeune princesse jouait un jour dans le château. Par hasard, elle a rencontré une bonne vieille en train de[11] filer.

- Que faites-vous là, ma bonne femme ? a dit la Princesse.

- Je file, lui a répondu la vieille.

- Comment le faites-vous? a dit la princesse. Et elle a pris le fuseau, elle s'est percée la main, et elle est tombée évanouie.

Le roi s'est souvenu de la prédiction des fées et il a mis la princesse dans le plus bel appartement du palais, sur un lit en broderie d'or et d'argent.

Au bout de cent ans, le fils d'un roi d'une autre famille royale est allé à la chasse. Il a vu un grand château dans la forêt, et il a demandé ce que c'était.[12] Les uns[13]

---

6. Freely adapted from Charles Perrault, *Contes de ma mère l'Oye* (Mother Goose Tales), first published in 1697. For the original see Charles Perrault, *Contes,* © Éditions Rencontre, 1968, pp. 181–193.

7. *tout d'un coup:* all of a sudden

8. *qui n'avait pas été:* who had not been. Pluperfect tense. See chapter 17, section 17.1.

9. *se percera la main:* will pierce her hand. *mourra:* will die. Future tense of *se percer* and *mourir.* For the future tense, see chapter 12.

10. *viendra:* will come. Future tense of venir.

11. *en train de:* in the midst of

12. *ce que c'était:* what it was

13. *Les uns:* some

disaient que les sorciers y faisaient leur sabbat. Les autres disaient qu'un ogre y demeurait. Mais un vieux paysan lui a dit :

« Dans ce château dort une princesse, la plus belle du monde; elle va y dormir cent ans, et le fils d'un roi va la réveiller » .

Le prince est entré dans le château et il a vu sur un lit une princesse qui paraissait avoir seize ans, et qui avait quelque chose de lumineux et de divin. Il s'est approché et il s'est mis à genoux auprès d'elle. Puis il lui a donné un baiser d'amour et la princesse s'est éveillée, mettant fin à[14] l'enchantement.

---

14. *mettant fin à:* putting an end to

ADDITIONAL FORMS OF THE NEGATIVE

9.1. GENERAL PATTERN

Although ne . . . pas is the basic form of the negative in French, translated as *not* in English, French has many other negative expressions, as does English. One may *no longer* do something, one may *never* do something, one may do *nothing,* and so on. In French, whatever the negative expression may be, it (almost) always begins with *ne* preceding the verb. After the verb, *pas* may be replaced by any of the following more specific words of negation:

	NEGATION	ENGLISH TRANSLATION	PART OF SPEECH
	aucun, -e	no (thing), none of	preceding adjective
	guère	hardly, scarcely	adverb
	jamais	never	adverb
	ni . . . ni	neither . . . nor	conjunction
ne + verb +	*nul, -le*	no (thing)	preceding adjective
	nul	no one	pronoun
	personne	no one	pronoun
	plus	no longer	adverb
	point	not, not at all	adverb
	rien	nothing	pronoun

But be careful—when used *without ne,* some of these words have a positive meaning:

aucun, -e	any
jamais	ever
la personne	the person

Whenever you come across a *ne* in a sentence, the first thing you have to do is find the other half that accompanies it: *ne* is an indication that a negation is on the way, but only the second word tells you what the specific negative expression is.

Elle *ne* va *plus* à l'école.	She *no longer* goes to school.
Il *ne* lit *jamais* les journaux sur la Toile.	He *never* reads the newspapers on the Web.
Il *ne* mange *aucun* dessert.	He *doesn't* eat *any* desert.
Je *n*'aime *ni* le café *ni* le thé.	I like *neither* coffee *nor* tea / I *don't* like *either* coffee or tea.

In the *passé composé,* the *ne* precedes the auxiliary verb (or, in the case of reflexive verbs, it precedes the reflexive pronoun); and the other part of the negative phrase follows the auxiliary verb, preceding the past participle:

Elle *n'est plus* allée à l'école.	She *no longer* went to school.
Il *n'a jamais* lu les journaux sur la Toile.	He *never* read the newspapers on the Web.
Il *n'a pas* mangé *aucun* dessert.	He *didn't* eat *any* desert.
Je *n'ai pas* bu *ni* le café *ni* le thé.	I *didn't* drink *either* coffee or tea/I drank *neither* coffer nor tea.

9.2. IRREGULARITIES IN VARIOUS FORMS OF THE NEGATIVE

9.2.1. WORD ORDER

The basic sentence order of *ne* + verb + other half of negative phrase can change when the negative word that accompanies *ne* is a noun that is the subject of the sentence. As nouns, *personne, rien,* or *nul* may function as subjects of sentences, in which case they will be placed at the very beginning of the sentence and will be followed by the *ne,* which in turn will be followed by the verb:

Personne ne *va au spectacle ce soir.*	No one is going to the show this evening.
Rien n'*est impossible à ceux qui travaillent fort.*	Nothing is impossible for those who work hard.
Nul n'*est censé ignorer la loi.*	No one is supposed not to know the law. (ignorance of the law is no excuse)

Similarly, if one of the negative preceding adjectives (*aucun, aucune; nul, nulle*) modifies a noun that is the subject of the sentence, the preceding negative adjective will come first, then the subject, followed by the *ne* and then the verb:

Aucun *livre ne traite de ce sujet.*	*No* book deals with this subject.
Nul *bonheur* n'existe *sans la faculté d'oubli.*[1]	*No* happiness exists without the ability to forget.

With infinitives, the two parts of the negative stay together and are both placed before the verb:

Ne pas *fumer.*	*No* smoking. (*Literally:* not to smoke)
C'est difficile de ne jamais *voir son pays natal.*	It is difficult never to see one's native country (again).

Non pas together, and alone, means *not:*

Le problème de l'Homme est celui de la Culture: non pas *un mouvement linéaire, mais un double mouvement centripète et centrifuge.*[2]

The problem of Man is that of Culture: *not* a linear movement but a double movement, centripetal and centrifugal.

As responses to questions, *personne* and *rien* can be used alone, as single words without *ne,* to signify *no one* and *nothing:*

Que fait-il? Rien.	What is he doing? Nothing.
Qui est dans la maison? Personne.	Who is in the house? No one.

9.2.2. *NE . . . QUE* MEANS ONLY

When *ne* is not accompanied by any of the previously mentioned negative words, it may be accompanied by *que.* Together, *ne . . . que* means *only:* memorize this four-word rule now. The *que* may be at a distance from the *ne* and/or from the verb; place the *only* at that place in the sentence where the *que* is found.

Il n'a qu'une sœur.
He has only one sister. (or: He has but one sister.)

Cet aspect de la théorie n'est qu'une petite parenthèse dans sa pensée.
This aspect of the theory is only a small parenthesis in his (her) thought.

---

1. Abbreviation of a famous line from Nietzsche in *La généalogie de la morale (The Genealogy of Morals)*: "Nul bonheur, nulle sérénité, nulle espérance, nulle fierté, nulle jouissance de l'instant présent ne pourrait exister sans la faculté d'oubli." http://www.webphilo.com/textes/voir.php?numero=453061508, retrieved November 26, 2011.
2. Loosely borrowed from the translation passage by Léopold Senghor at the end of chapter 11.

Les touristes n'utilisent que des bicyclettes pour faire le tour de la ville.
The tourists use only bicycles to tour the city.

Les touristes n'utilisent des bicyclettes que pour faire le tour de la ville.
The tourists use bicycles only for touring the city.

Associated with this use of *que*, the phrase *rien que* means *nothing but:*

La vérité, rien que *la vérité.*   The truth, *nothing but* the truth.

9.2.3. *NE FAIRE QUE*

Ne faire que followed by an infinitive means *to do nothing but,* or *to do* something *incessantly.*

Il ne fait que travailler.   He does nothing but work/He works all the time.
Elle ne fait que parler avec ses amies.   She does nothing but talk with her friends.

9.2.4. *NE . . . PLUS . . . QUE*

Ne . . . plus . . . que means *no longer . . . (anything) except.* Occasionally, *ne* will be accompanied by both *plus* and *que* in order to express the meaning of *no longer . . . except.* In these cases, we usually need to insert an extra word—*anything*—into the sentence so that it fully makes sense in English.

Il ne travaille plus que sur son projet.   He no longer works on anything except his project.

Mon ami ne pense plus qu'à sa famille.   My friend no longer thinks of anything except his family.

The word *que* has multiple functions and meanings in French, as will be seen in chapter 11, section 11.6 and chapter 16, section 16.1.1. Only consider the *que* as part of a *ne . . . que, ne faire que,* or *ne . . . plus . . . que* construction if there is no other negative word that accompanies the *ne* in the sentence.

9.2.5. VERBS THAT CAN USE *NE* ALONE TO EXPRESS THE NEGATIVE

Sometimes verbs in French are able to use *ne* all by itself, without any complement such as *pas, rien, jamais, plus,* etc., to fully indicate the negative. The four verbs that regularly do this are *cesser* (to cease), *oser* (to dare), *pouvoir* (to be able), and *savoir* (to know). You can remember them by their acronym, *COPS.* However, other verbs following the pronouns *qui, que,* or *quel* may occasionally also use *ne* without *pas* (as in Article III of the translation passage at the end of this chapter). Thus the following sentences are translated in the negative, even though they seem to be missing half of the negative construction:

Il ne pouvait venir ce soir.	He couldn't come this evening.
Il ne savait ce qu'il disait.	He didn't know what he was saying.
Elle ne cesse de parler.	She doesn't (ever) stop talking.
Il n'osait dire la vérité.	He didn't dare say the truth.

Translation Exercise A

1. Nous n'avons pas eu de vacances cet été.
2. Elle ne joue plus du piano.
3. Personne n'a répondu à ma question.
4. Elle ne lave jamais le plancher.
5. Il ne lisait rien d'intéressant dans le journal.
6. Je ne mange jamais de viande.
7. Les choses ne sont plus très simples.
8. Elle ne finit jamais ses devoirs. Elle ne finit jamais rien.
9. Il ne parlait guère de sa jeunesse.
10. Aucun des acteurs ne jouait le rôle attendu.[3]
11. Il ne perd aucune occasion de poser des questions difficiles.
12. L'inefficacité énergétique des ordinateurs ne trouble personne.
13. On ne trouve nulle part ailleurs un cas pareil.
14. Personne n'est resté en ville pendant les vacances.
15. Ils ne se sont plus souvenus de leur histoire collective.
16. Nous ne sommes intelligents collectivement que grâce aux différents savoirs transmis de génération en génération.
17. La majorité des Roms en Italie possède un passeport yougoslave, qui ne correspond plus à aucun[4] pays existant.
18. La compétition mondiale autour des ressources minérales ne peut[5] qu'aller plus loin.

---

3. *attendu:* expected. Past participle of attendre.
4. *aucun:* any
5. *peut:* present tense of *pouvoir*, to be able (see chapter 10, section 10.2., -oir verbs)

9.3. TRANSLATION PASSAGE

DÉCLARATION DES DROITS DE L'HOMME ET DU CITOYEN DE 1789[6]

Article premier: Les hommes naissent[7] et demeurent libres et égaux en droits. Les distinctions sociales ne peuvent[8] être fondées que sur l'utilité commune.

Article II: Le but de toute association politique est la conservation des droits naturels et imprescriptibles de l'homme. Ces droits sont la liberté, la propriété, la sûreté et la résistance à l'oppression.

Article III: Le principe de toute Souveraineté réside essentiellement dans la Nation. Nul corps, nul individu ne peut exercer d'autorité qui n'en émane expressément.

Article IV: La liberté consiste à pouvoir faire tout ce qui[9] ne nuit[10] pas à autrui : ainsi l'exercice des droits naturels de chaque homme n'a de bornes que celles[11] qui assurent aux autres Membres de la Société, la jouissance de ces mêmes droits. Ces bornes ne peuvent être déterminées que par la Loi.

Article V: La Loi n'a le droit de défendre[12] que les actions nuisibles à la Société. Tout ce qui n'est pas défendu par la Loi ne peut être empêché, et nul ne peut être contraint à faire ce qu'elle n'ordonne pas.

---

6. http://www.assemblee-nationale.fr/histoire/dudh/1789.asp . Retrieved November 20, 2011

7. *naissent:* present tense of *naître,* to be born

8. *peuvent:* present tense of *pouvoir,* to be able.

9. *ce qui:* that which. See chapter 16, section 16.1.5.

10. *nuit:* present tense of *nuire,* to be harmful to

11. *celles:* those (f. pl.). See chapter 11, section 11.3.

12. *défendre:* to prohibit

MORE IRREGULAR YET COMMON VERBS

THE PRESENTATION OF French verbs in chapter 2 as divided into the three families of -*er*, -*re*, and -*ir* verbs oversimplifies the diversity of French verbs. Closer inspection reveals the existence of a great many variations within the -*re* and -*ir* families. One important variation within the family of -*ir* verbs involves the verbs *venir* and *tenir*, along with a large group of verbs that are constituted by *venir* or *tenir* with different prefixes added to them. Another important variation within -*ir* verbs is the family of verbs that end in -*oir*, although even these verbs vary among themselves as to how they are conjugated. Some of the most commonly used of all these verbs follow, so that you can begin to familiarize yourself with them and to recognize them when you come across them. All the main verbs presented in this chapter (*venir, tenir,* and all the -*oir* verbs) should be conjugated in written form in all tenses learned thus far, even if this assignment is done over the next few classes or study sessions. A fuller account of these and other irregular verbs will be given in chapter 24, once all the verb tenses have been presented.

10.1. *VENIR* (TO COME) AND *TENIR* (TO HOLD)

These two verbs are twins that are conjugated exactly the same way in every tense, and both are irregular in their conjugation of the present tense. They are important because they are very commonly used, and because they constitute the main component of a large group of verbs composed of the addition of a prefix to one or the other of them (see the following chart). All the verbs of this group are conjugated in all tenses in exactly the same way.

Pay special attention to the third person singular of the present tense of *venir* and *tenir*. This form seems to end in -*ent*, when in reality it ends in –*t*, which just happens to be preceded by the letters -*en*-. Because of this, the third person singular of these verbs can easily be mistaken for the third person plural form. The translator must be alert to this possible misidentification so as to translate the verb in the correct person. This becomes even more important when *venir* or *tenir* is embedded in a verb that includes a prefix: For *il obtient* you will need to recognize the embedded *tient* as the third person singular of *tenir* in the present tense, in order to know that what you should look up in the dictionary is *ob + tenir*, or *obtenir*, to obtain. Similarly, for *elle devient*, you'll need to recognize the embedded *vient* as the third person singular of *venir* in the present tense, in order to know that what you should look up in the dictionary is *de + venir*, or *devenir*, to become. Memorize *venir/tenir* in the present tense now.

VENIR (TO COME)	ENGLISH	*TENIR* (TO HOLD)	ENGLISH
je viens	I come, I am coming	*je tiens*	I hold, I am holding
tu viens	you come, you are coming	*tu tiens*	you hold, you are holding
il/elle/on vient	he/she/one comes, is coming	*il/elle/on tient*	he/she/one holds, is holding
nous venons	we come, we are coming	*nous tenons*	we hold, we are holding
vous venez	you come, you are coming	*vous tenez*	you hold, you are holding
ils/elles viennent	they come, they are coming	*ils/elles tiennent*	they hold, they are holding
past participle:	*venu* came	*tenu*	held

The following verbs are made up of *venir* and *tenir* plus a prefix:

convenir	to suit, to agree	*contenir*	to contain
devenir	to become	*entretenir*	to look after, sustain
parvenir	to attain, to reach	*maintenir*	to maintain
prévenir	to inform, to warn	*obtenir*	to obtain
provenir	to come from	*retenir*	to retain
revenir	to return	*soutenir*	to support
se souvenir de	to remember		

10.2. *-OIR* VERBS

Often grouped as a single family, these verbs have important similarities as well as significant variations among them. Note that some (*pouvoir, vouloir, savoir, devoir*) are not commonly used in the continuous present in English. In these cases, no continuous present tense form is given in the translations. Practice figuring out how the *imparfait* of each verb here is formed by following the protocol set out in chapter 5, and learn to recognize the past participles of these verbs, which all end in -*u*.

POUVOIR	TO BE ABLE (TO DO SOMETHING)	*VOULOIR*	TO WANT
je peux/je puis[1]	I can, I am able	*je veux*	I want
tu peux	you can, you are able	*tu veux*	you want
il/elle/on peut	he/she/one can, is able	*il/elle/on veut*	he/she/one wants
nous pouvons	we can, we are able	*nous voulons*	we want
vous pouvez	you can, you are able	*vous voulez*	you want
ils/elles peuvent	they can, they are able	*ils/elles veulent*	they want
past participle: *pu* — able		*voulu* — wanted	

VOIR	TO SEE	*RECEVOIR*	TO RECEIVE
je vois	I see, I am seeing	*je reçois*	I receive, I am receiving
tu vois	you see, you are seeing	*tu reçois*	you receive, you are receiving
il/elle/on voit	he/she/one sees, is seeing	*il/elle/on reçoit*	he/she/one receives, is receiving
nous voyons	we see, we are seeing	*nous recevons*	we receive, we are receiving
vous voyez	you see, you are seeing	*vous recevez*	you receive, you are receiving
ils/elles voient	they see, they are seeing	*ils/elles reçoivent*	they receive, they are receiving
past participle: *vu* — saw		*reçu* — received	

SAVOIR	TO KNOW	*DEVOIR*	TO HAVE TO (DO SOMETHING); TO OWE
je sais	I know	*je dois*	I have to, I owe
tu sais	you know	*tu dois*	you have to, you owe
il/elle/on sait	he/she/one knows	*il/elle/on doit*	he/she/one has to, owes

---

1. *Je puis:* less common, more literary form. Used in questions in the place of *peux: Puis-je,* May I.

nous savons	we know	*nous devons*	we have to, we owe
vous savez	you know	*vous devez*	you have to, you owe
ils/elles savent	they know	*ils/elles doivent*	they have to, they owe

| past participle: | *su* | | knew | *dû (due, dus, dues)*[2] | had to; owed |

Translation Exercise A

1. Hier soir, ils ont vu la pièce de théâtre de Molière.
2. Les règles établies par l'administration doivent être respectées.
3. Il peut nous amener chez nous après le cours.
4. Les deux gouvernements parviennent à un compromis.
5. Cendrillon devait rentrer chez elle avant minuit.
6. Ils veulent aller au Musée canadien des civilisations.
7. Elle reçoit une augmentation de salaire cette année.
8. Il obtient son diplôme avec les autres étudiants.
9. Ils demandent si[3] les grandes industries peuvent soutenir des rapports durables avec la nature.
10. Elle sait faire de très bonnes pâtisseries.
11. Je vois, j'entends, mais je ne comprends rien.
12. Pour entrer dans l'édifice, on doit montrer sa carte d'identité.
13. Lorsqu'il a vu le feu dans la cheminée, il ne savait pas quoi faire.
14. Si cela vous convient, on fait le tour de la ville cet après-midi.
15. Le géneral dit que l'OTAN[4] doit garder des armes nucléaires.

---

2. The past participle of *devoir* is *dû,* with a circumflex over the *u* in order to distinguish it from the contraction *du* (preposition *de* + definite article *le*). When *devoir* takes *avoir* as its past participle, the use of *dû* as a component of the *passé composé* is straightforward. However, when the past participle of *devoir* is used as an adjective (e.g., a predicate adjective), or when in the *passé composé* the verb is preceded by the direct object and the past participle must agree with that direct object, agreement endings must be added. Since the addition of the agreement endings *-e,-s,* or *-es* makes the past participle visibly different from the contraction *du*, in these cases the circumflex is not retained.
3. *si:* if
4. *l'OTAN:* NATO

IMPERSONAL PRONOUNS, DEMONSTRATIVE PRONOUNS, IMPERSONAL VERBS, AND AN INTRODUCTION TO THE WORD *QUE*

11.1. DEMONSTRATIVE PRONOUN *CE*

The demonstrative pronoun *ce* means *it* or *this,* and occasionally *he* or *she.* This demonstrative pronoun *ce* should not be confused with the demonstrative adjective *ce, cet, cette, ces,* meaning *this/these.* (A pronoun takes the place of a noun, whereas an adjective accompanies a noun and modifies it.) English also uses the word *this* both as an adjective and as a pronoun: *This* (adjective) *book is very heavy* vs. *This* (pronoun) *is very difficult.*) The demonstrative pronoun *ce* is used as the subject of *être* to form the very common phrases *c'est* (*it is, he is,* or *she is*) and *ce sont* (*it's them, it is they* [*who . . .*], or *they are*):

C'est vrai.	It's true.
C'est lui.	It's him.
C'est aujourd'hui jeudi.	It's Thursday today.
C'est un avocat.	He is a lawyer.
Ce sont mes amis qui m'attendent.	It's my friends who are waiting for me.
Ce sont les organisateurs qui font le travail.	It is the organizers who are doing the work.
Ce sont des enfants d'immigrants.	They are children of immigrants.

11.2. DEMONSTRATIVE PRONOUNS *CECI* AND *CELA*

The demonstrative pronoun *ceci* combines the impersonal pronoun *ce,* meaning *it* or *this,* with the suffix *-ci,* which means *here* or *close by. Ceci* refers to a thing close to the speaker and is translated as *this* or *this here.*

Prenez ceci.	Take this.
Qui a fait ceci?	Who did this?
Ceci est à moi.	This here is mine.

The demonstrative pronoun *cela* combines the demonstrative pronoun *ce*, meaning *it* or *this*, with the suffix *-là*, which means *over there*. *Cela* refers to something at a distance from the speaker and is translated as *it* or *that*, or even *that there* or *that over there*. *Cela* is often contracted to *ça*.

Donnez-moi cela.	Give me that/Give that to me.
Cela me rend très triste.	That makes me very sad.
Qui a dit cela?	Who said that?
Qu'est-ce que c'est que cela? (idiomatic)	What is that? (What [on earth] is that?)
C'est ça.	That's it.

11.3. DEMONSTRATIVE PRONOUN *CELUI*

The commonly used demonstrative pronoun *celui* means *that (one)* or *the one (that . . .)* and has four different forms, depending on its gender (masculine or feminine) and on its number (singular or plural):

	MASCULINE	FEMININE	ENGLISH TRANSLATION
Singular	*celui*	*celle*	the one / he / she / this / that
Plural	*ceux*	*celles*	the ones / they / these / those

As in:

J'ai mon livre et celui de mon frère.	I have my book and that of my brother (and my brother's).
Voici mes cahiers et ceux de mon ami.	Here are my notebooks and those of my friend.
Il apporte mes lettres et celles de mes sœurs.	He is bringing my letters and those of my sisters.
La crise financière de 2011 ressemble à celle de 1929.	The financial crisis of 2011 resembles that of 1929.

Followed by the relative pronouns *qui* or *que* (see chapter 16 for a full discussion of relative pronouns *qui* and *que*), these demonstrative pronouns mean: he who, she who, the one who, the one(s) which, those who, and so on:

Voyez-vous celui qui chante?	Do you see the one who is singing?
Voici ma plume et celle que vous cherchez.	Here is my pen and the one you are looking for.
Pour ceux qui vivent en Europe, cela n'est pas facile à accepter.	For those who live in Europe, this is not easy to accept.

To make clear distinctions or contrasts, the suffixes *-ci* (here) and *-là* (there) can be added to these demonstrative pronouns, which then mean: *this one here, these here; that one there, those there.*

Cet exercice-ci est court, mais celui-là *est long.*
This exercise here is short but that one there is long.

Cette porte est ouverte, mais celle-là *est fermée.*
This door is open but that one there is closed.

Ces journaux sont d'aujourd'hui; ceux-là *sont d'hier.*
These newspapers are today's; those over there are from yesterday.

Voulez-vous ceux-ci *ou* ceux-là?
Do you want these here or those there?

The suffix *-ci* added to these demonstrative pronouns can indicate "the latter," whereas the suffix *-là* added to them can indicate "the former":

J'ai rencontré François et son cousin; celui-ci *est professeur,* celui-là *est avocat.*
I met François and his cousin; the latter is a professor, the former is a lawyer.

11.4. THE IMPERSONAL PRONOUN *IL*

The impersonal *il* is used to mean "it" when referring to the hour of the day or the weather, and when followed by impersonal verbs:

Il est une heure.	It's one o'clock.
Il fait chaud.	It's hot.
Il neige.	It's snowing.
Il pleut.	It's raining.

11.5. IMPERSONAL VERBS

Several verbs in French are considered impersonal: they are used only in the third person singular (and very occasionally in the infinitive), with the impersonal subject pronoun *il*.

11.5.1. *IL Y A*: THERE IS, THERE ARE

The most important and common of these impersonal verbs is *il y a,* which means *there is* or *there are,* and which is conjugated just like *il a* (he has), except that the *y* is always included, transforming the meaning completely. This phrase is found everywhere throughout the French language, so you should memorize it now. The infinitive of *il y a* is *il y avoir. Il y a* is always conjugated in the singular (*il y a*) even though its meaning may be singular or plural. Obviously, it can be conjugated in all tenses, and in the affirmative or in the negative:

il y a	there is, there are
il n'y a pas	there isn't, there aren't
il y avait	there was, there were
il n'y avait pas	there wasn't, there weren't
il y a eu	there was, there were
il n'y a pas eu	there wasn't, there weren't

Il y a un beau jardin à côté de la maison.	There is a beautiful garden beside the house.
Il y a trois chaises dans la salle.	There are three chairs in the room.

11.5.2. *IL FAUT*: IT IS NECESSARY

Il faut is from the infinitive *falloir,* which means *to be necessary,* and occurs only in the impersonal third person singular. Although *il faut* can also be translated as *one must*, this translation can lead to confusion: the novice translator is easily tempted— wrongly—to think that the *il* of *il faut* refers to *he,* as in *he must.* But *il faut* in and of itself does not tell us who it is who must do something. This confusion is best avoided by translating *il faut* simply as *it is necessary.*

The negative of *il faut* does not mean that something is not necessary; on the contrary, it means that *it is necessary* that whatever follows does *not* happen. That is, *il faut,* whether in the affirmative or the negative, always carries the force of an injunction:

il faut	it is necessary, one must.
il ne faut pas	it is necessary NOT (to do something); one must not
il fallait	it was necessary

il ne fallait pas	it was necessary NOT (to do something)
il a fallu	it was necessary
il n'a pas fallu	it was necessary NOT (to do something)

Be careful not to confuse *il faut* (it is necessary) with *il fait* (he does, he makes).

When accompanied by an indirect object pronoun (see section 8.5.), *il faut* tells us *to whom* something is necessary. In these cases, rather than translating it as *it is necessary to me* or *it is necessary to him*, *il faut* can more easily be translated as *I have to/I must/I need; s/he has to / s/he must / s/he needs,* according to the indirect object pronoun used:

il me faut	I have to, I need (it is necessary to me)
il nous faut	We have to, we must, we need (it is necessary to us)
Il nous faut partir.	We must leave, we have to leave.
Il lui faut un nouveau parapluie.	He needs a new umbrella.
Il me faut lire cent pages de plus.	I have to read one hundred more pages.

Often, *il faut* can be followed by a noun or noun phrase that then becomes the subject of *il faut*. In other words, the noun or noun phrase that follows *il faut* becomes that which is necessary or needed:

Il faut plus d'ornements dans l'architecture de notre temps.	More ornaments are necessary in our current architecture.
Il nous fallait dix heures pour y aller.	We needed ten hours to get there./It took us ten hours to get there. (Ten hours were needed to get there.)
Il n'en fallait pas davantage.	Nothing more was needed. (No more of it was needed.)
Il a fallu dix mois pour faire les préparations.	Ten months were needed to make the preparations./It took ten months to make the preparations.
Il m'a fallu dix mois pour faire les préparations.	I needed ten months to make the preparations./It took me ten months to make the preparations.

11.5.3. OTHER IMPERSONAL VERBS

Other impersonal verbs include

il s'agit de	it has to do with, it concerns, it regards
il s'agissait de	it had to do with, it concerned, it was regarding

il paraît que	it seems that, rumor has it
il paraissait que	it seemed that
il vaut	it is worth
il valait	it was worth
il semble que	it seems that, it appears that
il semblait que	it seemed that
il se peut que	it is possible that
il se pouvait que	it was possible that
il reste _____	_____ *remains [or] There remains* _____
il restait _____	_____ *remained [or] There remained* _____

See section 20.2.4 for other impersonal verbs with *faire*.

11.6. THE VARIOUS USES OF *QUE*

The small word *que* in French has several different and often mutually exclusive meanings and grammatical uses. (When followed by a vowel, it is shortened to *qu'*.) As we've already seen, *que* can be used as part of a comparative construction with *plus, moins,* and so on, to mean *than* or *as*:

Elle est plus jolie que *sa sœur.*	She is prettier *than* her sister.
Elle est aussi jolie que *sa sœur.*	She is as pretty *as* her sister.

As we have further seen, *que* is used as part of the pair *ne ... que,* meaning *only.* But *que* is also commonly used as a subordinate conjunction (a conjunction that introduces a subordinate or dependent clause; i.e., a clause that cannot stand on its own), translated as *that:*

Il dit qu'il travaille très fort.
He says *that* he is working very hard.

Je sais qu'*il ne va pas à l'université.*
I know *that* he isn't going to university.

Il dit qu'il aime travailler dans la bibliothèque.
He says *that* he likes working in the library.

Il faut rappeler que *nous vivons une expérience exceptionnelle.*
It is necessary to remember *that* we are living through an exceptional experience. (We must remember *that* we are going through an exceptional experience.)

And importantly, *que* functions as a relative pronoun translated as *that, which,* or *whom,* and as an interrogative pronoun translated as *What?,* uses that will be addressed in greater detail in chapter 16. In its use as a relative or interrogative pronoun it is partnered with *qui,* which is translated as *that, which,* or *who.*

Le livre que j'achète est très intéressant.
The book *that* I'm buying is very interesting.

Le garçon qu'elle regarde est le fils de son voisin.
The boy *whom* she is watching is the son of her neighbor.

Les élèves qui persévèrent progressent très vite.
The students *who* persevere advance very quickly.

Que veut-il?
What does he want?

Translation Exercise A

1. C'est aujourd'hui lundi.
2. Il y a plusieurs espèces de fleurs dans le jardin.
3. Il dit que son frère est arrivé.
4. C'est mon frère qui va à la bibliothèque.
5. Les étudiants lisent les livres de Camus et ceux de Sartre.
6. Il reste deux mois avant les vacances.
7. Il nous reste deux mois avant les vacances.
8. Voici[1] des livres pour ceux qui lisent l'espagnol.
9. Il s'agit d'une histoire romantique.
10. Il ne reste que deux poèmes à lire.
11. Il y avait trente-deux étudiants dans la classe.
12. Ce sont les étudiants qui arrivent maintenant.
13. Pour celui qui sait regarder, tout est miracle.
14. Voici ma robe et celle que vous cherchez.
15. Il n'y a que deux partis politiques aux États-Unis.
16. Il est dix heures du matin.
17. Il faut souligner que cette étude est très compliquée.
18. Il lui fallait travailler rapidement pour finir à l'heure.[2]

---

1. *voici:* here is, here are; *voilà:* there is, there are
2. *à l'heure:* on time

19. Prenez ces pommes-ci; celles que vous mangez ne sont pas mûres.
20. Il ne faut pas fumer dans la salle.
21. Paris vaut bien une messe.[3]
22. Il faut cultiver notre jardin.[4]

11.7. TRANSLATION PASSAGE

Find and underline the demonstrative pronouns, then translate the entire passage.

NÉGRITUDE ET HUMANISME[5]

. . . le problème de l'Homme . . . est celui de la Culture. Celle-ci n'est plus or-nement, encore moins distraction, mais ce mouvement réel, sans rupture entre les idées et les faits, la pensée et l'acte, qui réalise[6] l'*Homme intégral;* non pas[7] un mouvement linéaire, mais oscillatoire, dialectique, un double mouvement cen-tripète et centrifuge: celui de la raison et du cœur, de la science et du mythe. En face de ceux qui nous demandaient de choisir entre l'Afrique noire et l'Europe, la stagnation et l'assimilation, nous avons découvert que . . . notre vocation de[8] colonisés est de surmonter les contradictions de la conjoncture, l'antinomie ar-tificiellement dressée entre l'Afrique et l'Europe, notre hérédité et notre éduca-tion. C'est de la greffe de celle-ci sur celle-là que doit naître notre liberté.[9] . . . Trop assimilés et pas assez assimilés? Tel est exactement notre destin de métis culturels. . . . En face des nationalismes, des racismes, des académismes, c'est le combat pour la *liberté de l'Âme*—de l'Homme.

LÉOPOLD SÉDAR SENGHOR

---

3. Famous saying attributed to Henri IV, the Protestant royal who converted to Catholicism in order to be accepted as King of France in the sixteenth century.
4. Famous last phrase of Voltaire's *Candide.*
5. Léopold Sédar Senghor, « De la liberté de l'âme ou Éloge du métissage », *Liberté 1: Négritude et Humanisme,* coll. *L'Histoire immédiate,* © Éditions du Seuil (Paris), 1964, pp.102–103. Reprinted by permission. Senghor (1906–2001), Senegalese poet and politician, was the first president of Senegal, a founding member of both the *Négritude* and the *Francophonie* movements, and the first African to be elected to the Académie Française, the prestigious institution that oversees French language usage.
6. From *réaliser,* to fulfill
7. *non pas:* not
8. *de:* as
9. *que doit naître notre liberté:* that our liberty must be born

THE FUTURE AND CONDITIONAL TENSES/*LE FUTUR SIMPLE ET LE CONDITIONNEL*

12.1. THE FUTURE AND CONDITIONAL STEM

The future and conditional tenses in French are presented together because they both use the same stem—the future/conditional stem—even though they have different tense endings. The basic future/conditional stem is the entire infinitive, with the exception of -*re* verbs, for which the future/conditional stem is the entire infinitive minus the final -*e*. However, many verbs exhibit irregular future/conditional stems. Some of the most common irregular stems are the following:

INFINITIVE	(ENGLISH)	FUTURE/CONDITIONAL STEM
avoir	to have	*aur-*
être	to be	*ser-*
aller	to go	*ir-*
faire	to do	*fer-*
venir	to come	*viendr-*
tenir	to hold	*tiendr-*
pouvoir	to be able	*pourr-*
vouloir	to want	*voudr-*
voir	to see	*verr-*
savoir	to know	*saur-*
devoir	to have to, to owe	*devr-*
falloir	to be necessary	*faudr-*
valoir	to be worth	*vaudr-*

In spite of all these irregularities, the future/conditional stem always ends in the letter *-r.* There are no exceptions to this rule.

12.2. THE FUTURE TENSE/*LE FUTUR SIMPLE:* ENDINGS

The future tense is formed by adding the following endings to the future/conditional stem, which should be memorized now:

1st *person sing.*	*-ai*
2nd *person sing.*	*-as*
3rd *person sing.*	*-a*
1st *person pl.*	*-ons*
2nd *person pl.*	*-ez*
3rd *person pl.*	*-ont*

Note that the endings for the first and second persons plural (the *nous* and *vous* endings) of the future tense are the same endings as those for the present tense. How will you tell the difference between the *nous* and *vous* forms of the present tense, on the one hand, and the future tense, on the other?

Look for the letter that precedes the tense ending. If that letter is *-r*, then you have most likely encountered the future tense. Even if the verb is irregular, its future/conditional stem will always end with an *-r.*

Once you recognize that you have encountered a verb in the future or conditional tense, you may still have to look it up in the dictionary to find out its meaning. If you can't deduce the infinitive form from the future/conditional stem in order to find it in the dictionary, the verb is probably irregular. In that case, go to the irregular verb index in your dictionary, where the verb will be listed alphabetically, and track it down in the *future* column.

Here is an example of the future tense, with *regarder,* to look at:

PRESENT TENSE	FUTURE TENSE	ENGLISH TRANSLATION OF FUTURE TENSE
je regard*e*	je regarder*ai*	I will look at
tu regard*es*	tu regarder*as*	you will look at
il/elle/on regard*e*	il/elle/on regarder*a*	he/she/one will look at
nous regard*ons*	nous regarder*ons*	we will look at
vous regard*ez*	vous regarder*ez*	you will look at
ils/elles regard*ent*	ils/elles regarder*ont*	they will look at

A few verbs make it more difficult to discern the difference between the present and future tenses. These are a handful of verbs like *préparer, considérer, comparer, ouvrir,* and *offrir,* which have an -*r* that *precedes* the infinitive ending in addition to the -*r* that is at the end of the infinitive ending. In these cases, you have to determine whether the -*r* that seems to precede the future tense ending is truly the final -*r* of the infinitive ending (and thus the verb is in the future tense) or whether it is an -*r* that precedes the infinitive ending (and thus the verb is in the present tense). Compare carefully the *nous* and *vous* forms of *préparer* in the present and future tenses:

PRESENT TENSE	FUTURE TENSE	ENGLISH TRANSLATION OF FUTURE TENSE
je prépare	je préparerai	I will prepare
tu prépares	tu prépareras	you will prepare
il/elle/on prépare	il/elle/on préparera	he/she/one will prepare
nous préparons	nous préparerons	we will prepare
vous préparez	vous préparerez	you will prepare
ils/elles préparent	ils/elles prépareront	they will prepare

12.3. THE NEAR FUTURE/*LE FUTUR PROCHE*

An alternative way of expressing something that is going to happen soon in the future is *le futur proche,* which corresponds to the *near future* in English. In both languages, instead of using the future tense, the *present* tense of *aller/to go* is used together with the infinitive. Novice translators should be alert to the fact that in this situation, *aller* must be translated into the *continuous* present, or the resulting translation won't make sense:

je vais dormir	I *am going* to sleep
ils vont manger	they *are going* to eat
elle va voir son ami	she *is going* to see her friend

12.4. THE CONDITIONAL TENSE/*LE CONDITIONNEL*

The conditional is generally considered a *tense* in English, whereas in French it is considered a *mood*, along with the indicative, imperative, and subjunctive moods. (See the introduction to chapter 19 for more on grammatical moods.) The French conditional tense/mood describes events that *would* take place under certain conditions, and therefore is always translated with the English word *would. Vouloir* is often used in the conditional tense to express a wish or a request more politely: *Je voudrais* (I would like) rather then the more blunt *je veux* (I want).

The conditional tense is formed with the same stem as the future tense: the entire infinitive, or, in the case of *-re* verbs, the entire infinitive minus the final *-e*; or the irregular stems given in section 12.1. To these stems are added the conditional tense endings, which are *the imparfait endings.* So you already know the conditional tense endings, having learned the *imparfait* endings earlier in chapter 5.

But having two different tenses, the *imparfait* and the conditional, that use the same endings makes it crucial to be able to differentiate the two. How can you be sure to distinguish between the *imparfait* and conditional tenses, since their endings are exactly the same? Once again, the key lies in the letter *-r*: the conditional endings are preceded by the letter *-r* that ends the irregular future/conditional stem, whereas the *imparfait* endings are not preceded by that final *-r*:

PRESENT TENSE	IMPARFAIT	CONDITIONNEL	ENGLISH TRANSLATION OF CONDITIONAL TENSE
je regarde	je regardais	je regarderais	I would look at
tu regardes	tu regardais	tu regarderais	you would look at
il/elle/on regarde	il/elle/on regardait	il/elle/on regarderait	he/she/one would look at
nous regardons	nous regardions	nous regarderions	we would look at
vous regardez	vous regardiez	vous regarderiez	you would look at
ils/elles regardent	ils/elles regardaient	ils/elles regarderaient	they would look at

Once again, as in the future tense, verbs like *préparer, considérer, comparer, ouvrir,* and *offrir* can trip you up, because the *-r* that precedes their infinitive endings can easily be confused with the final, infinitive *-r*:

PRESENT TENSE	IMPARFAIT	CONDITIONNEL	ENGLISH TRANSLATION OF CONDITIONAL TENSE
je prépare	je préparais	je préparerais	I would prepare
tu prépares	tu préparais	tu préparerais	you would prepare
Il/elle/on prépare	il/elle/on préparait	il/elle/on préparerait	he/she/one would prepare
nous préparons	nous préparions	nous préparerions	we would prepare
vous préparez	vous prépariez	vous prépareriez	you would prepare
ils/elles préparent	ils/elles préparaient	ils/elles prépareraient	they would prepare

Look closely at how similar the *nous* and *vous* forms are in the present, future, *imparfait*, and conditional tenses, so that you can be sure to see how to distinguish one from the others:

PRESENT	FUTURE	*IMPARFAIT*	CONDITIONAL
nous regard*ons*	nous regarder*ons*	nous regard*ions*	nous regarder*ions*
vous regard*ez*	vous regarder*ez*	vous regard*iez*	vous regarder*iez*
nous prépar*ons*	nous préparer*ons*	nous prépar*ions*	nous préparer*ions*
vous prépar*ez*	vous préparer*ez*	vous prépar*iez*	vous préparer*iez*

In all cases, these verb forms end in *-ons* or in *-ez*; the important question you must always ask is, "What *precedes* these endings?" Preceded by an *i*, they become *imparfait* endings (*-ions, -iez*). Preceded by an *r*, they become future tense endings (*-r-ons, -r-ez*). Preceded by an *i* that in turn is preceded by an *r*, they become conditional endings (*-r-ions, -r-iez*).

The verbs *avoir* and *être* must be memorized in the future and conditional tenses because of their irregularity, the ubiquity of their general use, and their use in compound tenses. Similarly, the verb *aller* must also be memorized in the future and conditional tenses, because its future/conditional stem begins with an entirely different letter than its infinitive. If you come across the future tense of *aller* (e.g., *il ira*), you may recognize that it is in the future tense and that it is probably irregular, but you will still not be able to find it anywhere in the dictionary because you will be looking for it alphabetically under the letter *i*, whereas it will be listed under *a* for *aller*.

AVOIR IN THE FUTURE TENSE

j'aur*ai*	I will have
tu aur*as*	you will have
il/elle/on aur*a*	he/she/one will have
nous aur*ons*	we will have
vous aur*ez*	you will have
ils/elles aur*ont*	they will have

AVOIR IN THE CONDITIONAL TENSE

j'aur*ais*	I would have
tu aur*ais*	you would have
il/elle/on aur*ait*	he/she/one would have
nous aur*ions*	we would have
vous aur*iez*	you would have
ils/elles aur*aient*	they would have

ÊTRE IN THE FUTURE TENSE

je ser*ai*	I will be
tu ser*as*	you will be
il/elle/on ser*a*	he/she/one will be
nous ser*ons*	we will be

ÊTRE IN THE CONDITIONAL TENSE

je ser*ais*	I would be
tu ser*ais*	you would be
il/elle/on ser*ait*	he/she/one would be
nous ser*ions*	we would be

| vous serez | you will be | vous seriez | you would be |
| ils/elles seront | they will be | ils/elles seraient | they would be |

ALLER IN THE FUTURE TENSE

ALLER IN THE CONDITIONAL TENSE

j'irai	I will go	j'irais	I would go
tu iras	you will go	tu irais	you would go
il/elle/on ira	he/she/one will go	il/elle/on irait	he/she/one would go
nous irons	we will go	nous irions	we would go
vous irez	you will go	vous iriez	you would go
ils/elles iront	they will go	ils/elles iraient	they would go

Remember, all impersonal verbs (see chapter 10, section 10.5.) can occur in the future and conditional tenses as well:

il y aura	there will be
il y aurait	there would be
il faudra	it will be necessary
il faudrait	it would be necessary

Translation Exercise A

1. il fait / ils feront / vous feriez / il faut faire
2. j'ai parlé / tu parles / ils parleront / il parlerait / vous parlez
3. je finis / vous finirez / ils finissent / elles finiraient / vous finissiez
4. il va / il ira / il allait / il irait / ils iraient / ils vont
5. elle a préparé / il préparait / ils prépareraient / vous préparez
6. ils trouvent / vous trouverez / elles trouveraient / elles trouvaient
7. je descends / je descendrais / je descendais / nous descendrions
8. je mets / nous mettions / vous mettrez / ils mettraient / ils ont mis
9. il joint / nous joignons / ils joignent / ils joignaient / ils joindront
10. sans rien dire / il dit / il disait / il dira / ils diraient
11. il réfléchit / on réfléchira / nous réfléchirions / ils réfléchissaient
12. il a / ils auront / elle aurait / ils avaient / ils ont eu
13. elle vient / elles viennent / il viendra / nous viendrons / ils viendraient

14. il y a / il y avait / il y a eu / il y aura / il y aurait
15. j'étudie / nous étudions / vous étudiiez / vous étudierez / ils étudieraient
16. il faut / il fallait / il faudra / il faudrait / il a fallu
17. je choisis / ils choisiront / nous choisissons / elles choisissaient / elles choisir-aient
18. je vois / il voyait / on verra / ils verront / elles verraient
19. il obtient / ils obtiennent / ils obtiendront / ils obtenaient / ils ont obtenu
20. je ne suis plus / ils ne seraient jamais / il n'était plus / sans être / elle sera / nous étions
21. tu savais / il sait / vous saurez / on saurait / tout le monde saura / ils sauront
22. il ralentit / ils ralentissent / on ralentissait / je ralentirai / ils ralentiraient
23. il ouvre / il a ouvert / il ouvrira / il ouvrirait / il ouvrait
24. il construit / il a construit / ils construisent / nous construirions
25. il offre / il offrira / nous offrons / nous offrirons / nous offrions / nous offririons

Translation Exercise B

1. Le ministre restera dans la capitale sept ans.
2. Ce soir nous donnerons un grand dîner pour tous nos amis.
3. La nouvelle réforme leur serait favorable.
4. Il a eu l'impression d'être dans un train qui ne s'arrêterait jamais.
5. Le constat des experts sur le caractère du changement climatique est que les températures ne cesseront pas d'augmenter.
6. Selon cette théorie, la dépendance serait en réalité le propre[2] de l'humain; et l'indépendance personnelle ne serait qu'une illusion.
7. Les gens veulent réaliser leurs rêves dans cette vie, mais souvent quelque chose viendra les briser.
8. Le nouveau projet de loi proposé par le gouvernement pourrait être rétroactif.
9. Le plus beau compliment serait de le voir comme un artiste inclassable.
10. Convaincus qu'ils ne tireront jamais bénéfice du système de retraite, les élites choisiront l'émigration.
11. Le principal avantage de ce système résiderait dans sa flexibilité envers ceux qui pourraient en profiter.

---

2. *le propre*: the characteristic

12. L'organisation pour la gestion globale de la biodiversité aura un mandat politique et supranational.

12.5. TRANSLATION PASSAGE

Underline all the verbs, and underline verbs in the future and conditional tenses twice, then translate the entire passage:

CAHIER D'UN RETOUR AU PAYS NATAL[3]

Partir. Mon cœur bruissait de générosités emphatiques. Partir . . . j'arriverais lisse et jeune dans ce pays mien et je dirais à ce pays dont[4] le limon[5] entre dans la composition de ma chair: « J'ai longtemps erré et je reviens vers la hideur désertée de vos plaies. »

Je viendrais à ce pays mien et je lui dirais: « Embrassez-moi[6] sans crainte . . . Et si je ne sais que parler, c'est pour vous que je parlerai ».

Et je lui dirais encore:

« Ma bouche sera la bouche des malheurs qui n'ont point de bouche, ma voix, la liberté de celles qui s'affaissent au cachot du désespoir ».

Et venant[7] je me dirais à moi-même:

« Et surtout mon corps aussi bien que[8] mon âme, gardez-vous[9] de vous croiser les bras en l'attitude stérile du spectateur, car la vie n'est pas un spectacle, car une mer de douleurs n'est pas un proscenium, car un homme qui crie n'est pas un ours qui danse . . . »

AIMÉ CÉSAIRE

---

3. Aimé Césaire, *Cahier d'un retour au pays natal,* © Présence Africaine (Paris), 1983, p. 22. Reprinted by permission. Césaire (1913–2008), African-Martinican francophone poet, author, and politician, was one of the founders of the *Négritude* movement of Francophone literature. His *Cahier d'un retour au pays natal* is considered a masterpiece of French literature of the twentieth century.

4. *dont*: whose. See chapter 16, section 16.4.

5. *limon*: silt, clay

6. *Embrassez-moi*: embrace me. Imperative of *embrasser* with direct object pronoun; see chapter 13, section 13.4.3.

7. *venant*: on the way; literally, *coming*, present participle of *venir.* See chapter 13, section 13.1.

8. *aussi bien que*: as well as

9. *gardez-vous de*: keep yourself from, be careful not to. Imperative of reflexive verb *se garder:* see next chapter.

PRESENT PARTICIPLES AND IMPERATIVES

13.1. PRESENT PARTICIPLES

The present participle in English always ends in *-ing* (singing, smiling, walking, etc.). In French, the present participle always ends in *-ant*. It is formed by taking the *nous* form of the present tense, dropping the *-ons*, and adding *-ant*.

chantant	singing
donnant	giving
finissant	finishing
ayant	having
étant	being
allant	going
sachant	knowing

Unlike in English, these present participles are never joined with subject pronouns to form the continuous or progressive form of a conjugated tense.

Present participles can be used as simple adjectives; as verbal adjectives forming subordinate clauses; or, preceded by the preposition *en*, as gerunds, adverbial participles also forming subordinate clauses.

1. Present participles are used as simple adjectives. Like all simple adjectives, in this usage present participles must agree with the noun that is modified:

un livre intéressant	an interesting book
des livres intéressants	some interesting books
une histoire intéressante	an interesting story
des histoires intéressantes	some interesting stories

2. Present participles are used as verbal adjectives, forming subordinate clauses. In this usage they do not agree with anything:

Mon ami, voyant *que j'étais confus, m'a expliqué la situation.*
My friend, seeing that I was confused, explained the situation to me.

N'étant ni étudiant ni professeur, je n'assistais pas au cours à l'université.
Being neither as student nor a professor, I was not attending classes at the university.

Tout étant *fait pour une fin, tout est nécessairement pour la meilleure fin.*[1]
Everything being made for an end, everything is necessarily for the best end.

Les étudiants venant *d'outre-mer devaient montrer qu'ils savaient parler anglais.*
The students coming from overseas had to show that they could speak English.

3. Present participles are used with the preposition *en* to form the gerund, an adverbial participle:

en allant   *en cherchant*   *en faisant*   *en écrivant*

In English, our gerunds can be preceded by a variety of prepositions: *in, while, by, through.* Therefore, the *en* directly preceding a present participle in French may be translated by any of these prepositions in English, according to whichever makes the most sense in the context given:

en allant   by going, while going, in going, through going

As in the following sentences:

Son frère s'est blessé en tombant *d'un arbre.*
His brother wounded himself by falling from a tree.

En explorant ces thèmes, les auteurs montrent la richesse d'une œuvre importante.
By exploring these themes, the authors demonstrate the wealth of an important work.

En attendant mon avion je regardais le monde autour de moi.
While waiting for my plane I was watching the people around me.

It is important to remember never to translate a present participle as the fully fledged present tense.

---

1.   Famous line from Voltaire's *Candide.*

13.2. IMPERATIVES

The imperative is the form of a verb used to make an order. For example: *Eat your dinner!* (*Eat* is the imperative form.) *Be good! Hurry up!* In English, we have only one form for the imperative: the second person, singular and/or plural. That means that whenever we utter a command or an order in English, we are implicitly addressing someone as *you*. We form the imperative by taking the *you* form of the verb in the present tense and dropping the subject or subject pronoun.

PRESENT TENSE SENTENCE (STATEMENT FORM)	IMPERATIVE FORM
You do your homework.	Do your homework!
You take your car in to get the oil changed.	Take your car in to get the oil changed!

In French, the imperative is formed in much the same way, but the two different forms of the second person—second person singular and second person plural—result in two corresponding forms of the imperative. As in English, the imperative is formed by taking the present tense of the second person, the *tu* or *vous* forms, and then dropping the subject or subject pronoun *tu* or *vous,* keeping only the conjugated verb form itself. In addition, French has another form for the imperative that we lack in English: the first person plural (*nous,* we). This form, too, is made by taking the present tense of the *nous* form and dropping the *nous.* It is translated into English with the words "let us" or "let's." Thus there are three forms of the imperative for every verb in French:

PRESENT TENSE STATEMENT	TRANSLATION	IMPERATIVE FORM	TRANSLATION
Tu fais tes devoirs.	You do your homework.	*Fais tes devoirs!*	Do your homework!
Nous faisons nos devoirs.	We do our homework.	*Faisons nos devoirs!*	Let's do our homework!
Vous faites vos devoirs.	You do your homework	*Faites vos devoirs!*	Do your homework!

The *tu* form of -*er* verbs tends to drop the final –*s* of its present tense ending when forming the imperative:

Tu lui donnes le cadeau.	You give him the gift.
Donne-lui le cadeau.	Give him the gift.

Not only *avoir* and *être,* but several other verbs as well have irregular forms for the imperative. When the imperative form is irregular, it is usually borrowed from the present subjunctive form of that verb. (See chapter 19 for the subjunctive forms of verbs.) Some irregular imperatives:

	IMPERATIVE OF *AVOIR*		IMPERATIVE OF *ÊTRE*		IMPERATIVE OF *ALLER*	
(tu)	*aie!*	have!	*sois!*	be!	*va!*	go!
(nous)	*ayons!*	let's have!	*soyons!*	let's be!	*allons!*	let's go!
(vous)	*ayez!*	have!	*soyez!*	be!	*allez!*	go!

	IMPERATIVE OF *VOULOIR*		IMPERATIVE OF *SAVOIR*	
(tu)	*veuille!*	Please, kindly	*sache!*	know!
(nous)	*veuillons!*	Let's please (do . . .)	*sachons!*	let's know!
(vous)	*veuillez!* *	Please, kindly	*sachez!*	know!

*Veuillez is often found in the closing line of a formal letter, as in: *Veuillez agréer, Monsieur, l'expression de mes sentiments distingués.* (Approximately: Kindly, sir, accept the expression of my best regards. Although this is over the top in English, it is not unusual in formal written French and is translated in English as *yours truly* or *sincerely yours.*)

For other representative models of the imperative, see Verb Chart II and Irregular Verb Chart II in the appendix at the back of the book.

13.3. NEGATIVE IMPERATIVES

In general, negative imperatives are formed by placing the *ne* right before the verb and the *pas* or other negative form right after:

Ne mange pas le gâteau.	Don't eat the cake.
N'oubliez pas de sortir la poubelle.	Don't forget to take out the garbage.
N'ouvrons pas les fenêtres quand il fait froid.	Let's not open the windows when it's cold out.

13.4. IMPERATIVES WITH DISJUNCTIVE PRONOUNS AND OBJECT PRONOUNS; AND REFLEXIVE IMPERATIVES

13.4.1. DISJUNCTIVE (PREPOSITIONAL) PRONOUNS

Disjunctive pronouns are used to form the imperative while using direct and/or indirect object pronouns, and to form the imperatives of reflexive verbs. Disjunctive pronouns are pronouns that can stand alone. They are also known as prepositional pronouns because they are the same pronouns that are used to follow prepositions.

Before going any further in learning about imperatives, learn the disjunctive pronouns and their uses:

SUBJECT PRONOUNS	DISJUNCTIVE PRONOUNS	ENGLISH TRANSLATION OF DISJUNCTIVE PRONOUNS
je	*moi*	me/to me/for me
tu	*toi*	you/to you/for you
il/elle/on	*lui/elle/soi*	him/her/one; to him/to her/to one; for him/for her/for one
nous	*nous*	us/to us/for us
vous	*vous*	you/to you/for you
ils/elles	*eux/elles*	them/to them/for them

13.4.2. USES OF DISJUNCTIVE (OR PREPOSITIONAL) PRONOUNS

DESCRIPTION: DISJUNCTIVE PRONOUNS ARE USED	CORRESPONDING EXAMPLE		
a. With imperatives using object pronouns, and with reflexive imperatives (see sections 13.4.3.and 13.4.4)	*donnez-le-*moi give it to me	*levez-*vous get up	*souviens-*toi remember
b. After a comparison	*Il est plus grand que* moi. He is taller than me (than I am).		
c. After *ce* and *être*	*C'est* lui. It's him.	*Ce sont* eux. It's them.	
d. After prepositions	*contre* moi against me	*sans* elle without her	*entre* nous among us
	avec toi with you	*pour* vous for you	*chez* lui at his home/ at his place
e. Alone (as the answer to a question)	*Qui a écrit la lettre?* Moi. Who wrote the letter? Me. (I did)		
f. For added emphasis (not translated into English)	*Les Brésiliens, eux, ils savent jouer au « foot ».* The Brazilians (really) know how to play soccer.		
g. With *être* and *à* to denote possession	*Le stylo est à moi.* The pen is mine.	*Le livre est à lui.* The book is his.	
h. With *-même* to express -self (-selves)	*Il l'a fait lui-même.* He did it himself.	*On doit le faire soi- même.* One must do it oneself.	

13.4.3. IMPERATIVES USING DISJUNCTIVE, DIRECT, OR INDIRECT OBJECT PRONOUNS

In positive commands, direct object pronouns and/or indirect object pronouns *follow* the verb and are linked to the verb with a hyphen. In addition, the object pronouns *me* and *te* are replaced by the disjunctive pronouns *moi* and *toi*.

Écoutez- moi!	Listen to me.
Donnez-les-moi.	Give them to me.
Envoyez-la-leur.	Send it to them.
Faisons nos devoirs. Faisons-les.	Let's do our homework. Let's do it.
Montrez-les-lui.	Show them to him.
Parlez-lui.	Speak to him.

However, in negative commands, the *ne* and any direct or indirect object pronouns *precede* the verb as in regular sentences, and *me* and *te* remain as is.

Ne me regardez pas.	Don't look at me.
Ne lui donne pas le livre.	Don't give the book to him.

With -*er* verbs, when the second person singular imperative is followed by the pronouns *y* or *en*, the final -s is not dropped from the verb:

Vas-y	Go there!
Parles-en	Talk about it.

13.4.4. IMPERATIVE FORMS OF REFLEXIVE VERBS

The imperative form of reflexive verbs begins by following the general rule for forming the imperative: The subject pronoun is dropped. The reflexive pronoun, however, is then replaced by the *disjunctive* pronoun, which is placed *after* the verb, to which it is attached with a hyphen. Compare the following reflexive statements with their corresponding imperative forms:

Statement:	*Tu te lèves.*	You get up.	*Nous nous souvenons*	We remember.
Imperative:	*Lève-toi!*	Get up!	*Souvenons-nous!*	Let's remember!

Statement:	*Vous vous dépêchez.*	You hurry up.	*Tu t'assieds.*	You sit down.
Imperative:	*Dépêchez-vous!*	Hurry up!	*Assieds-toi!*	Sit down!

In the negative form of the imperative for reflexive verbs, the reflexive pronoun is not changed into the disjunctive pronoun, and it remains placed in front of the verb:

Negative statement:	*Tu ne te laves pas les mains maintenant.*
	You don't wash your hands now.
Negative imperative:	*Ne te lave pas les mains maintenant!*
	Don't wash your hands now!
Negative statement:	*Vous ne vous souvenez pas de ces temps difficiles.*
	You don't remember those difficult times.
Negative imperative:	*Ne vous souvenez pas de ces temps difficiles.*
	Don't remember those difficult times.

Translation Exercise

Locate the present participle and/or the imperative form in each sentence, then translate.

1. Faites tous vos devoirs avant de retourner en classe.
2. Soyons honnêtes: les examens sont beaucoup trop difficiles.
3. Écoute-moi quand je te parle.
4. Ne me quitte pas!
5. « Sois sage! », elle disait à son enfant.
6. En parlant lentement, il lui expliquait la complexité de sa théorie.
7. Donne-lui le livre qu'il cherche.
8. Lisez les journaux français pour apprendre la langue plus vite.
9. Mange vite ton déjeuner avant de partir.
10. Taisez-vous! Les enfants dorment.
11. Étant d'un tempérament plus scientifique qu'artistique, il parle des faits et non des émotions.
12. Allons au concert ce soir: allons-y.
13. Ne me demande pas de faire l'impossible.
14. Ne t'inquiète pas.
15. Dépêche-toi, nous sommes déjà en retard.
16. Levez-vous quand le juge entre dans le palais de justice.
17. Asseyez-vous dans l'autobus après avoir acheté votre billet.
18. En traduisant un livre, il est interdit d'en trahir l'esprit original.
19. « À la claire fontaine, m'en allant promener, j'ai trouvé l'eau si belle que je m'y suis baigné . . . »[2]
20. Dans un entretien accordé à un journal quotidien, le politicien a changé d'opinion, expliquant qu'il soutenait les efforts internationaux en faveur de la paix.

---

2. First line of a famous French folksong. See http://www2.cpdl.org/wiki/index.php/A_la_claire_Fontaine_ (Traditional)

13.5. TRANSLATION PASSAGE

JOURNAUX DE GUERRE ET DE PRISON[3]

Ô mon Dieu! Ne punissez pas la nation métisse. À cause de Jésus, Marie, Joseph, faites-lui miséricorde. Voyez comme elle est charitable, comme elle est douce et facile à conduire. Considérez favorablement, ô mon Dieu, les grands ouvrages que[4] fait la nation métisse pour votre plus grande gloire, pour l'honneur de la religion, pour le salut des âmes, pour le bien de la société.

Ô mon Dieu! Je vous en prie,[5] pour l'amour de Jésus, de Marie, de Joseph et de saint Jean-Baptiste, ne vous fâchez pas contre la nation métisse canadienne-française.

Tournez plutôt votre colère contre vos ennemis, Ô mon Dieu. Châtiez-les Terriblement; châtiez-les extraordinairement selon votre miséricorde infinie pour vos enfants.

Ô mon Dieu! Vous m'avez dit charitablement: je vais me fâcher contre elle. Daignez vous fâcher contre la police montée. Ô, fâchez-vous contre elle! Je l'accuse devant vous, au nom du Christ qu'elle blasphème, au nom de la Vierge qu'elle outrage, au nom du Saint-Esprit qu'elle offense en blasphémant contre le saint sacrement du Baptême. Punissez épouvantablement la police montée . . . Pour l'amour de Jésus-Christ, pour l'amour de Marie, pour l'amour de saint Joseph, Sauvez-nous, merveilleusement.

LOUIS RIEL

---

3. Louis Riel: *Journaux de guerre et de prison (Wartime and Prison Notebooks)*, présentation, notes et chronologie métisse 1604–2006, Ismène Toussaint, © Editions Internationales Alain Stanké (Outrement, Québec), 2005, p. 50. Reprinted by permission. Excerpt from the journals of Louis Riel, founder of the Canadian province of Manitoba, leader of the Métis (mixed-race) people of the Canadian prairies and leader of two rebellions on their behalf against the Canadian government in the mid-nineteenth century, for which he was eventually arrested, tried, and executed.

4. *que:* that. *que fait la nation métisse:* that the Métis nation does. For this use of *que* as a relative pronoun, see chapter 16, section 16.1.4.

5. *Je vous en prie:* please; I pray of you.

THE PASSIVE VOICE

THE PASSIVE VOICE can be represented in a number of ways in French. As we have seen, the passive voice can be expressed by using the past participle as a predicate adjective and by the use of reflexive verbs. In addition, the third person indefinite, *on,* often causes a sentence to be translated into the passive voice.

14.1. THE PASSIVE VOICE FORMED BY THE PAST PARTICIPLE AS A PREDICATE ADJECTIVE

Review the use of past participles as predicate adjectives in section 6.3. The passive voice is often expressed by a past participle used as a predicate adjective with a copula verb. We have seen how the predicate adjective *follows the verb,* rather than following the noun. However, because the past participle is being used as an adjective, it still agrees with the noun in number and gender. This construction can take place in any tense:

Le gâteau est mangé.	(passive voice in the present tense)	The cake is eaten.
Le gâteau a été mangé.	(passive voice in the *passé composé)*	The cake was eaten.
La maison est construite.	(passive voice in the present tense)	The house is constructed.
La maison sera construite.	(passive voice in the future tense)	The house will be constructed.

This is a very common way in which the passive voice is formed in French. However, as mentioned in chapter 7 on the *passé composé,* care must be taken not to confuse the passive voice formed with the past participle as a predicate adjective, on the one hand, with the *passé composé* of verbs that take *être* as their auxiliary verb, which use the past participle as a complement to the auxiliary verb, on the other hand (see and review section 7.7.). This potential confusion arises in all compound tenses and will be addressed again in detail in chapter 17, which discusses other compound tenses.

14.2. USE OF REFLEXIVE VERBS TO FORM THE PASSIVE VOICE

While there are several ways in which reflexive verbs may be translated (see chapter 4), it is very common to use the reflexive verb to express the passive voice in French (as in section 4.2.6.). Indeed, in many cases the best translation of a reflexive verb in French may well be the passive voice in English. For instance:

Je m'appelle Jean.	Literally:	*I call myself John.*
	Better:	*I am called John* or *My name is John.*
Il s'intéresse aux sciences politiques.	Literally:	*He interests himself in political science.*
	Better:	*He* is interested *in political science.*
La bibliothèque se trouve près du parc.	Literally:	*The library finds itself near the park.*
	Better:	*The library* is found *near the park.*
	Better still:	*The library is near the park.**

*As mentioned in chapter 4, *se trouver* is translated as a *locative* form of *to be*, referring to the *location* where something *is*.

14.3. THE TRANSLATION OF THE SUBJECT PRONOUN *ON* AND ITS USE TO FORM THE PASSIVE VOICE

The third person subject pronoun *on* literally means *one*. Although the use of *one* as the subject in a sentence in English is limited and tends to sound pedantic, *on* is used *all the time* in French, in formal and casual speech and writing. *On* derives from the French *homme*, signifying humankind or the universal person. Thus *on* is used in French to indicate the nonspecific general case, whereas in English we are more likely to use the third (or first) person plural (*they* or *we*)—or the passive voice—to indicate the nonspecific general case. Become familiar with the possibility of translating a sentence with *on* into the passive voice, as well as into the first or third persons plural.

On parle français à Montréal.	Literally:	*One speaks French in Montreal.*
	Better:	*They speak French in Montreal.* (if the speaker is not a member of the generality referred to)
	Or:	*We speak French in Montreal.* (if the speaker is a member of the generality referred to)
	Or, in the passive voice:	*French* is spoken *in Montreal.*
On donne deux heures aux élèves pour écrire l'examen.	Literally:	*One gives the students two hours to write the exam.*
	Better:	*They give the students two hours to write the exam.*
	Or, in the passive voice:	*The students* are given *two hours to write the exam*
Ceci est un phénomène que l'on ne retrouve qu'en France.	Literally:	*This is a phenomenon that one finds only in France.*
	Better:	*This is a phenomenon that we/they find only in France.*
	Best, in the passive voice:	*This is a phenomenon that* is found *only in France.*

Translation Exercise A

Give the translation that sounds best in English:

1. Il s'appelle Bruno.
2. On nous donne deux heures pour écrire l'examen.
3. Ils s'inquiètent de ce déséquilibre.
4. Ces organisations ne sont pas liées au gouvernement.
5. La bibliothèque se trouve au centre-ville.
6. On a imposé des conditions difficiles aux étudiants.
7. Ses arguments s'appliqueront à des situations diverses.
8. Le coût humain ne se justifie pas.
9. Sa nouvelle idée était accueillie avec scepticisme.
10. Cette tendance s'observe davantage chez les femmes.
11. Dans ce livre on trouvera des contributions de plusieurs auteurs.
12. En été, on adore entendre la musique en plein air.
13. Quarante-cinq millions d'Américains s'expriment en espagnol.

14. Ma sœur et moi, on parlait de notre mère pendant[1] des heures.

15. Le chœur est composé de plusieurs voix.

16. Le gouvernement va se serrer la ceinture.[2]

17. Le programme de musique est consacré aux œuvres de Mozart.

18. La saison des fraises s'allonge d'année en année.

19. Les deux premiers ministres se sont rencontrés hier dans la capitale.

20. « Après les examens, on souhaite obtenir les meilleurs résultats », a dit le directeur.

14.4. TRANSLATION PASSAGE

ESSAI SUR LE DON: FORME ET RAISON DE L'ÉCHANGE DANS LES SOCIÉTÉS ARCHAÏQUES[3]

Le commerce *kula* est d'ordre noble.[4] Il semble être réservé aux chefs, ceux-ci étant à la fois[5] les chefs des flottes, des canots, et les commerçants et aussi les donataires[6] de leurs vassaux, en l'espèce de[7] leurs enfants, de leurs beaux-frères, qui[8] sont aussi leurs sujets, et en même temps les chefs de divers villages inféodés. Il s'exerce de façon noble, en apparence purement désintéressée et modeste. On le distingue soigneusement du simple échange économique de marchandises utiles qui[9] porte le nom de *gimwali*. Celui-ci se pratique, en effet, en plus du *kula*, dans les grandes foires primitives que[10] sont les assemblées du *kula* intertribal

---

1. *pendant:* literally, "during." Here "for."

2. *se serrer la ceinture:* on the model of *il se lave les mains.* See chapter 4, section 4.3.2.

3. Marcel Mauss, *Essai sur le don: Forme et raison de l'échange dans les sociétés archaïques,* © Presses Universitaires de France (Paris), 2007, pp. 107–108. Reprinted by permission. Originally published in *l'Année Sociologique,* seconde série (1924–1925). Mauss (1872–1950) was one of the fathers, along with Durkheim, of French sociology, remembered above all for this "Essay on the Gift," one of the seminal essays of social anthropology.

4. *d'ordre noble:* aristocratic, of a noble order. Cf. « noblesse oblige. »

5. *à la fois:* at the same time

6. *donataires:* beneficiaries

7. *en l'espèce de:* in this particular case

8. *qui:* who. See chapter 16 for an explanation of this and other relative pronouns.

9. *qui:* which. See chapter 16, sections 16.1.2 and 16.1.3.

10. *que:* which. Again, see chapter 16, sections 16.1.2 and 16.1.4. for this use of *que* as the direct object (and not the subject) of the clause it introduces

ou dans les petits marchés du *kula* intérieur: il se distingue par un marchandage très tenace des deux parties, procédé indigne du *kula.* On dit d'un individu qui ne conduit pas le *kula* avec la grandeur d'âme nécessaire, qu'il le « conduit comme un *gimwali* ». En apparence, tout au moins, le *kula*—comme le *potlatch* nord-ouest américain—consiste à donner, de la part des uns,[11] à recevoir, de la part des autres, les donataires d'un jour étant les donateurs de la fois suivante. Même, dans la forme la plus entière, la plus solennelle, la plus élevée, la plus compétitive du *kula,* celle des grandes expéditions maritimes, des *Uvalaku,* la règle est de partir sans rien avoir à échanger, même sans rien avoir à donner, fût-ce[12] en échange d'une nourriture, qu'on refuse même de demander. On affecte de ne faire que[13] recevoir. C'est quand la tribu visiteuse hospitalisera,[14] l'an d'après, la flotte de la tribu visitée, que les cadeaux seront rendus avec usure.

MARCEL MAUSS

---

11. *des uns:* of some
12. *fût-ce:* even if it might be
13. *ne faire que:* to do nothing but. See chapter 9, section 9.2.3.
14. *hospitalisera:* will be hospitable to

15

LE PASSÉ SIMPLE/THE SIMPLE PAST, OR THE PAST HISTORIC

IN FRENCH, THE *passé simple,* or the simple past, is a literary tense: it is used only in writing and formal speech. The *passé composé* is the common way to express the past tense in conversational French; it is also used in written French when the writer wants to write in the idiom of everyday speech. The *passé simple* is used in written French to give a more elegant tone to the text. The *passé simple,* also called the *passé défini* in French, is known in English as the *simple* (i.e., one word) *past,* the *past historic* tense, the *past definite*, the *preterit*, or the *past indicative*.

The *passé simple* has three main forms: one for all *-ER* verbs, and two others that apply to members of both the families of *-RE* and *-IR* verbs. Memorize all three families of endings as you learn them.

15.1. THE *PASSÉ SIMPLE* OF *-ER* VERBS

To form the *passé simple* of -ER verbs, the -ER is removed from the infinitive, and the following endings are added (the example of *aller* is given alongside the endings):

1st person sing.	-ai	j'allai	I went
2nd person sing.	-as	tu allas	you went
3rd person sing.	-a	il/elle/on alla	he/she/one went
1st person pl.	-âmes	nous allâmes	we went
2nd person pl.	-âtes	vous allâtes	you went
3rd person pl.	-èrent	ils/elles allèrent	they went

Note that the first three endings for the singular are the same as the first three endings singular in the future tense. How can you tell the difference, then, between the future tense and the *passé simple* of -ER verbs in the singular form? The answer, of course, rests with the all-important letter -*r* that ends each future/conditional stem, and therefore that must precede the ending for the verb to be in the future tense.

If the endings -*ai,* -*as,* or -*a* are not preceded by the letter -*r* in an -ER verb, then the verb is in the *passé simple.* For instance:

il arrivera	*il arriva*	*il ira*	*il alla*	*il regardera*	*il regarda*
he will arrive	he arrived	he will go	he went	he will look at	he looked at

But continue to watch out for verbs such as *préparer, considérer,* and *comparer* that have an *r before* the infinitive -*er*:

il préparera	*il prépara*	*il considérera*	*il considéra*
he will prepare	he prepared	he will consider	he considered

15.2. THE *PASSÉ SIMPLE* OF -*RE* AND -*IR* VERBS

There are two other sets of endings for the *passé simple.* Neither set of endings applies exclusively to -*RE* or to -*IR* verbs: some members of each set of endings apply to some -*RE* and to some -*IR* verbs.

The first of these two sets of endings is based on the vowel *i*:

		FINIR	*DIRE*	*FAIRE*
1st person sing.	-*is*	je finis	je dis	je fis
2nd person sing.	-*is*	tu finis	tu dis	tu fis
3rd person sing.	-*it*	il finit	il dit	il fit
1st person pl.	-*îmes*	nous finîmes	nous dîmes	nous fîmes
2nd person pl.	-*îtes*	vous finîtes	vous dîtes	vous fîtes
3rd person pl.	-*irent*	ils finirent	ils dirent	ils firent

Once again we are faced with a translation problem, because the *passé simple* in the singular forms of some verbs such as *finir* and *dire* are the *same words* as the singular forms of these verbs in the *present tense.* Fortunately, this is not the case with most verbs that take the -*is* endings in the *passé simple,* but you still need to be aware of this possibility. There is truly no way to tell the difference between the present tense and the *passé simple* of these few verbs. The only indicator is the context itself: what tense(s) is the previous phrase or sentence in? If the previous phrase or sentence has been in any of the past tenses— *passé simple, passé composé, imparfait,* or, as we'll see in the next chapter, the *plus-que-parfait*—then the verb in question will be translated in the *passé simple.* If, on the other hand, the previous phrase or sentence has featured verbs in the present tense, the future, or the conditional tense, then the verb will be translated in the present tense.

Other -*RE* and -*IR* verbs form their *passé simple* with the following endings, based on the letter *u:*

	ENDINGS	*COURIR*	*CONNAÎTRE*	*RECEVOIR*
1ˢᵗ person sing.	-*us*	je cour*us*	je conn*us*	je reç*us*
2ⁿᵈ person sing.	-*us*	tu cour*us*	tu conn*us*	tu reç*us*
3ʳᵈ person sing.	-*ut*	il cour*ut*	il conn*ut*	il reç*ut*
1ˢᵗ person pl.	-*ûmes*	nous cour*ûmes*	nous conn*ûmes*	nous reç*ûmes*
2ⁿᵈ person pl.	-*ûtes*	vous cour*ûtes*	vous conn*ûtes*	vous reç*ûtes*
3ʳᵈ person pl.	-*urent*	ils cour*urent*	ils conn*urent*	ils reç*urent*

Notice that all three possible *passé simple* third person plural endings end in either -*èrent,* -*irent,* or -*urent.* Let your eye become alert to the possibility of a five-letter ending. It is unfortunately very easy to look at this ending and see only the -*ent,* quickly mistaking the tense for the present tense. Some will notice the *r* that precedes the -*ent* and may mistakenly think that they have found the future tense, forgetting that the third person plural future tense ending is -*ont,* and not -*ent.* It is all the more important to learn to take in -*èrent,* -*urent,* and -*irent* as entire endings, because many irregular verbs lose not only the infinitive ending, but almost the entire infinitive form except for the first, or first two, letters, before adding the *passé simple* endings. This means that several verbs have endings significantly longer than the stem itself, especially in the third person plural. Unless you memorize the *passé simple* endings, you will be tempted to translate the third person plural of these verbs (incorrectly) in the present tense, rather than in the simple past:

AVOIR	*ÊTRE*	*FAIRE*	*SAVOIR*	*PRENDRE*	*METTRE*	*DEVOIR*
j'*eus*	je *fus*	je *fis*	je *sus*	je *pris*	je *mis*	je *dus*
tu *eus*	tu *fus*	tu *fis*	tu *sus*	tu *pris*	tu *mis*	tu *dus*
il *eut*	il *fut*	il *fit*	il *sut*	il *prit*	il *mit*	il *dut*

nous eûmes	nous fûmes	nous fîmes	nous sûmes	nous prîmes	nous mîmes	nous dûmes
vous eûtes	vous fûtes	vous fîtes	vous sûtes	vous prîtes	vous mîtes	vous dûtes
ils eurent	ils furent	ils firent	ils surent	ils prirent	ils mirent	ils durent

Notice how the third person plural of all the preceding verbs has a five-letter ending preceded by a stem of only one or two letters. The first three of these, *avoir, être,* and *faire,* should be memorized in the *passé simple* now.

Venir, tenir, and all the verbs that are based on them follow an irregular model of the *passé simple,* which should also be memorized now:

VENIR	TENIR
je vins	je tins
tu vins	tu tins
il/elle/on vint	il/elle/on tint
nous vînmes	nous tînmes
vous vîntes	vous tîntes
ils/elles vinrent	ils/elles tinrent

Impersonal verbs too can turn up in the *passé simple:*

il y eut	there was, there were
il fallut	it was necessary

Translation Exercise A

1. il allait / il va / il est allé / il alla / il ira / il irait
2. nous faisons / nous ferons / nous avons fait / ils firent/ ils feraient
3. je veux / je voulais / je voudrais / je voudrai / je voulus / veuillez
4. elles prépareront / elles ont préparé / elles préparent / elles prépareraient
5. vous pouvez / vous pourrez / vous pouviez / vous pourriez / vous avez pu
6. il sait / ils sauront / il savait / il a su / il sut / ils savent / il saura / il saurait
7. elle prit / elle prend / elle prendra / elle prenait / elle prendrait
8. il vient / il vint / il venait / il viendra / il est venu / nous venions
9. ils ont / ils avaient / ils auraient / ils auront / ils eurent
10. j'écris / j'écrivais / j'ai écrit / j'écrivis / j'écrirai
11. il voit / il verra / il voyait / il a vu / il verrait / il vit
12. je vis / je vivais / je vivrai / je vivrais / j'ai vécu / je vécus

13. tu conduis / tu conduisais / tu conduiras / tu conduirais / tu conduisis

14. il a ouvert / il ouvrait / il ouvre / il ouvrira / il ouvrirait / il ouvrit

15. elle connaît / elle connaissait / elle a connu / elle connut / elle connaîtra

16. ils joignent / ils joindront / ils ont joint / ils joignaient / ils joignirent

17. je me souviens / je me souvenais / je me souvins / je me suis souvenu / je me souviendrai

18. il oublie / il a oublié / il oubliera / il oublierait / il oubliait / nous oubliions / il oublia

19. soyons / nous sommes / nous fûmes / nous serons / nous étions / nous avons été

20. il devient / il devint / il devenait / il est devenu / il deviendra / ils deviennent / ils devinrent

21. nous considérons / nous considérions / nous considérerions / nous considérerons / nous avons considéré

22. il y eut / il y avait / il y a / il y a eu / il y aura / il y aurait

Translation Exercise B

1. Il vit un de ses camarades dans la rue.

2. Elle entra dans le jardin avec sa fille.

3. Leurs progrès furent considérables.

4. Quand il rentra quelques minutes plus tard, il trouva son ami assis sur le fauteuil.

5. Il lui fallut quelques jours pour finir le travail.

6. Après son discours il n'y eut plus rien à dire.

7. Il se souvint de longues journées d'été passées en plein soleil sur la plage au bord de la mer.

8. C'est à la fin du dix-neuvième siècle que les interprétations évolutionnistes fleurirent.

9. Une fois arrivée[1] à la salle, elle fut bien surprise de ne voir personne.

10. Les jours qui précédèrent la cérémonie furent pleins d'intérêt.

11. Il marcha longtemps et le soir il se coucha au milieu des champs.

12. Toutes sortes de procédés furent employés pour empêcher les travailleurs de se mettre en grève.

13. Ces économistes parlèrent pour la première fois des spéculations récentes.

14. Les journalistes élargirent le champ de leurs observations parce qu'ils voulurent résoudre toutes les questions qui restèrent sans réponse.

15. Le gouvernement affirma la législation sur les droits civiques et le droit de vote.

16. En 1989 eut lieu[2] la chute du mur de Berlin, événement qui marqua la fin de la guerre froide.

---

1. *Une fois arrivée:* Once having arrived
2. *eut lieu:* from *avoir lieu,* to take place. See chapter 20, section 20.2.3.

15.3. TRANSLATION PASSAGE

MARIA CHAPDELAINE[3]

Le jour de l'an[4] n'amena aucun visiteur. Vers le soir, la mère Chapdelaine, un peu déçue, cacha sa mélancolie sous la guise d'une gaieté exagérée.

— Quand même[5] il ne viendrait personne, dit-elle, ce n'est pas une raison pour nous laisser pâtir. Nous allons faire de la tire.[6]

Les enfants poussèrent des cris de joie et suivirent des yeux les préparatifs avec un intérêt passionné. Du sirop de sucre et de la cassonade furent mélangés et mis à cuire; quand la cuisson fut suffisamment avancée, Télesphore rapporta du dehors un grand plat d'étain rempli de belle neige blanche. Tout le monde[7] se rassembla autour de la table, pendant que[8] la mère Chapdelaine laissait tomber le sirop en ébullition goutte à goutte sur la neige, où il se figeait à mesure[9] en éclaboussures sucrées, délicieusement froides.

Chacun fut servi à son tour, les grandes personnes imitant plaisamment l'avidité gourmande des petits; mais la distribution fut arrêtée bientôt, sagement, afin de réserver un bon accueil à la vraie tire, dont[10] la confection ne faisait que[11] commencer. Car il fallait parachever la cuisson, et, une fois la pâte prête,[12] l'étirer longuement pendant qu'elle durcissait. Les fortes mains grasses de la mère Chapdelaine manièrent cinq minutes durant l'écheveau[13] succulent qu'elles allongeaient et repliaient sans cesse; peu à peu leur mouvement se fit plus lent, puis une dernière fois la pâte fut étirée à la grosseur du doigt et coupée avec des ciseaux, à grand effort, car elle était déjà dure. La tire était faite.

LOUIS HÉMON

---

3. Louis Hémon, *Maria Chapdelaine*, preceded by a chronology, bibliography, and preface prepared by Pierre Pagé (Montreal: Bibliothèque Canadienne-Française, Fides, 1970), pp. 121–122, © Bernard Grasset, 1924. *Maria Chapdelaine* has remained one of the most famous novels of French Canada since it was first published in 1913.
4. *Le jour de l'an:* New Year's day
5. *Quand même*: Even though
6. *tire*: taffy
7. *Tout le monde:* Everyone
8. *pendant que:* while
9. *à mesure:* immediately
10. *dont*: of which. See chapter 16, section 16.4.
11. *ne faisait que:* was barely beginning. See chapter 9, section 9.2.3, for a more literal translation.
12. *une fois la pâte prête:* once the mixture was ready
13. *l'écheveau:* skein, mass

RELATIVE AND INTERROGATIVE PRONOUNS AND ADJECTIVES

16.1. RELATIVE PRONOUNS *QUI* AND *QUE*

16.1.1. THE MANY USES OF *QUE*

As indicated earlier (in chapter 11, section 11.6) the small word *que* has a wide variety of grammatical uses and meanings in French. This is because it is derived from several different Latin words—*qui, quia, quid*—all of which had different grammatical functions, yet all of which came to be condensed into the single French word *que*.

As we've already seen, *que* can be used as part of a comparative construction to mean *than* or *as*:

Elle est plus jolie que *sa sœur.*	She is prettier *than* her sister.
Elle est aussi jolie que *sa sœur.*	She is as pretty *as* her sister.

Que can also be used as a conjunction, meaning *that*, often introducing indirect speech:

Il dit qu'*il travaille très fort.*	He says *that* he is working very hard.
Il faut que *tu rentres avec elle ce soir.*	It is necessary *that* you return with her this evening.

Or it can be used as a conjunction meaning *whether* or *may* (usually accompanied by the subjunctive; see Chapter 19):

Que-tu l'aimes ou non.	Whether you like him or not.
Que Dieu vous bénisse.	May God bless you.

It is also used as an exclamatory adverb, meaning *how*:

Que *c'est beau!*   How pretty it is!

16.1.2. RELATIVE PRONOUNS *QUI* AND *QUE*

One of the most important—and tricky—uses of *que* in French is its use, along with *qui*, as a relative pronoun. Relative pronouns, in French as in English, introduce relative, or subordinate, clauses, as opposed to independent clauses. An independent clause is one that can stand alone, even if it is taken out of the context of the entire sentence:

I like the book that you have written.

In this sentence, the first part, "I like the book," is an independent clause that can stand alone without the rest of the sentence. On the other hand, dependent, subordinate, or relative clauses cannot stand on their own without the rest of the sentence. The second part of the preceding sentence, "that you have written," is a relative clause that cannot stand on its own. It is introduced by the relative pronoun *that*. In English, our relative pronouns are *that, which, who,* or *whom*. (The relative pronoun *what*, as in "I like what you are writing," can be expressed in French only with the compound relative pronouns for *that which*: see "Compound relative pronouns *ce qui* and *ce que*," section 16.1.5.) The difference between *who* and *whom* as relative pronouns in English is that *who* is the *subject* of the clause it introduces, whereas *whom* is the *object* of the clause it introduces:

I saw the man whom you are going to marry.	(*whom* introduces the relative clause but it is the object of that clause; *you* is the subject of the relative clause.)
I saw the man who is going to marry you.	(*who* introduces the relative clause of which it is the subject.)

In French, *qui* and *que* may refer to people or to things. They, too, differ according to whether the relative pronoun is the subject or the object of the relative clause it introduces. The relative pronoun *qui* is always the subject of the clause it introduces, whereas the relative pronoun *que* is always the object of the clause it introduces.

English is most comfortable with the *subject-verb-object* word order. But French subordinate clauses often mix this order up in ways that can seem counterintuitive to the English speaker, so it is important to memorize the following rules concerning the translation of the relative pronouns *qui* and *que*.

16.1.3. THE RELATIVE PRONOUN *QUI*

The relative pronoun *qui* means *who, which,* or *that.* It is always the *subject* of the clause it introduces. Immediately after translating *qui*, go directly to the verb and translate it (even if there are other words in between *qui* and the verb).

L'homme qui vous attendait est parti.	The man who was waiting for you has left.
C'est mon cousin qui a fait cela.	It's my cousin who did that.
Les enfants qui nous ont parlé vont à cette école.	The children who spoke to us go to this school.
Voilà les élèves qui ont gagné le prix.	Here are the students who won the prize.

16.1.4. THE RELATIVE PRONOUN *QUE*

The relative pronon *que* means *whom, which,* or *that.* It is always the *object* of the clause it introduces. Immediately after translating *que*, find the subject of the clause—go directly to the next noun or noun phrase and translate it. Then come back and translate any words you have had to jump over in order to go directly to the subject.

Sentences with the relative pronoun *que* often follow an inverted word order, where the verb follows the *que* directly. If you don't remember the preceding rule, you will be sorely tempted to translate *que*—incorrectly—as the subject, rather than as the object, of the clause it introduces. This may give you a good English sentence, but unfortunately, it will be the wrong English sentence, and you will have no way of knowing that its meaning is incorrect. Hence the need to memorize this rule of translation.

L'homme que vous attendiez est parti.	The man whom you were waiting for has left.
C'est mon cousin que vous avez vu dans le jardin.	It's my cousin whom you saw in the garden.
Il était éprouvé par le chagrin que lui causait la mort de son père.	He was stricken by the grief that the death of his father was causing him.
Elle a parlé du rôle qu'a joué la découverte de l'art africain dans le développement de la sensibilité moderne.	She spoke of the role that the discovery of African art played in the development of the modern sensibility.

Note that *que* is shortened to *qu'* when followed by a vowel, but *qui* is never shortened.

16.1.5. THE COMPOUND RELATIVE PRONOUNS *CE QUI* AND *CE QUE*

The two compound relative pronouns *ce qui* and *ce que*, which mean *that which,* are used to express the relative pronoun *what.* *Ce qui* is always the subject of the relative clause it introduces:

Dites-moi ce qui est arrivé.	Tell me what (that which) happened.
Elle aime ce qui est beau.	She likes what (that which) is beautiful.

Ce que is always the object of the relative clause it introduces:

Vous n'aimez pas ce qu'elle a dit.	You don't like what (that which) she said.
Ce que l'on[1] raconte de moi n'est pas vrai.	What (that which) one says of me is not true / What they say about me is not true. / What is said about me is not true.
Je n'entends pas ce que vous dites.	I don't hear what (that which) you are saying.

Translation Exercise A

1. L'homme qui descend de l'autobus est un avocat.
2. L'homme que regardent les enfants est leur grand-père.
3. Les amis qui sont venus voir les feux d'artifice[2] sont arrivés en retard.
4. L'accord que cherchent les politiciens n'est pas facile à trouver.
5. Il nous faut exposer en détail ce que le gouvernement a fait.
6. L'autobus qu'ont pris mes amis est arrivé à Chicago hier soir.
7. Ce qui nous intéresse, c'est[3] l'origine des mythes qui nous étaient inconnus.
8. C'est sur ces faits que repose son analyse politique.
9. Il discutait de la différence entre ce qui est permis et ce qui est répressif, ce qui est juste et ce qui ne l'est pas.
10. Les problèmes que connaît le Canada cette année ne sont pas dus[4] à une crise intérieure.

---

1. For the use of *l'* before *on,* see chapter 2, section 2.2. The *l'* has no meaning or grammatical function.
2. *feux d'artifice:* fireworks
3. Both the *Ce* at the beginning of the sentence and the *c'* of *c'est* are the subject of this sentence. This use of a doubled or redundant subject is a common feature in French; the redundant subject is not translated into English.
4. *dus:* past participle of *devoir* in the masculine plural, agreeing with *Les problèmes.* See chapter 10, section 10.2., footnote 2.

11. Les nouvelles qu'ont rapportées les journaux au sujet des armes de destruction massive étaient fausses.

12. Ce que nous voyons dans les médias, c'est le pouvoir d'influencer la pensée des citoyens ordinaires.

13. Il faut prendre conscience de l'ampleur du gaspillage que représente l'extension du périmètre des villes vers les zones agricoles.

14. Cette ordonnance, que beaucoup d'associations attendaient depuis longtemps, est une grande avancée en matière de sécurité.

15. C'est à cette situation que doivent être attribués les conflits territoriaux.

16. La dette climatique pourrait atteindre des milliards de dollars, ce qui pourrait constituer une raison pour le gouvernement de changer ses décisions politiques.

16.2. USES OF THE ADJECTIVE *QUEL*

The adjective *quel* means *which,* and can be used as a relative, interrogative, prepositional, and exclamatory adjective. (Note that this is an adjective and not a pronoun.) As a relative adjective with *que,* it can be followed by the subjunctive to mean *whichever* or *whatever* (see chapter 19 for the subjunctive). Like all adjectives, it has to agree with the noun it modifies, and therefore has four possible forms:

	MASCULINE	FEMININE
Singular	*quel*	*quelle*
Plural	*quels*	*quelles*

These adjectives can introduce relative clauses:

Il faut savoir quels règlements sont en vigueur.	It is necessary to know which rules are in force.
Quelle que soit notre heure de départ, on sera en retard.	Whatever time we may leave, we will be late.

They can follow prepositions:

On voit en quelle mesure la découverte est importante.	We see to what degree the discovery is important.
Il ne sait pas à quelle heure commence le concert.	He doesn't know at what time the concert begins.

And, most commonly, they are used as interrogative adjectives:

Quel livre a-t-il?	Which book does he have?
Quel est ton avis?	What is your opinion?
Quelle heure est-il?	What time is it?
Quels sont les meilleurs étudiants?	Which are the best students?

They are also used as exclamatory adjectives:

Quelle belle photo!	What a beautiful photo!
Quelle chance j'ai eu!	How lucky I was!

16.3. THE RELATIVE AND PREPOSITIONAL PRONOUN *LEQUEL;* THE PREPOSITIONAL PRONOUN *QUI*

16.3.1. THE RELATIVE PRONOUN *LEQUEL*

The relative pronoun *lequel* means *which,* or *which one(s)*. It is formed from the adjective *quel* preceded by the definite article. This pronoun also has four possible forms, depending on the number and gender of the noun to which it refers. Both the endings and the definite article change with each form:

	MASCULINE	FEMININE
Singular	*lequel*	*laquelle*
Plural	*lesquels*	*lesquelles*

Dis-moi lequel *tu aimes le mieux.*	Tell me which one you like best.
J'ai lu plusieurs livres, lesquels *me paraissaient intéressants.*	I read several books which seemed interesting to me.

16.3.2. THE PREPOSITIONAL PRONOUNS *LEQUEL* AND *QUI*

The pronouns *lequel* and *qui* are also used to follow prepositions, as is the prepositional pronoun *qui*. Following prepositions, *lequel* is used for things and *qui* is used for persons. Note that the prepositional pronoun *qui* has a completely different function and meaning than the relative pronoun *qui*. The relative pronoun *qui* is always the subject of the relative clause it introduces and means *that, which,* or *who.* The prepositional pronoun *qui,* on the other hand, is used after a preposition and can only be translated as *whom.*

Nous avons une petite maison derrière laquelle il y a un jardin.
We have a little house behind which there is a garden.

Il parlait aux étudiants parmi lesquels plusieurs venaient d'outre-mer.
He was speaking to the students, among whom many came from overseas.

C'est une personne sur qui je peux toujours compter.
This is a person on whom I can always count.

Elle connaît le monsieur avec qui je parlais.
She knows the gentleman with whom I was speaking.

Since *lequel, laquelle, lesquels,* and *lesquelles* are each composed of the definite article + *quel,* when any of these masculine or plural pronouns are preceded by the prepositions *à* or *de,* the *à* or *de* will contract with the *le* or *les* within the pronoun itself:

à lequel→auquel   *à lesquel(le)s→auxquel(le)s*
de lequel→duquel   *de lesquel(le)s→desquel(le)s*
à laquelle remains as is
de laquelle remains as is

Quels sont les gens auxquels vous écrivez?
Who are the people to whom you are writing?

C'est un homme énigmatique autour duquel beaucoup d'autres se groupent.
He's a mysterious man around whom many others are gathered.

La société considère ses membres comme des coopérateurs vis-à-vis desquels elle a des devoirs.
Society regards its members as collaborators towards which it has some obligations.

16.4. THE RELATIVE PRONOUN *DONT*

The relative pronoun *dont* (which has absolutely nothing to do with the English word *don't*) is used to mean *of which, of whom,* or *whose.* It always introduces a relative clause, the subject of which generally follows it. If you translate *dont* as *of which* or *of whom* first, you may get an awkward-sounding sentence, but you will grasp its meaning; from there you can go on to put it into more idiomatic English:

Le spectacle dont *il parle est formidable.*
The show of which *he speaks is fantastic.*

Le garçon dont *je connais le père retourne chez lui.*
The boy of whom *the father I know is returning home.*
The boy whose *father I know is returning home.*

Voici un autre roman de Victor Hugo; j'ai perdu celui dont *je vous ai parlé.*
Here is another novel by Victor Hugo; I lost the one of which *I spoke to you.*
Here is another novel by Victor Hugo; I lost the one which *I told you about.*

Dont can also be used to give an example of a member of a group previously mentioned, as though to mean: *one of whom* (or *which*) *is* (or *was*), even though the verb corresponding to the *is* or *was* is not expressed in French:

Il avait plusieurs collègues, dont *mon professeur.*
He had several colleagues one of whom (was) *my professor.*

Translation Exercise B

1. Quel a été l'événement majeur de l'année passée?
2. L'autre est le miroir dans lequel on se découvre soi-même.
3. Le politicien a une faille cachée à laquelle il ne pourra pas échapper.
4. Dites-nous quels sont vos employeurs préférés.
5. Avec qui travaillez-vous ce soir?
6. Quels sont les problèmes globaux les plus nuisibles ?
7. Il m'a jeté un de ces regards auxquels on ne répond pas.
8. Quelles études ont-ils suivies ?
9. Le président a commis une faute dont il a du mal[5] à se remettre.
10. Ce sont des questions essentielles auxquelles chacun de nous devrait[6] pouvoir répondre.
11. Ce sont des fonctions dont le juge est spécialement chargé.
12. Le film nous invite à réfléchir sur les raisons pour lesquelles nous devons faire attention aux questions du réchauffement climatique.
13. Il faut établir quelles sont les causes qui ont influencé les faiblesses du système financier.

---

5. *mal:* difficulty
6. *devrait:* should. See chapter 20, section 20.1.3.

14. La famille est le centre autour duquel se développent les dynamiques interperson-
nelles.
15. Il s'agit d'une association bénévole, dont le but est de mieux répondre aux crises
médicales.

16.5. THE INTERROGATIVE PRONOUNS *LEQUEL, QUI,* AND *QUE*

16.5.1. THE INTERROGATIVE PRONOUN *LEQUEL*

The relative pronoun *lequel* can also function as an interrogative pronoun meaning
Which? or *Which one?* or *Who?* or *Whom?*

Lequel voulez-vous?	Which one do you want?
Laquelle est sa sœur?	Which one is her sister?
Lesquels veut-il?	Which ones does he want?

16.5.2. THE INTERROGATIVE PRONOUNS *QUI?* AND *QUE?*

Qui and *que* also function as principal interrogative pronouns meaning *Who?* or *What?*
However, their usage as interrogative pronouns differs entirely from their usage as
relative pronouns. Whereas the *relative* pronoun *qui* is used when it is the *subject* of
the clause it introduces, regardless of whether it is a person or a thing, the *interroga-*
tive pronoun *qui* is used only for a person, regardless of whether the person is the
subject or object of the question. And whereas the *relative* pronoun *que* is used as
the *object* of the clause it introduces, regardless of whether it refers to a person or
a thing, the *interrogative* pronoun *que* is used only for things, regardless of whether
they are the subjects or objects of the question.

The interrogative pronoun *qui* always refers to a person; it can be the subject *or*
the object of the question:

Qui chante?	Who is singing?
Qui cherchez-vous?	Whom are you looking for?
Qui a parlé?	Who spoke?
Qui aime-t-il?	Whom does he love?

The interrogative pronoun *que* always refers to a thing:

Que veut- il?	What does he want?
Que mangez- vous?	What are you eating?

16.6. QUESTIONS FORMED WITH BOTH INTERROGATIVE AND RELATIVE PRONOUNS *QUI* AND *QUE*

Questions in French are very commonly expressed by adding *to* the interrogative pronoun the words "*est-ce*," and then the relative pronoun introducing the rest of the question. The first, interrogative, pronoun is *qui* or *que*, depending on whether it refers to a person or a thing; the second, relative, pronoun is *qui* or *que*, depending on whether it is the subject or the object of the clause it introduces. The literal translation for the more complex questions follows, but in the end these more complex questions are commonly translated as the simple question in English.

SIMPLE QUESTION	TRANSLATION	MORE COMMON BUT MORE COMPLEX QUESTION	LITERAL TRANSLATION
Qui chante?	Who sings?	*Qui est-ce qui chante?*	Who is it who is singing?
Qui a parlé?	Who spoke?	*Qui est-ce qui a parlé?*	Who is it who spoke?
Qui cherchez-vous?	Whom are you looking for?	*Qui est-ce que vous cherchez?*	Who is it that you are looking for?
Qui aime-t-il?	Whom does he love?	*Qui est-ce qu'il aime?*	Who is it that he loves?
Que mange-t-il?	What does he eat?	*Qu'est-ce qu'il mange?*	What is it that he is eating?
Que lisez-vous?	What are you reading?	*Qu'est-ce que vous lisez?*	What is it that you are reading?
Que veut-il?	What does he want?	*Qu'est-ce qu'il veut?*	What is it that he wants?
Que se passe-t-il?	What is happening?	*Qu'est-ce qui se passe?*	What is it that is going on?

The question *Who is it?* is rendered in French as *Qui est-ce?* The simple *Qu'est-ce que* without a following relative clause is often used to mean *What is?* as in *Qu'est ce que la francophonie?* for *What is 'Francophonie?'* (the global community of French-speaking peoples and nations). In addition, the simple questions made by inverting the subject and object as shown in section 2.8, are often reconfigured by placing the words *Est-ce que* in front of the un-inverted sentence:

SIMPLE QUESTION	SAME QUESTION USING *EST-CE QUE*	ENGLISH TRANSLATION
Va-t-il au cinéma?	*Est-ce qu'il va au cinéma?*	Is he going to the movies?
Vient-elle avec nous?	*Est-ce qu'elle vient avec nous?*	Is she coming with us?
Avez-vous mon livre?	*Est-ce que vous avez mon livre?*	Do you have my book?

Translation Exercise C

1. Est-ce qu'il est content de te voir?
2. Que réclament les étudiants qui sont en grève?
3. Qu'est-ce que le médecin a conseillé ?
4. Qui a écrit cet essai sur l'internet?
5. Qu'est-ce qui peut expliquer les événements d'hier?
6. Qui est-ce qui peut expliquer les événements d'hier?
7. Quelle est la plus belle image du monde?
8. De quelle maladie souffre-t-il?
9. Lesquels des acteurs nominés pour les Oscars préférez-vous?
10. Qui pourrait dénoncer ces gens qui fuient leur pays en temps de guerre?
11. À qui donnera-t-on le premier prix?
12. De tous ces artistes, lesquels sont les plus fameux?
13. Lequel des deux est le plus grand écrivain: celui qui raconte des choses originales ou celui qui transforme des mots communs en phrases poétiques?
14. Que peuvent nous apprendre les journaux sur l'opinion politique populaire?
15. Qu'est-ce qu'un logiciel libre?[7] Un logiciel libre est un logiciel qui est fourni avec l'autorisation pour quiconque de l'utiliser, de le copier, et de le distribuer.

16.7. TRANSLATION EXERCISE

Parse this passage: Classify each word according to its part of speech. Find all the relative and interrogative pronouns and translate them according to the guidelines given in this chapter. For nouns, pronouns, and adjectives, give number and gender. For verbs, give tense, person, number, and gender. (Be careful to distinguish *que* as a relative pronoun from *que* as the partner to a preceding *ne*, meaning *only*.) Identify all reflexive verbs as such and indicate whether they should be translated in the active or passive voice. Then translate the entire section.

---

7. *un logiciel libre:* freeware

L'INVENTION DU QUOTIDIEN: ARTS DE FAIRE[8]

S'[9]il est vrai que partout s'étend et se précise le quadrillage[10] de la « surveillance »,[11] il est d'autant plus[12] urgent de déceler comment une société entière ne s'y[13] réduit pas; quelles procédures populaires (elles aussi « minuscules » et quotidiennes) jouent avec les mécanismes de la discipline et ne s'y conforment que pour les tourner; enfin quelles « manières de faire »[14] forment la contrepartie, du côté des consommateurs (ou « dominés »?), des procédés muets qui organisent la mise en ordre sociopolitique.

Ces « manières de faire » constituent les mille pratiques par lesquelles des utilisateurs se réapproprient l'espace organisé par les techniques de la production socioculturelle. Elles posent des questions analogues et contraires à celles que traitait le livre de Foucault: analogues, puisqu'il s'agit de distinguer les opérations quasi microbiennes qui prolifèrent[15] à l'intérieur des structures technocratiques et en détournent le fonctionnement par une multitude de « tactiques » articulées sur les « détails » du quotidien; contraires, puisqu'il ne s'agit plus de préciser comment la violence de l'ordre se mue en technologie disciplinaire, mais d'exhumer les formes subreptices[16] que prend la créativité dispersée, tactique et bricoleuse[17] des groupes ou des individus pris désormais dans les filets de la « surveillance ». Ces procédures et ruses de consommateurs composent, à la limite, le réseau d'une anti-discipline qui est le sujet de ce livre.

MICHEL DE CERTEAU

---

8. Michel de Certeau, *L'Invention du quotidien.* Volume I: *Arts de faire,* © Éditions Gallimard (Paris) 1990, pp. xxxix–xl. Reprinted by permission.
9. *s'* short for *si:* if. See chapter 22, section 22.7.
10. *quadrillage:* grid
11. *surveillance:* discipline, surveillance. cf. Foucault's *Surveiller et punir,* translated into English as *Discipline and Punish.*
12. *d'autant plus:* all the more
13. *y:* to it. Refer to chapter 8, section 8.7, for this use and translation of the indirect pronoun *y.*
14. *manières de faire:* ways of doing, ways of operating
15. *prolifèrent:* this looks like the *passé simple,* but actually it is the present tense of *proliférer,* to proliferate. (The *passé simple* form of this verb would be: *ils proliférèrent.*)
16. *subreptices:* surreptitious
17. *bricoleuse* (fem. of *bricoleur,* handyman): makeshift

MORE COMPOUND TENSES

THE *PASSÉ COMPOSÉ,* which was presented in chapter 7, is the first of several compound tenses in French. Compound tenses are those tenses whose verb forms are made up of two words, as opposed to simple tenses, which are made up of one word only. By now you have learned the seven rules pertaining to the formation of the *passé composé.* Now is a good time to check back to chapter 7 to review these rules, making sure that you know them all by memory, because all but one of the rules concerning the *passé composé* apply in their entirety to all the other compound tenses we will learn in this chapter. The one rule that changes from one compound tense to another is the tense of the auxiliary verb: the *passé composé* is formed with an auxiliary verb *in the present tense* plus a past participle, whereas other compound tenses are formed with an auxiliary verb *in a different tense,* plus a past participle. Other than that, every other rule already learned about the *passé composé* applies to all the other compound tenses.

17.1. *LE PLUS-QUE-PARFAIT/*THE PLUPERFECT

The name of this tense, "more-than-perfect," refers to the idea of a "perfect" tense, that is, a tense whose action has been completed. The *plus-que-parfait,* or the *pluperfect* as it is called in English, refers to something that happened *further in the past than,* or *before,* the action in the perfect, or past, tense. In English, the pluperfect is always expressed with the auxiliary verb *had*: I *had* sung, I *had* seen. Sentences in the pluperfect refer to something that happened before the time of the simple or compound past:

Before I went to the store, I *had* researched where all the sales were.

In French, the *plus-que-parfait* is formed with an auxiliary verb in the *imparfait*, plus a past participle. All the other rules concerning the *passé composé* apply to the pluperfect. Thus, *avoir* and *être* in the *imparfait* are the auxiliary verbs for the *plus-que-parfait*. Any verb that takes *être* in the *passé composé* will take *être* in the *plus-que-parfait*; and all the rules of agreement pertaining to the *passé composé* apply to the pluperfect as well.

Examples of verbs in the *plus-que-parfait* taking *avoir* as their auxiliary:

j'avais fini	I had finished
tu avais regardé	you had looked at
il/elle/on avait dormi	he/she/one had slept
nous avions cherché	we had looked for
vous aviez écrit	you had written
ils/elles avaient touché	they had touched

Remember, the *imparfait* of *avoir* is translated as *had: j'avais*, I had. Never mix up *have* and *had* in your translations of compound tenses! they are completely different auxiliary verbs, resulting in completely different tenses, and must always be translated accordingly:

J'ai *ouvert la porte.*	I opened the door, *or* I *have* opened the door.	*passé composé*
J'avais *ouvert la porte.*	I *had* opened the door.	*plus-que-parfait* / pluperfect

Again, as with the *passé composé*, with verbs that take *avoir* as their auxiliary, if the direct object precedes the verb, the past participle must agree in number and gender with the direct object:

Il avait mangé les pommes.	He had eaten the apples.
Il les avait mangées.	He had eaten them.

Remember as well that to translate the pluperfect of verbs that take *être*, *être* must be translated as though it were *avoir* (because we have only the one auxiliary verb in English, *to have*):

j'étais venu(e)	I had come
tu étais tombé(e)	you had fallen
il/elle/on s'était levé(e)	he/she/one had arisen
nous étions allé(e)s	we had gone
vous vous étiez amusé(e)(s)	you had enjoyed yourself/selves
ils/elles étaient arrivé(e)s	they had arrived

Another issue to be kept in mind is, once again, the difference between the use of *être* as an auxiliary verb in a compound tense and the use of *être* with a past participle that is functioning as a predicate adjective (as discussed in chapter 7, section 7.7). These two situations look identical but are translated into two completely different tenses. When *être* in any tense is part of a compound tense (i.e., when it is used as an auxiliary verb with past participles of members of the family of twenty verbs that take *être*, or with the past participles of any reflexive verbs), it is translated not literally but as a form of *to have*, as though it were *avoir*. On the other hand, when *être* in any tense is followed by a past participle of any verb that is *neither* one of the twenty verbs that take *être* as their auxiliary verb *nor* a reflexive verb, the past participle is being used as a *predicate adjective* and *être* in whatever tense it appears is translated literally.

Le garçon était tombé. The boy **had** fallen.	*Tomber* is one of the twenty verbs that take *être* as their auxiliary verb, so this is a compound tense, and *était* must be translated as a form of *avoir*: **had**
Le gâteau était mangé. The cake **was** eaten.	*Manger* is *not* one of the twenty verbs that take *être* as their auxiliary verb, nor is it a reflexive verb; therefore *mangé* is *not* part of a compound tense. Rather, *mangé* is a past participle used as a predicate adjective, and *était* must be translated literally: **was.**

17.2. *LE FUTUR ANTÉRIEUR*/THE FUTURE PERFECT

Le futur antérieur, or the future perfect, is the tense that tells what *will have happened* by a certain time in the future. For example:

By the year 2050, greenhouse gases *will have risen* to a very high level.

In French, the future perfect is formed with an auxiliary verb (*avoir* or *être*) in the future tense, followed by a past participle. Again, all the other rules given in chapter 7 concerning the *passé composé* apply equally to the future perfect:

j'aurai fini	I will have finished
tu auras écrit	you will have written
il/elle/on aura répondu	he/she/one will have answered

nous aurons parlé	we will have spoken
vous aurez conduit	you will have driven
ils/elles auront vendu	they will have sold

Again, in these compound tenses with verbs that take *être*, *être* must be translated as though it were *avoir:*

je serai sorti(e)	I will *have* gone out
tu seras descendu(e)	you will *have* gone down
il/elle/on sera rentré(e)	he/she/one will *have* returned
nous serons arrivé(e)s	we will *have* arrived
vous vous serez levé(e)(s)	you will *have* gotten up
ils/elles seront allé(e)s	they will *have* gone

And again, if the direct object precedes the verb with verbs that take *avoir* as their auxiliary, the past participle must agree with the direct object:

Il aura mangé les pommes.	He will have eaten the apples.
Il les aura mangées.	He will have eaten them.

We must consider once more the difference between verbs that take *être* as an auxiliary verb in the future *perfect* tense and those taking *être* in the future tense followed by a past participle used as a predicate adjective:

Le garçon sera tombé. The boy **will have** fallen.	*tomber* is one of the twenty verbs that take *être* as their auxiliary verb, so this is a compound tense, and *sera* must be translated as a form of *avoir:* **will have**
Le gâteau sera mangé. The cake **will be** eaten.	*manger* is *not* one of the twenty verbs that take *être* as their auxiliary verb, nor is it a reflexive verb; therefore *mangé* is not part of a compound tense. Rather, *mangé* is a past participle used as a predicate adjective, and *sera* must be translated literally: **will be.**

17.3. *LE CONDITIONNEL PASSÉ*/THE CONDITIONAL PERFECT

The *conditionnel passé*, or the conditional perfect, refers to what I *would have done* under a certain set of circumstances:

If I had known you were coming, I would have *baked a cake.*

The conditional perfect is formed with the auxiliary verb in the conditional tense, followed by a past participle. If the auxiliary verb is *être*, it must be translated as though it were *avoir:*

j'aurais fait	I would have made
tu aurais fini	you would have finished
il/elle/on serait venu(e)	he/she/one would have come
nous nous serions dépêché(e)s	we would have hurried up
vous seriez devenu(e)(s)	you would have become
ils/elles auraient donné	they would have given

Here again, if the direct object precedes the verb with verbs that take *avoir* as their auxiliary, the past participle must agree with the direct object:

Il aurait mangé les pommes.	He would have eaten the apples.
Il les aurait mangées.	He would have eaten them.

Verbs in the conditional perfect that take *être* as their infinitive must be distinguished from *être* in the future tense with the past participle used as a predicate adjective:

Le garçon serait tombé. The boy **would have** fallen.	*Tomber* is one of the twenty verbs that take *être* as their auxiliary verb, so this is a compound tense, and *serait* must be translated as a form of *avoir:* **would have**
Le gâteau serait mangé. The cake **would be** eaten.	*Manger* is not one of the twenty verbs that take *être* as their auxiliary verb, nor is it a reflexive verb; therefore *mangé* is not part of a compound tense. Rather, it is a past participle used as a predicate adjective, and *serait* must be translated literally: **would be.**

17.4. *LE PASSÉ ANTÉRIEUR*

The *passé antérieur* is a literary tense; that is, a tense that is written but not spoken. It is made up of an auxiliary verb (*avoir* or *être*) in the *passé simple,* plus a past participle. It differs only slightly in meaning from the *plus-que-parfait*: it is more precise in time than the pluperfect, allowing the author to pinpoint a more specific moment in his narration. But because we lack this precise temporal nuance in English, the *passé antérieur* is simply translated into the English pluperfect. Like the *passé simple,* it has a more elegant, or less colloquial, tone, than the *plus-que-parfait*. Again, *être* used as an auxiliary verb in the *passé antérieur* must be translated as though it were *avoir*:

j'eus écrit	I had written
tu fus arrivé(e)	you had arrived
il/elle/on eut regardé	he/she/one had looked at
nous eûmes cherché	we had looked for
vous vous fûtes levé(e)(s)	you had gotten up
ils/elles furent allé(e)s	they had gone

If the direct object precedes the verb with verbs that take *avoir* as their auxiliary, the past participle must agree with the direct object:

Il eut mangé les pommes.	He had eaten the apples.
Il les eut mangées.	He had eaten them.

And verbs in the *passé antiérieur* with *être* as their infinitive must be distinguished from *être* in the *passé simple* with the past participle used as a predicate adjective:

Le garçon fut tombé.	*Tomber* is one of the twenty verbs that take *être* as their
The boy **had** fallen.	auxiliary verb, so this is a compound tense, and *fut* must be translated as a form of *avoir:* **had**
Le gâteau fut mangé.	*Manger* is not one of the twenty verbs that take *être* as their
The cake **was** eaten.	auxiliary verb nor is it a reflexive verb, therefore *mangé* is not part of a compound tense. Rather, *mangé* is a past participle used as a predicate adjective, and *fut* must be translated literally: **was**

You can see how crucial it is to have *avoir* and *être* memorized in every single tense. Unless you have these two verbs at your fingertips in all tenses, you will not be able to recognize and correctly translate compound tenses when you encounter them. Take the time to reconsolidate your knowledge of these two verbs in all tenses now.

Translation Exercise A

1. il a regardé / il aura regardé / il eut regardé / il aurait regardé/ il avait regardé
2. je suis arrivée / je fus arrivée / je serai arrivée / j'étais arrivée / je serais arrivée
3. elle voudrait/ elle aurait voulu/ elle voudra / elle aura voulu / elle avait voulu / elle voulait

4. ils sont allés / ils seront allés / ils allaient / ils seraient allés / ils furent allés

5. il est devenu membre / il sera devenu membre/ il était devenu membre / il serait devenu membre

6. le gâteau est mangé / le gâteau sera mangé / le gâteau était mangé /le gâteau serait mangé

7. ils vinrent / ils sont venus / ils furent venus / ils étaient venus / ils viendraient / ils seraient venus

8. elle avait commencé / elle aura commencé / elle commencera / elle eut commencé /

9. il eut fallu / il avait fallu / il a fallu / il aura fallu / il aurait fallu / il fallut

10. on a su / on sut / on aura su / on aurait su / on avait su / on eut su

11. je dus / je devais / j'ai dû / j'eus dû / j'aurais dû / j'aurai dû / je devrais

12. nous sommes descendus / nous fûmes descendus / nous étions descendus / nous serions descendus

13. il est rassuré / il était rassuré / il sera rassuré / il serait rassuré / il fut rassuré

14. il est tombé / il sera tombé / il était tombé / il serait tombé / il fut tombé

15. elles sont rentrées / elles furent rentrées / elles étaient rentrées / elles seront rentrées

16. ils ont fait / ils eurent fait / ils avaient fait / ils auront fait / ils auraient fait/ ils faisaient/ ils firent

17. j'ouvre / j'ai ouvert / j'ouvris / j'aurai ouvert / j'avais ouvert / j'aurais ouvert / j'eus ouvert

18. il écrit / il écrivit / il avait écrit / il eut écrit / il aura écrit / il a écrit

19. il prit / il aura pris / il a pris / il prendrait / il aurait pris / il avait pris / il eut pris

20. il y a / il y avait / il y aura / il y aura eu / il y aurait eu / il y avait eu / il y aurait

Translation Exercise B

1. J'avais fini mon travail lorsqu'il m'a appelé.
2. Si je lui avais envoyé une invitation, il serait venu chez nous aujourd'hui.
3. Si j'eus mis trois gâteaux sur la table, il en aurait mangé un.
4. Je serai parti quand il viendra la semaine prochaine.
5. Je serais ravi de faire votre connaissance.
6. Demain matin, il aura écrit les lettres à ses collègues.
7. Demain matin, il les aura écrites.
8. Elle aurait voulu s'échapper de sa vie provinciale.
9. Avant de partir en voyage, il avait pris un repas copieux.

10. Il n'aurait osé rêver d'un tel honneur. (refer back to chapter nine, section 9.2.5.)

11 S'il avait eu le temps, il serait resté plus longtemps.

12. La cathédrale de Notre-Dame de Paris fut achevée en 1245.

13. Je me suis retrouvé face à des obstacles aussi grands que ceux que j'avais voulu éviter.

14. Je ne vous aurais jamais parlé de mon passé, si vous ne me l'aviez pas demandé.

15. Comme ils étaient de l'autre côté de la montagne, mes cris ne leur seraient pas parvenus.

16. Il lui promit d'examiner son affaire aussitôt que le marchand serait revenu.

17. Si elle savait ce que son fils avait fait, la femme aurait été heureuse.

18. Cette idée ne me serait jamais venue sans avoir lu le livre.

17.5. TRANSLATION PASSAGE

ESSAI SUR LE GOÛT[1]

Notre manière d'être est entièrement arbitraire; nous pouvions avoir[2] été faits comme nous sommes, ou autrement. Mais, si nous avions été faits autrement, nous aurions senti autrement; un organe de plus ou de moins dans notre machine aurait fait une autre éloquence, une autre poésie; une contexture[3] différente des mêmes organes aurait fait encore une autre poésie: par exemple, si la constitution de nos organes nous avait rendus capables d'une plus longue attention, toutes les règles qui proportionnent[4] la disposition du sujet à la mesure de notre attention, ne seraient plus; si nous avions été rendus capables de plus de pénétration, toutes les règles qui sont fondées sur la mesure de notre pénétration, tomberaient de même;[5] enfin toutes les lois établies sur ce que notre machine est d'une certaine façon, seraient différentes, si notre machine n'était pas de cette façon.

Si notre vue avait été plus faible et plus confuse, il aurait fallu[6] moins de mou-lures[7] et plus d'uniformité dans les membres[8] de l'architecture: si notre vue avait

---

1. Montesquieu, *Essai sur le goût,* © Éditions Payot & Rivages (Paris), 1993, pp. 12–13. Montesquieu (1689–1755) was one of the great philosophers of the French Enlightenment.
2. *nous pouvions avoir:* we could have. See chapter 20, Modal Verbs, section 20.1.2.
3. *contexture:* arrangement
4. *proportionnent:* from *proportionner,* to accommodate
5. *de même:* in the same way
6. *il aurait fallu:* for this use of *falloir,* see chapter 11, section 11.5.2.
7. *moulures:* patterns, designs
8. *membres:* parts, elements

été plus distincte, et notre âme capable d'embrasser plus de choses à la fois, il aurait fallu dans l'architecture plus d'ornements; si nos oreilles avaient été faites comme celles de certains animaux, il aurait fallu réformer[9] bien de nos instruments de musique. Je sais bien que les rapports que les choses ont entre elles auraient subsisté;[10] mais le rapport qu'elles ont avec nous ayant changé, les choses qui, dans l'état présent, font un certain effet sur nous, ne le feraient plus; et comme la perfection des arts est de nous présenter les choses telles qu'elles nous fassent[11] le plus de plaisir qu'il est possible, il faudrait qu'il y eût[12] du changement dans les arts, puisqu'il y en aurait dans la manière la plus propre à nous donner du plaisir.

MONTESQUIEU

---

9. *réformer:* to alter
10. *subsisté:* remained, from *subsister,* to remain
11. *qu'elles nous fassent:* literally, that they might make for us. Present subjunctive, third person plural, of *faire;* see chapter 19, sections 19.1. and 19.2.1.
12. *qu'il y eût:* imperfect subjunctive of *il y a;* see chapter 19, section 19.2.2. *Il faudrait qu'il y eût:* it would be necessary that there had been (i.e., there would have to have been).

THE CAUSATIVE *FAIRE*

18.1. THE CAUSATIVE *FAIRE*, AN IDIOMATIC CONSTRUCTION

The causative *faire* is an idiomatic construction that expresses the idea of one person having something done by another person. The subject of the sentence is the person who has the intention, while the person who actually carries out the work—the agent, so to speak—is represented by a noun preceded by *par* or *à,* or else by the indirect object pronoun. In English, we express the causative *faire* by using the verbs *to have* or *to cause:*

They will have their house painted this summer.
They will have their house painted by the painters.
They will have them paint their house.

They is the subject of this sentence, but clearly, *they* won't be doing the painting themselves: *they* will *have* the painters do the work for them. *They* have the intention; the painters will actually carry out the work. *The painters*—the actual agents of the action—are expressed by the indirect object in French, which in turn is expressed by *par* or *à* (or *au* or *aux*) plus a noun or pronoun. When this agent of action in the causative *faire,* expressed as the indirect object, is replaced by a pronoun, the pronoun will be the indirect object pronoun (refer to the list of indirect object pronouns in chapter 8, section 8.5). The French versions of the preceding sentences look like this:

Ils feront peindre leur maison cet été.
Ils feront peindre leur maison par les peintres.
Ils leur feront peindre leur maison.

(Be careful to distinguish *leur* as a possessive pronoun, as in *leur maison;* and *leur* as in indirect object pronoun, as in *ils leur feront peindre.*)

IMPORTANT *Whenever the verb* faire—*in any tense whatsoever—is immediately followed by an infinitive, we have an instance of the causative* faire.

Since it is constructed idiomatically, the causative *faire* cannot be translated in a straightforward manner. When you encounter *faire* in any tense followed by an infinitive, follow this protocol:

1. Translate the subject of the sentence
2. Translate *faire* as a form of *to cause* or *to have* in the same tense as you find *faire*. Although English commonly uses *to have* as the operative word in this construction, starting off by translating *faire* as a form of *to cause* will often give you a clearer sense of the meaning of the sentence.
3. Skip over the infinitive that follows *faire.*
4. Translate the next noun structure.
5. Go back and translate the infinitive. If the infinitive is a transitive verb, translate it in the passive voice.
6. In most cases, translate any preposition (*à, au, aux, par*) as *by,* that is, as indicating the agent of the action. (Occasionally, *à* may retain its original meaning, as when someone has something done *for* someone rather than *by* them).
7. Translate any remaining words as the agent of the action.

Example: L'institutrice fera réciter les poèmes aux étudiants.

1.	*L'institutrice*	The instructor
2.	*fera*	will cause
3.	*réciter*	*skip over this infinitive*
4.	*les poèmes*	the poems
5.	*réciter*	*now go back and translate this infinitive. Because it is a transitive verb, it is translated in the passive voice:* to be recited
6.	*aux*	by the (*here the indirect object functions as the agent of the action*)
7.	*étudiants*	students

The instructor will cause the poems to be recited by the students. Or, now that we know what the meaning is, *The instructor will have the poems recited by the students.* As this is still somewhat awkward in English, we are free to put the sentence into a more idiomatic English: *The instructor will have the students recite the poems.*

Whenever you encounter the causative *faire,* translate it according to the preceding protocol first. Only then, once you have figured out the meaning, should you go ahead and put the sentence into more idiomatic English. If you begin by first reaching for an idiomatic translation, chances are that you will mix up the meaning of the sentence.

The causative *faire* can, of course, use both direct and indirect object *pronouns*, rather than nouns:

Il fait lire le livre aux étudiants.
He causes the book to be read by the students.   *or*
He is having the book read by the students.   *or*
He is having the students read the book.

Il leur fait lire le livre.
He causes the book to be read by them.   *or*
He is having the book read by them.   *or*
He is having them read the book.

Il le leur fait lire.
He is causing it to be read by them.   *or*
He is having it read by them.   *or*
He is having them read it.

18.1.1 CONVENTIONAL OR FIXED FORMS OF THE CAUSATIVE *FAIRE*

There are several forms of the causative *faire* that are used so frequently that they have come to be translated together as idiomatic phrases:

faire arriver	to deliver	*faire venir*	to summon
faire intervenir	to involve	*faire voir*	to show
faire manger	to feed		
faire parvenir	to send		
faire remarquer	to point out		
faire savoir	to inform		

Translation Exercise A

1. Mes cousins ont fait bâtir une belle maison.
2. Il leur faisait lire ce livre.
3. L'idée fut si fantastique qu'elle le fit rire.

4. Il fera transporter l'ordinateur demain après-midi.

5. Elle lui fit manger un morceau du fromage.

6. Il m'avait fait beaucoup souffrir.

7. La mère a fait manger le repas par ses enfants.

8. Elle l'a fait manger par ses enfants.

9. Elle le leur a fait manger.

10. On le fit siéger au conseil municipal.

11. Le gouvernement veut faire produire des produits biologiques[1] à ces fermiers.

12. Le président a fait connaître ses opinions aux citoyens.

13. Le médecin le fit guérir à ses dépens.

14. Les expéditeurs se sont chargés de faire arriver les paquets en deux jours.

15. Son discours fit naître une grande curiosité dans mon esprit.

16. Le professeur fait traduire des phrases en anglais aux élèves.

17. Quand elle est tombée malade, on a fait venir le médecin.

18. La création de l'Union européenne a fait naître d'immenses espoirs.

19. Une musique d'orchestre se fit entendre de l'intérieur de la salle.

20. Les autorités firent prévaloir leur interprétation de la situation.

18.2. TRANSLATION PASSAGE

Find the causative *faire* in these two passages, underline and translate them, then translate both passages.

LES FORMES ÉLÉMENTAIRES DE LA VIE RELIGIEUSE[2]

Or c'est précisément ce que nous avons tenté de faire et nous avons vu que cette réalité, que les mythologies se sont représentées[3] sous tant de formes différentes, mais qui est la cause objective, universelle et éternelle de ces sensations *sui generis* dont est faite l'expérience religieuse, c'est la société. Nous avons montré quelles forces morales elle développe et comment elle éveille ce sentiment d'appui, de sauvegarde, de dépendance tutélaire qui attache le fidèle à son culte.

---

1. *produits biologiques:* organic produce
2. Emile Durkheim, *Les Formes élémentaires de la vie religieuse,* © Presses Universitaires de France (Paris), 1960 [1912], pp. 597-98. Reprinted by permission. Durkheim (1858–1917) is considered the father of modern sociology.
3. *se sont représentées:* have reconfigured; have represented

C'est elle qui l'élève au-dessus de lui-même: c'est même elle qui le fait. Car ce qui fait l'homme, c'est cet ensemble de biens intellectuels qui constitue la civilisation, et la civilisation est l'œuvre de la société. Et ainsi s'explique le rôle prépondérant du culte dans toutes les religions, quelles qu'elles soient.[4] C'est que[5] la société ne peut faire sentir son influence que si elle est un acte, et elle n'est un acte que si les individus qui la composent sont assemblés et agissent en commun. C'est par l'action commune qu'elle prend conscience de soi et se pose;[6] elle est avant tout une coopération active. Même les idées et les sentiments collectifs ne sont possibles que grâce à des mouvements extérieurs qui les symbolisent, ainsi que[7] nous l'avons établi. C'est donc l'action qui domine la vie religieuse par cela seul que c'est la société qui en est la source.

EMILE DURKHEIM

18.3. TRANSLATION PASSAGE

TRISTES TROPIQUES[8]

En manifestant, par notre vocation, la prédilection qui nous pousse vers des formes sociales et culturelles très différentes de la nôtre—surestimant celles-là aux dépens de celle-ci—nous ferions preuve d'une inconséquence radicale; comment pourrions-nous proclamer ces sociétés respectables, sauf en nous fondant sur les valeurs de la société qui nous inspire l'idée de nos recherches? Incapables à jamais d'échapper aux normes qui nous ont façonnés, nos efforts pour mettre en perspective les différentes sociétés, y compris[9] la nôtre, seraient encore une façon honteuse de confesser sa supériorité sur toutes les autres.

. . . Aucune société n'est parfaite. Toutes comportent par nature une impureté incompatible avec les normes qu'elles proclament, et qui se traduit concrètement

---

4. *quelles qu'elles soient:* whatever they may be. Present subjunctive of *être:* see chapter 19.
5. *C'est que:* This is because
6. *se pose:* presents itself, from *se poser*
7. *ainsi que:* as
8. Claude Lévi-Strauss, *Tristes Tropiques,* © Librairie Plon (Paris), 1955, pp. 444, 446. Reprinted by permission.
9. *y compris:* including

par une certaine dose d'injustice, d'insensiblité, de cruauté. Comment évaluer cette dose? L'enquête ethnographique y parvient.[10] Car, s'il est vrai que la comparaison d'un petit nombre de sociétés les fait apparaître très différentes entre elles, ces différences s'atténuent quand le champ d'investigation s'élargit. On découvre alors qu'aucune société n'est foncièrement bonne; mais aucune n'est absolument mauvaise. Toutes offrent certains avantages à leurs membres, compte tenu[11] d'un résidu d'iniquité dont l'importance paraît approximativement constante et qui correspond peut-être à une inertie spécifique qui s'oppose, sur le plan de la vie sociale, aux efforts d'organisation.

CLAUDE LÉVI-STRAUSS

---

10. *y parvient:* gets us there; comes to the rescue (more literally: arrives at or reaches [that evaluation])
11. *compte tenu:* considering, taking into account (more literally: having taken into account)

19

LE SUBJONCTIF/THE SUBJUNCTIVE

WHEREAS ENGLISH HAS three grammatical *moods*—the indicative, the imperative, and the subjunctive—French counts four grammatical *moods*: the indicative, imperative, conditional, and subjunctive. With the exception of the imperative, all the tenses that have been discussed thus far are part of what is called in English the *indicative mood,* which expresses statements that are presented as factual. Questions and negative statements are also part of the indicative mood.

The *subjunctive mood* expresses a *subj*ective or hypothetical perspective regarding facts or opinions as they are desired, commanded, imagined, doubted, feared, hoped for, or viewed as the subject of uncertainty. In English, the subjunctive mood is rarely used. It occurs from time to time without most anglophones being aware when they are actually using it. For instance,

Indicative:	She knows that the frog *is* only an amphibian.
Subjunctive:	She wishes that the frog *were* really a prince.
Indicative:	The king *lives* well.
Subjunctive:	Long *live* the king!
Indicative:	She never *arrives* on time.
Subjunctive:	It is important that she *arrive* before nightfall.
Indicative:	When *I move*, I will lose my security deposit.
Subjunctive:	If *I were to move* tomorrow, I would lose my security deposit.

However, most of the time in English we simply use various tenses of the indicative—the present, the conditional, or the future—where French would use the subjunctive:

I wish that you *would* pick up the laundry today.
I hope that he *will* arrive before nightfall.
If I *moved* tomorrow, I would lose my security deposit.

French, on the other hand, makes use of the subjunctive very frequently. Because English does not use the subjunctive as frequently, we often translate the French subjunctive into the closest tense of the indicative in English.

19.1. WHEN IS THE SUBJUNCTIVE USED IN FRENCH?

The subjunctive is used often in French, usually in subordinate or relative clauses (but occasionally in independent clauses) to express something that is desired, commanded, doubted, feared, possible, uncertain, and so on. It is generally preceded by a verb expressing desire, command, doubt, and so on, followed by a subordinate clause in the subjunctive. The subjunctive clause is usually introduced by the relative pronoun *que*, meaning *that*, as in, *I wish that . . .* or *I fear that . . . .* If there is no preceding independent clause, the *que* expresses the idea of *may*, *let,* or *whether* something might or might not be the case.

The following conditions in which the subjunctive is used are too numerous and complex to be memorized. They are provided as a reference for the sake of clarifying the use of the subjunctive:

1. The subjunctive is used in clauses depending on verbs that express a wish, desire, or command. The subject of the main clause is a different person from the subject of the dependent clause:

Ma mère désire que vous dîniez avec nous ce soir.	My mother wants you to dine with us this evening.
Mon père veut que j'aille à l'université.	My father wants me to go to university.

But note:

Ma mère désire dîner.	My mother wants to dine.
Il veut aller à l'université.	He wants to go to university.

(In these last 2 sentences, the subject of the first verb is the same person as the subject of the second verb, so the subjunctive is not used.)

2. The subjunctive is used in independent clauses expressing a wish or an order, where *que* is often translated with the English words *may* or *let*.

Que Dieu vous bénisse.	May God bless you.
Qu'elle aille vivre quelque part ailleurs!	May she go live somewhere else!

Occasionally, there is no *que* at all; the *que* is merely implied:

Dieu le veuille!	May God grant it.
Vive la reine!	Long live the queen!

3. The subjunctive is used to express uncertainty or supposition, where *que* is translated as whether; or, when preceded by *quel* or *quoi*, as *whatever* or *whoever*:

Qu'il s'agisse d'une situation contemporaine ou historique . . .
Whether it has to do with a contemporary or historical situation . . .

Quels que soient vos intérêts . . .
Whatever your interest is [whatever your interests may be] . . .

Quoi qu'il mange, il ne grossit pas.
Whatever he eats, he doesn't get fat.

Le nouveau professeur, quel qu'il soit, aura beaucoup à faire.
The new professor, whoever he may be, will have a lot to do.

4. The subjunctive is used in clauses depending on expressions of emotion, such as joy, sorrow, shame, fear:

Elle est contente que je parte.	She is happy that I am leaving.
Je regrette que le dîner ne soit pas prêt.	I'm sorry that dinner is not ready.
Il a honte que je sache.	He is ashamed that I know.
*Elle a peur que le chien ne lui fasse mal.**	She is afraid that the dog might hurt her. She is afraid lest the dog hurt her.

*Verbs of fearing and sometimes verbs of doubting take a redundant (and therefore not translated) *ne* before the verb in the dependent clause, similar in meaning to the English "lest."

5. The subjunctive is used in clauses depending on certain impersonal expressions indicating necessity, importance, probability etc.

*Il faut que je finisse mes devoirs.**	It is necessary that I finish my homework (I have to finish my homework).
Il est important que Jean vienne chez moi.	It is important that John come to my place.
Il est possible qu'il pleuve.	It is possible that it may rain.

* This can equally be expressed as: *Il me faut finir mes devoirs* (see chapter 11, section 11.5.2.).

6. The subjunctive is used in clauses depending on verbs of thinking, believing or hoping, when used negatively or interrogatively:

Pensez-vous qu'elle soit belle?	Do you think she is beautiful?
Je ne crois pas qu'il soit à la maison.	I don't believe that he is at the house.
Croyez-vous que nous ayons beaucoup d'argent?	Do you believe that we have a lot of money?

7. The subjunctive is used in clauses that depend on a superlative adjective, or on *seul* (only), *premier* (first), or *dernier* (last):

Marie est la plus jolie demoiselle que je connaisse.
Mary is the prettiest young woman that I know.

Charles est le meilleur acteur que nous ayons.
Charles is the best actor that we have.

François est le seul ami que vous ayez.
François is the only friend that you have.

8. The subjunctive is used in relative clauses which have an indefinite antecedent:

Elle désire un mari qui ait beaucoup d'argent.
She wants a husband who has a lot of money.

Il n'y a personne qui sache faire cela.
There is no one who knows how to do that.

Je cherche un homme qui sache parler trois langues.
I am looking for a man who knows how to speak three languages.

but:

Je connais un homme qui sait parler trois langues.
I know a man who knows how to speak three languages.*

* That is, when the antecedent is no longer indefinite, the sentence reverts to the indicative.

9. The subjunctive is used in dependent clauses introduced by certain conjunctions, such as *avant que ... ne* (before), *pour que, afin que* (in order that); *bien que, quoique* (although); *jusqu'à ce que* (until); *pourvu que* (provided that). Note that the conjunction *avant que* (before) is often followed by a redundant *ne*, which is not translated:

Bien qu'il soit malade, il va à l'école.
Even though he is sick, he's going to school.

Je viendrai avant que vous ne partiez pour Paris.
I will come before you leave for Paris.

J'attendrai jusqu'à ce que vous ayez fini la lettre.
I will wait until you have finished the letter.

Il est parti avant que nous n'ayons mangé.
He left before we had eaten.

19.2. THE FOUR TENSES OF THE SUBJUNCTIVE

The tenses of the subjunctive, unlike those of the indicative, do not have a precise temporal meaning; that is, they do not necessarily refer to a specific time in the present, past, or future. Although the tenses of the indicative must be translated strictly according to the models given in the previous chapters, there is much more leeway in translating the subjunctive. Occasionally, the French subjunctive is translated into the corresponding subjunctive tense in English. Most of the time, however, the subjunctive is simply translated into the nearest available corresponding indicative tense, because we use the subjunctive so rarely in English. (So if you don't recognize the subjunctive, you still have a good chance of translating it correctly!) Occasionally, we may add a *may, might,* or *would* to indicate the uncertainty that is at the heart of the subjunctive—but only if the sentence demands it. Because the subjunctive is almost always found in a relative clause introduced by the relative pronoun *que,* the word *que* is included in the following conjugations.

19.2.1. *LE SUBJONCTIF PRÉSENT*

The *present subjunctive*—(that) I speak, (that) I (will/would/may/might) speak—is usually formed by taking the third person plural form of the present indicative tense (the *ils* form), dropping the *-ent* ending, and adding the present subjunctive endings: *-e, -es, -e, -ions, -iez, -ent.*

INFINITIVE	PARLER	FINIR	PARTIR	METTRE
3rd person pl. pres. indicative:	parl-ent	finiss-ent	part-ent	mett-ent
que je (j')	parle	finisse	parte	mette
que tu	parles	finisses	partes	mettes
qu' il/elle/on	parle	finisse	parte	mette
que nous	parlions	finissions	partions	mettions
que vous	parliez	finissiez	partiez	mettiez
qu' ils/elles	parlent	finissent	partent	mettent

As you can see, in the present subjunctive, the endings for the first three persons singular and the ending for the third person plural are the same as the present indicative tense endings. The endings for the first and second persons plural, however, are the same as the first and second persons plural endings of the *imparfait*. This gives the distinctive "shoe" or "boot" form that characterizes the present subjunctive: the first three persons singular together with the third person plural follow one pattern (the present tense endings), while the *nous* and *vous* forms follow another pattern (the *imparfait* endings):

que je parle	que nous parlions
que tu parles	que vous parliez
qu'il/elle/on parle	qu'ils/elles parlent

Some verbs adopt a completely irregular subjunctive stem but still use the same pattern of subjunctive endings as indicated earlier:

	FAIRE	SAVOIR	POUVOIR
que je (j')	fasse	sache	puisse
que tu	fasses	saches	puisses
qu' il/elle/on	fasse	sache	puisse
que nous	fassions	sachions	puissions
que vous	fassiez	sachiez	puissiez
qu' ils/elles	fassent	sachent	puissent

With some irregular verbs not only the endings but also the stems themselves follow the same "boot" pattern. Either, as with *aller* and *vouloir*, an irregular stem is introduced for the first three persons in the singular and the third person plural—while the *nous* and *vous* forms revert to the expected stem corresponding to the *imparfait* form—or, as in *prendre, venir, voir, devoir, boire*, the regular subjunctive stem (the third person present indicative minus the -*ent*) is kept for the first three persons singular and the third person plural, while an irregular stem is used for the *nous* and *vous* forms, which continue to mimic the corresponding *imparfait* forms:

que j'aille	que nous allions
que tu ailles	que vous alliez
qu'il/elle/on aille	qu'ils/elles aillent

que je prenne	que nous prenions
que tu prennes	que vous preniez
qu'il/elle/on prenne	qu'ils/elles prennent

	ALLER	VOULOIR	PRENDRE	VENIR	VOIR	DEVOIR	BOIRE
que je (j')	aille	veuille	prenne	vienne	voie	doive	boive
que tu	ailles	veuilles	prennes	viennes	voies	doives	boives
qu' il/elle/on	aille	veuille	prenne	vienne	voie	doive	boive
que nous	allions	voulions	prenions	venions	voyions	devions	buvions
que vous	alliez	vouliez	preniez	veniez	voyiez	deviez	buviez
qu' ils/elles	aillent	veuillent	prennent	viennent	voient	doivent	boivent

And, of course, *avoir* and *être* are completely irregular and must be memorized:

	AVOIR	*ÊTRE*
que je (j')	aie	sois
que tu	aies	sois
qu' il/elle/on	ait	soit
que nous	ayons	soyons
que vous	ayez	soyez
qu' ils/elles	aient	soient

The present subjunctive is most commonly translated into the present indicative in English:

Ma mère désire que vous dîniez avec nous ce soir.	My mother wants you to eat with us tonight.
Mon père veut que j'aille à l'université.	My father wants me to go to university.
Quoi qu'il mange, il ne grossit pas.	Whatever he eats, he doesn't get fat.

19.2.2. *L' IMPARFAIT DU SUBJONCTIF*

The *imperfect subjunctive* is a literary verb form used in formal writing. It is formed by taking the third person singular of the *passé simple* (without the final -*t* in the case of

-re and *-ir* verbs) and adding the imperfect subjunctive endings: *-sse, -sses, -ˆt, -ssions, -ssiez, -ssent*:

	AVOIR	ÊTRE	ALLER	FAIRE	FINIR	DEVOIR
Third person s. of *passé simple*:	eu-	fu-	alla-	fi-	fini-	du-
que je (j')	eusse	fusse	allasse	fisse	finisse	dusse
que tu	eusses	fusses	allasses	fisses	finisses	dusses
qu' il/elle/on	eût	fût	allât	fît	finît	dût
que nous	eussions	fussions	allassions	fissions	finissions	dussions
que vous	eussiez	fussiez	allassiez	fissiez	finissiez	dussiez
qu' ils/elles	eussent	fussent	allassent	fissent	finissent	dussent

	POUVOIR	PRENDRE	SAVOIR	VENIR	VOIR	VOULOIR
Third person s. of *passé simple*:	pu-	pri-	su-	vin-	vi-	voulu-
que je (j')	pusse	prisse	susse	vinsse	visse	voulusse
que tu	pusses	prisses	susses	vinsses	visses	voulusses
qu'il/elle/on	pût	prît	sût	vînt	vît	voulût
que nous	pussions	prissions	sussions	vinssions	vissions	voulussions
que vous	pussiez	prissiez	sussiez	vinssiez	vissiez	voulussiez
qu'ils/elles	pussent	prissent	sussent	vinssent	vissent	voulussent

The imperfect subjunctive is found in a dependent clause when the independent clause is already in a past tense. It is translated by whatever past tense fits best into the sentence at hand, at times using the conditional *would* or *might* to indicate the uncertainty represented by the subjunctive:

Elle n'était pas sûre qu'il voulût venir.	She wasn't sure that he wanted to come.
Marie voulait que Jean lui envoyât une lettre.	Marie wished that John sent/had sent/would send/her a letter.
Elle n'était pas sûre que Jean voulût la voir.	She wasn't sure that John wanted to see her.

19.2.3. *LE SUBJONCTIF PASSÉ*

The *past subjunctive* is a compound tense in which the auxiliary verb is in the present subjunctive, followed by the past participle. Verbs take the same auxiliary verb (*avoir* or *être*) as they do in all other compound tenses and follow the same rules of agreement that govern all compound tenses.

	AVOIR	ÊTRE	FINIR	DONNER	ALLER
que je (j')	aie eu	aie été	aie fini	aie donné	sois allé(e)
que tu	aies eu	aies été	aies fini	aies donné	sois allé(e)
qu'il/elle/on	ait eu	ait été	ait fini	ait donné	soit allé(e)
que nous	ayons eu	ayons été	ayons fini	ayons donné	soyons allé(e)s
que vous	ayez eu	ayez été	ayez fini	ayez donné	soyez allé(e)(s)
qu'ils/elles	aient eu	aient été	aient fini	aient donné	soient allé(e)s

When the past subjunctive is used in the subordinate clause, its action took place before the action of the verb in the main clause. The past subjunctive is translated either as the past tense or pluperfect tense in English:

Elle est contente qu'il soit venu.	She is happy that he came.
Elle était contente qu'il soit venu.	She was happy that he had come.

19.2.4. *LE SUBJONCTIF PLUS-QUE-PARFAIT*

The *pluperfect subjunctive* is a rarely used compound tense in which the auxiliary verb (*avoir* or *être*) is in the imperfect subjunctive, followed by the past participle. As always, this tense too follows the rules of agreement governing all compound tenses.

	AVOIR	ÊTRE	FINIR	DONNER	ALLER
que je (j')	eusse eu	eusse été	eusse fini	eusse donné	fusse allé(e)
que tu	eusses eu	eusses été	eusses fini	eusses donné	fusses allé(e)
qu'il/elle/on	eût eu	eût été	eût fini	eût donné	fût allé(e)
que nous	eussions eu	eussions été	eussions fini	eussions donné	fussions allé(e)s
que vous	eussiez eu	eussiez été	eussiez fini	eussiez donné	fussiez allé(e)(s)
qu'ils/elles	eussent eu	eussent été	eussent fini	eussent donné	fussent allé(e)s

It is translated as the pluperfect or the conditional perfect: (that) I *had* given; (that) I *would have* finished:

Ô toi que j'eusse aimée, ô toi qui le savais! [1]
O you whom I would have loved, O you who knew it!
(or) You, whom I might have loved, who know it too!

---

1. Final line of the poem *À une passante* by Charles Baudelaire.

Translation Exercise A

1. Dieu le veuille!
2. Quoi que fît le père, le fils restait inquiet.
3. Aussi nombreuses qu'en soient les variétés, l'amour est partout le même.
4. Le juge a ordonné que cette femme soit mise en liberté.
5. Pour qu'une morale professionnelle puisse s'établir, il faut que la corporation devienne une institution responsable.
6. Y a-t-il quelqu'un ici qui ait des livres à vendre?
7. De tous les mots qui puissent être dits, il employait les plus effroyables.
8. Dans ses recherches historiques, il étudie comment fonctionnaient les anciennes institutions avant qu'eussent été développés les modèles institutionnels modernes.
9. Il faut que ces nouvelles organisations puissent fonctionner sans violer la Constitution.
10. Elle n'admet pas qu'il puisse y avoir quoi que ce soit[2] de déraisonnable dans ses croyances.
11. Voulez-vous que nous fassions un repas à la mode de mon pays?
12. « Qu'on me laisse aller et que je n'aille pas en prison! » a dit le refugié.
13. Il n'y a plus personne qui veuille travailler sept jours par semaine.
14. Il ignorait que vous eussiez quitté l'édifice.

19.3. TRANSLATION PASSAGE

Underline all verbs in the subjunctive and identify their tenses before translating the following passages.

LE BOURGEOIS GENTILHOMME[3]

....

Maître de philosophie: Je vous expliquerai à fond toutes ces curiosités.

Monsieur Jourdain: Je vous en prie.[4] Au reste il faut que je vous fasse une confidence. Je suis amoureux d'une Personne de grande qualité, et je souhaiterais que vous m'aidassiez à lui écrire quelque chose dans un petit Billet que je veux laisser tomber à ses pieds.

---

2. *quoi que ce soit:* anything (i.e., whatever it might be)
3. Molière, *Le Bourgeois Gentilhomme*, Act II, scene iv, from *Molière Œuvres Complètes, Tome II*, © Editions Gallimard (Paris) 2010 [1671]), p. 283.
4. *Je vous en prie:* Please do. Literally, I pray it of you.

Maître de philosophie: Fort bien.

Monsieur Jourdain: Cela sera galant, oui.

Maître de philosophie: Sans doute. Sont-ce des Vers que vous lui voulez écrire ?

Monsieur Jourdain: Non, non, point de Vers.

Maître de philosophie: Vous ne voulez que de la Prose ?

Monsieur Jourdain: Non, je ne veux ni Prose, ni Vers.

Maître de philosophie: Il faut bien que ce soit l'un, ou l'autre.

Monsieur Jourdain: Pourquoi ?

Maître de philosophie: Par la raison, Monsieur, qu'il n'y a pour s'exprimer, que la Prose, ou les Vers.

Monsieur Jourdain: Il n'y a que la Prose, ou les Vers ?

Maître de philosophie: Non, Monsieur: Tout ce qui n'est point Prose, est Vers; et tout ce qui n'est point Vers, est Prose.

Monsieur Jourdain: Et comme[5] l'on parle qu'est-ce que c'est donc que cela?[6]

Maître de philosophie: De la Prose.[7]

Monsieur Jourdain: Quoi? Quand je dis: « *Nicole, apportez-moi mes Pantoufles, et me donnez mon Bonnet de nuit* », c'est de la Prose?

Maître de philosophie: Oui, Monsieur.

Monsieur Jourdain: Par ma foi, il y a plus de quarante ans que[8] je dis de la Prose, sans que j'en susse rien; et je vous suis le plus obligé du monde, de m'avoir appris cela.

MOLIÈRE

---

5. *comme:* as; here, best translated as "when."

6. *Qu'est-ce que c'est (donc) que cela:* What is that (then)? See chapter 11, section 11.2. for this highly idiomatic expression.

7. *De la prose:* Prose. Recall this usage of the partitive pronoun *de*, explained in chapter 1, section 1.7.

8. *Il y a ... que je dis:* It's been...that I've been speaking. For this idiomatic expression of time, see chapter 21, section 21.2.

19.4. TRANSLATION PASSAGE

PENSÉES[9]

....

Nous ne tenons jamais au temps présent. Nous rappelons le passé; nous anticipons l'avenir comme trop lent à venir, comme pour hâter son cours; ou nous rappelons le passé pour l'arrêter comme trop prompt,[10] si imprudents que nous errons dans des temps qui ne sont point nôtres, et ne pensons point au seul qui nous appartient, et si vains que nous songeons à ceux qui ne sont rien, et échappons sans réflexion le seul qui subsiste. C'est que[11] le présent, d'ordinaire, nous blesse. Nous le cachons à notre vue parce qu'il nous afflige, et s'il nous est agréable nous regrettons de le voir échapper. Nous tâchons de le soutenir par l'avenir, et pensons à disposer[12] les choses qui ne sont pas en notre puissance pour un temps où nous n'avons aucune assurance d'arriver.

Que chacun examine ses pensées. Il les trouvera toutes occupées au passé ou à l'avenir. Nous ne pensons presque point au présent; et si nous y pensons, ce n'est que pour en prendre la lumière pour disposer de l'avenir. Le présent n'est jamais notre fin.

Le passé et le présent sont nos moyens; le seul avenir est notre fin. Ainsi nous ne vivons jamais, mais nous espérons de vivre, et nous disposant toujours à être heureux, il est inévitable que nous ne le soyons jamais.

BLAISE PASCAL

---

9. Blaise Pascal, *Pensées,* © Éditions du Seuil (Paris), 1962 [1670], ed. L. Lafuma, #47 (Brunschvicg #172). Pascal (1623–1662), mathematician, physicist, inventor, Catholic theologian, and a member of the Jansenist movement, is regarded as one of the finest masters of French prose; his *Pensées,* reflections on religious faith, are considered his greatest work.
10. *comme trop prompt:* as though it passes too swiftly (literally: as too swift)
11. *C'est que:* This is because
12. *disposer:* to arrange

MODAL VERBS AND OTHER COMMON IDIOMATIC VERBAL CONSTRUCTIONS

20.1. MODAL VERBS

Modal verbs are auxiliary verbs that express possibility, obligation, necessity, or desirability, such as (in English) *can, could, should, would, might, must,* and *ought.* By "auxiliary" we mean the fact that modal verbs do not stand on their own; rather, they are used in conjunction with a second, main, verb. Modal verbs should not be confused with the auxiliary verbs *avoir* and *être,* which are used to create new, compound tenses such as the *passé composé,* the *plus-que-parfait,* and so on. Instead, modal verbs may be in any tense, and rather than creating new tenses, they introduce the sense of possibility, obligation, or necessity to the meaning of the main verb. A modal verb can have different meanings in different contexts in French, as it can in English. Some English examples of modal verbs are the following:

1. You *should* not do that.
2. She *should* be here by 7:30. (Note the different meanings of *should* in sentences 1 and 2. In sentence 1, *should* is a directive or an admonishment, whereas in sentence 2, *should* conveys expectation.)
3. *Could* you pick me up when I've finished?
4. I *couldn't* find the book I was looking for. (Note the different tenses of *could* in sentences 3 and 4. In sentence 3, *could* implies a question about a possibility in the future, whereas in sentence 4, *couldn't* is in the past.)
5. *Would* you be so kind as to assist me?
6. *Wouldn't* he have finished his work by then?

In French, there are four major verbs that can be considered to have modal functions: *vouloir, pouvoir, devoir,* and *savoir.*

20.1.1. *VOULOIR*

The meaning of *vouloir* is *to want* something. Followed by an infinitive, its meaning is modal. In most tenses this does not pose any major problem for the translator:

Je veux manger une pomme.	I want to eat an apple.
Je voulais manger une pomme.	I wanted to eat an apple.

It is only in the conditional tense that the modal use of *vouloir* causes it to be translated differently from a straightforward form of the verb *to want. Vouloir* in the conditional tense is generally translated as *would like* and is often used in the place of the present tense as a more polite way to formulate what one *wants*—that is, what *one would like:*

Je voudrais lui parler directement.	I would like to talk to him directly.
Elle voudrait prendre un taxi pour se rendre chez elle.	She would like to take a taxi home.

20.1.2. *POUVOIR*

Pouvoir means *to be able* and is often used as a modal verb to mean *can, could,* or *would.* Note the different nuances *pouvoir* takes on when used as a modal verb:

Je peux vous voir ce soir à dix-huit heures.	I can see you this evening at 6:00 PM.[1]
Tu peux perdre tes devoirs.	You could/might lose your homework.
Il pouvait travailler toute la journée.	He could/he was able to work all day.
Nous pouvions avoir été faits comme nous sommes, ou autrement.[2]	We could have been made as we are, or otherwise.
Ils ne pouvaient pas trouver l'enfant.	They couldn't find the child.
Ils n'ont pas pu trouver l'enfant.	They were not able to find the child
Il pourrait travailler toute la journée.	He could/ he would be able to work all day long.
Elle pourrait venir si elle le voulait.	She could come if she wanted to.

---

1. Francophone countries tell time on the twenty-four-hour system rather than on the twelve-hour system common in anglophone usage. Therefore, 6 PM becomes 18h in French.
2. From Montesquieu, *Essai sur le goût;* see chapter17, section 17.5.

20.1.3. *DEVOIR*

The basic meaning of *devoir* is *to have to* do something, or *to owe* someone something. In the *imparfait* and conditional tenses *devoir* is generally used as a modal verb. As a modal verb, the meaning of *devoir* shifts from meaning *to have to* to meaning *should, ought,* or *supposed to*.

Il doit partir.	He has to leave/he must leave.
Il devrait partir	He should leave.
Il devait partir, mais il est resté.	He was supposed to leave, but he stayed.
Ils doivent lui parler.	They have to talk to him.
Ils devaient y aller avec moi.	They were supposed to go there with me.
Ils devraient lui parler.	They should talk to him.

The *passé composé* of *devoir* is used to say that something *must have* happened or *had to* happen:

Il a dû sortir de l'édifice vers trois heures.	He must have left the building by three o'clock.
J'ai dû voyager toute la nuit.	I had to travel all through the night.

The conditional perfect of *devoir* is used to say that something *should have* happened.

Tu aurais dû manger.	You should have eaten.
J'aurais dû travailler plus fort.	I should have worked harder.

20.1.4. *SAVOIR*

The verb *savoir* in any tense followed by an infinitive means *to know how* to do something. Since knowing how to do something implies that one is able to do that thing, *savoir* is often used in the place of *pouvoir,* to mean *to be able:*

Je sais parler trois langues.	I know (how to)/I can speak three languages.
Il saura compléter le rapport.	He will be able to finish the report.
Nous ne saurions pas soutenir votre réclamation.	We could not support your claim.
Il a su faire de la petite entreprise de son père un géant mondial.	He was able to make a world-wide giant from his father's small business.

Translation Exercise A

1. Il devrait arriver une demi-heure en avance.
2. On doit s'arrêter au coin de la rue.

3. Il ne pouvait rien faire.

4. Est-ce que je pourrais parler avec le professeur?

5. J'aurais dû lui dire que je venais le voir ce soir.

6. Elle ne savait pas nager.

7. Je voudrais vous rejoindre cet après-midi.

8. Il a dû finir sa lecture du nouveau roman.

9. Il a pu lire le livre, mais il n'a rien compris.

10. La situation politique pourrait mettre un terme aux négociations déjà fragiles entre les deux pays.

11. Je ne saurais comment vous remercier pour ce magnifique cadeau.[3]

12. Ils ont commencé à construire une route qui devrait permettre aux fermiers d'aller directement vendre leurs produits au marché.

13. La crise financière aurait dû nous apprendre deux ou trois choses.

14. Ces élections ne devraient pas avoir d'effets dramatiques sur la croissance mondiale.

15. Plusieurs des pays anciennement colonisés ont su d'un mariage forcé faire un mariage de raison, et parlent leur langue ancestrale aussi bien que la langue importée.

20.2. OTHER IDIOMATIC VERBAL CONSTRUCTIONS

The following verbs have common idiomatic usages that cannot be translated literally.

20.2.1. *VENIR DE*

There is no single word that can translate the English word *just*, as in, *I just saw the most wonderful movie.* Instead, the verb *venir* in the present tense (or in the *imparfait*) is followed by *de,* which is then followed by the infinitive form of the main verb. This forms the "immediate past": the *venir de* in the present tense is translated as the English word *just*, and the verb in the infinitive is put into the past tense in English. If *venir de* is in the *imparfait* in French, the main (infinitive) verb is put into the pluperfect in English:

Il vient de lire ce livre.	He just read this book.
Il venait d'écrire une lettre.	He had just written a letter.

---

3. See chapter 9, section 9.2.5 for the use of *ne* without *pas*.

Il vient de dîner.	He just ate dinner.
Il venait de dîner.	He had just eaten dinner.

20.2.2 *TENIR À*

The verb *tenir* by itself means *to hold.* When followed by the preposition *à,* the verb *tenir* means to hold something in one's mind or heart, in the sense of believing in, valuing, or being eager or anxious to do something:

Il tient à visiter Paris.	He is eager to visit Paris.
Nous tenons à notre avis.	We value/ hold on to / believe strongly our opinion.

Tenir à can also mean *to be due to* or *to partake of:*

Cela tient à des causes particulières.	This is due to particular causes.

20.2.3. *AVOIR* FOR STATES OF MIND AND BODY

Many states of mind and body that in English are expressed with the verb *to be* (I *am* hungry, you *are* afraid, he *is* wrong) are expressed with *avoir* in French. The *avoir* must be translated into the corresponding tense of *to be* in English:

avoir faim	to be hungry
avoir soif	to be thirsty
avoir chaud	to be warm
avoir froid	to be cold
avoir besoin de	to need (something)
avoir lieu	to take place
avoir raison	to be right
avoir tort	to be wrong
avoir sommeil	to be sleepy
avoir peur (de)	to be afraid (of)
avoir honte (de)	to be ashamed (of)
avoir mal à	to have an ache or pain
avoir beau (+ infinitive)	to do something in vain

Avoir is also used to express age:

Quel âge a-t-il?	How old is he?	*Il a trente ans.*	He is thirty years old.
Quel âge avez-vous?	How old are you?	*J'ai vingt-cinq ans.*	I'm twenty-five years old.

20.2.4. *FAIRE* AS AN IMPERSONAL VERB FOR THE STATE OF THE WEATHER OR THE ENVIRONMENT

The verb *faire* is used with the impersonal pronoun *il* to express the state of the environment or atmosphere. As in all impersonal verbs, the *il* that precedes *faire* in these expressions is always translated as *it,* and never as *he.* Although the following definitions refer to the weather outdoors, these expressions could also be used upon entering a building or other indoor environment:

Il fait beau.	It's nice out./The weather is good.
Il fait mauvais.	It's awful out./The weather is bad.
Il fait chaud.	It's hot out.
Il fait froid.	It's cold.
Il fait nuit.	It's nighttime; it's dark out.
Il fait jour.	It's daytime.
faire partie de . . .	to be a part of
faire semblant de . . .	to pretend to

20.2.5. *ALLER* FOR GREETINGS

The verb *aller* is the common verb used in greetings:

Comment allez-vous?	*Je vais très bien, merci*	How are you? I'm fine, thank you.
Comment ça va?	*Ça va bien, merci.*	How's it going? (more casual) Fine, thanks.
Il ne va pas bien.		He isn't well.
Comment vont les affaires?		How is business?

Translation Exercise B

Translate with reference to sections 20.2.1–5:

1. Les enfants ont faim.
2. Je viens de lire un roman policier très choquant.
3. Il fait très chaud ce soir.
4. Elle a peur des serpents.
5. Il a honte de ce qu'il a fait.
6. Le professeur n'a pas raison; il a tort.
7. Il faisait nuit quand elle est rentrée chez elle.
8. Les étudiants tiennent à réussir leurs examens.

9. Il a mal aux dents.

10. Il fait partie du parti socialiste.

11. Il vient d'écrire les dernières pages de sa thèse.

12. Le concert aura lieu demain.

13. Elle ne va pas très bien ces jours-ci.

14. Un vieil homme venait de tomber sur le trottoir.

15. Son enfant aîné a deux ans; le petit a onze mois.

20.3. TRANSLATION PASSAGE

DE LA DÉMOCRATIE EN AMÉRIQUE[4]

Dans les démocraties, on écoute les pièces de théâtre, mais on ne les lit point. La plupart de ceux qui assistent aux[5] jeux de la scène n'y cherchent pas les plaisirs de l'esprit, mais les émotions vives du cœur. Ils ne s'attendent point à y trouver une œuvre de littérature, mais un spectacle, et, pourvu que l'auteur parle assez correctement la langue du pays pour se faire entendre, et que ses personnages excitent la curiosité et éveillent la sympathie, ils sont contents; sans rien demander de plus à la fiction, ils rentrent aussitôt[6] dans le monde réel.[7] Le style y est donc moins nécessaire; car, à la scène, l'observation de ces règles échappe davantage.

Quant aux vraisemblances,[8] il est impossible d'être souvent nouveau, inattendu, rapide, en leur restant fidèle. On les néglige donc, et le public le pardonne. On peut compter qu'il ne s'inquiétera point des chemins par où vous l'avez conduit, si vous l'amenez enfin devant un objet qui le touche. Il ne vous reprochera jamais de l'avoir ému en dépit des règles . . . .

Les Américains mettent au grand jour[9] les différents instincts que je viens de peindre, quand ils vont au théâtre. Mais il faut reconnaître qu'il n'y a encore qu'un petit nombre d'entre eux qui y aillent. Quoique les spectateurs et les spectacles se

---

4. Alexis de Tocqueville, « Quelques Observations sur le théâtre des peuples démocratiques », *De la démocratie en Amérique,* Vol. 2, first part, chapter 19. © Librairie Philosophique J. Vrin (Paris, 1990 [1848]), pp. 81–82.

5. *assistent à (aux):* attend

6. *aussitôt:* immediately

7. *le monde réel:* real life

8. *vraisemblances:* plausibilities (of the plots)

9. *mettent au grand jour:* display very broadly

soient prodigieusement accrus depuis quarante ans aux États-Unis, la population ne se livre[10] encore à ce genre d'amusement qu'avec une extrême retenue.

Cela tient à des causes particulières que le lecteur connaît déjà, et qu'il suffit de lui rappeler en deux mots.

Les puritains, qui ont fondé les républiques américaines, n'étaient pas seulement ennemis des plaisirs ; ils professaient de plus une terreur toute spéciale pour le théâtre. Ils le considéraient comme un divertissement abominable, et, tant que leur esprit a régné sans partage, les représentations dramatiques ont été absolument inconnues parmi eux. Ces opinions des premiers pères de la colonie ont laissé des traces profondes dans l'esprit de leurs descendants.

L'extrême régularité d'habitudes et la grande rigidité de mœurs qui se voient aux États-Unis ont d'ailleurs été jusqu'à présent peu favorables au développement de l'art théâtral.

ALEXIS DE TOCQUEVILLE

20.4. TRANSLATION PASSAGE

LE PLAISIR DU TEXTE[11]

Toute une petite mythologie tend à nous faire croire que le plaisir (et singulièrement le plaisir du texte) est une idée de droite. A droite, on expédie d'un même mouvement vers la gauche tout ce qui est abstrait, ennuyeux, politique et l'on garde le plaisir pour soi: soyez les bienvenus parmi nous, vous qui venez enfin au plaisir de la littérature! Et à gauche, par morale (oubliant les cigares de Marx et de Brecht), on suspecte, on dédaigne tout « résidu d'hédonisme ». A droite, le plaisir est revendiqué *contre* l'intellectualité, la cléricature: c'est le vieux mythe réactionnaire du cœur contre la tête, de la sensation contre le raisonnement, de la « vie » (chaude) contre « l'abstraction » (froide): l'artiste ne doit-il pas, selon le précepte sinistre de Debussy, « *chercher humblement à faire plaisir* »? A gauche, on oppose la connaissance, la méthode, l'engagement, le combat, à la « simple

---

10. *se livre:* engage in, avail itself of.
11. Roland Barthes, *Le Plaisir du texte,* © Éditions du Seuil (Paris), 1973, coll. *Tel Quel,* new edition 2000, pp. 38–39. Reprinted by permission.

délectation » (et pourtant: si la connaissance elle-même était *délicieuse?*). Des deux côtés, cette idée bizarre que le plaisir est chose *simple,* ce pour quoi on le revendique ou le méprise. Le plaisir, cependant, n'est pas un *élément* du texte, ce n'est pas un résidu naïf; il ne dépend pas d'une logique de l'entendement et de la sensation; c'est une dérive, quelque chose qui est à la fois révolutionnaire et asocial et ne peut être pris en charge par aucune collectivité, aucune mentalité, aucun idiolecte. Quelque chose de *neutre?* On voit bien que le plaisir du texte est scandaleux: non parce qu'il est immoral, mais parce qu'il est *atopique.*

ROLAND BARTHES

CHANGES OF TENSE WITH IDIOMS OF TIME

21.1. *DEPUIS*

Depuis means either *since,* when followed by a specific time, or *for* (in the sense of *for a certain amount of time*) when followed by an amount of time. It indicates an action that began in the past but is still continuing at the time of narration. *Depuis* is accompanied by the present tense or by the *imparfait.* When it is accompanied by the present tense, the present tense in French must be translated into English as the "has been" form of the verb. When *depuis* is accompanied by the *imparfait,* the *imparfait* must be translated as the "had been" form of the verb:

Georges lit son roman depuis un mois.	George has been reading his novel for a month.
Georges lit son roman depuis lundi.	George has been reading his novel since Monday.
Georges lisait son roman depuis un mois.	George had been reading his novel for a month.
Georges lisait son roman depuis lundi.	George had been reading his novel since Monday.

21.2. *IL Y A . . . QUE, ÇA FAIT . . . QUE, VOILÀ . . . QUE*

Il y a ... que, ça fait ... que, and *voilà ... que* can take the place of *depuis,* causing the same alteration in the translation of the present or *imparfait* tenses; that is, the present is translated as the "has been" form of the verb, and the *imparfait* is translated as the "had been" form of the verb.

Il y a longtemps que je t'aime.
It's been a long time that I've loved you. (more literal translation)
I have loved you for a long time. (better English)

Il y avait longtemps qu'il travaillait sur ce chapitre.
It had been a long time that he had been working on this chapter. (more literal translation)
He had been working on this chapter for a long time. (better English)

Ça fait longtemps que j'habite à Chicago.
It's been a long time that I've been living in Chicago. (more literal translation)
I have been living in Chicago for a long time. (better English)

Cela faisait une heure que je vous attendais.
It had been an hour that I had been waiting for you. (more literal translation)
I had been waiting for you for an hour. (better English)

Voilà deux jours qu'il est malade.
It's been two days that he's been sick. (more literal translation)
He has been sick for two days. (better English)

BUT: *Il y a,* when *not* accompanied by *que* yet followed by an expression of time, means *ago,* and there is no alteration in the translation of the verb tense that follows:

Mon oncle est arrivé il y a trois jours.
My uncle arrived three days ago.

Je l'ai vue il y a quinze minutes.
I saw her fifteen minutes ago.

Le train est parti il y a cinq minutes.
The train left five minutes ago.

Translation Exercise A

1. Le nombre d'infractions est stable depuis les années 2000.
2. Dans le G-20 qu'il préside depuis novembre, le président a lancé des initiatives géopolitiques.
3. Nous travaillons depuis dix ans pour que les vaccins arrivent à tout le monde.
4. Il occupe le siège de conseiller municipal depuis 1986.
5. Je l'ai rencontré il y a dix ans.
6. Il y a un an que les enfants nous demandent de leur faire une surprise.
7. Il y avait un an que sa mère était morte.
8. Ça fait déjà un mois que nous parlons ensemble.

9. Voilà deux heures qu'il est parti.

10. Voilà une semaine qu'elle vous attend.

21.3. TRANSLATION PASSAGE

MÉDITATIONS MÉTAPHYSIQUES:

PREMIÈRE MÉDITATION: DES CHOSES QUE L'ON PEUT RÉVOQUER EN DOUTE[1]

Il y a déjà quelque temps que je me suis aperçu que, dès mes premières années, j'avais reçu quantité de fausses opinions pour véritables, et que ce que j'ai depuis fondé sur des principes si[2] mal[3] assurés, ne pouvait être que fort douteux et incertain; de façon qu'il me fallait entreprendre sérieusement une fois en ma vie de me défaire[4] de toutes les opinions que j'avais reçues jusques alors en ma créance, et commencer tout de nouveau dès les fondements, si je voulais établir quelque chose de ferme et de constant dans les sciences. Mais cette entreprise me semblant être fort grande, j'ai attendu que j'eusse atteint un âge qui fût si mûr, que je n'en pusse espérer d'autre après lui, auquel je fusse[5] plus propre[6] à l'exécuter; ce qui m'a fait différer si longtemps, que désormais je croirais commettre une faute, si j'employais encore à délibérer le temps qu'il me reste pour agir.

Maintenant donc que mon esprit est libre de tous soins, et que je me suis procuré un repos assuré dans une paisible solitude, je m'appliquerai sérieusement et avec liberté à détruire généralement toutes mes anciennes opinions.

RENÉ DESCARTES

---

1. René Descartes, *Méditations métaphysiques,* © Presses Universitaires de France (Paris), 1961 [1642], pp. 25–26. Reprinted by permission.

2. *si:* so. See chapter 22, section 22.7 for uses of *si.*

3. *mal:* badly. See chapter 3, section 3.2.2, for this irregular comparative form of *mauvais,* bad.

4. *me défaire:* to rid myself

5. *auquel je fusse:* at which I would be. This is the imperfect subjunctive in French, but the flexibility of subjunctive tenses dictates that the most syntactically appropriate English tense be used, which in this case is the conditional.

6. *propre:* suitable, able

21.4. TRANSLATION PASSAGE

DU CÔTÉ DE CHEZ SWANN[7]

....

Il y avait déjà bien des années que, de Combray, tout ce qui n'était pas le théâtre et le drame de mon coucher, n'existait plus pour moi, quand un jour d'hiver, comme je rentrais à la maison, ma mère, voyant que j'avais froid, me proposa de me faire prendre, contre mon habitude, un peu de thé. Je refusai d'abord et, je ne sais pourquoi, me ravisai. Elle envoya chercher un de ces gâteaux courts et dodus appelés Petites Madeleines qui semblent avoir été moulés dans la valve rainurée[8] d'une coquille de Saint-Jacques.[9] Et bientôt, machinalement, accablé par la morne journée et la perspective d'un triste lendemain, je portai à mes lèvres une cuillerée du thé où j'avais laissé s'amollir un morceau de madeleine. Mais à l'instant même où la gorgée mêlée des miettes du gâteau toucha mon palais, je tressaillis, attentif à ce qui se passait d'extraordinaire en moi. Un plaisir délicieux m'avait envahi, isolé, sans la notion de sa cause. Il m'avait aussitôt rendu les vicissitudes de la vie indifférentes, ses désastres inoffensifs, sa brièveté illusoire, de la même façon qu'opère l'amour, en me remplissant d'une essence précieuse: ou plutôt cette essence n'était pas en moi, elle était moi. J'avais cessé de me sentir médiocre, contingent, mortel. D'où avait pu me venir cette puissante joie? Je sentais qu'elle était liée au goût du thé et du gâteau, mais qu'elle le dépassait infiniment, ne devait pas être de même nature. D'où venait-elle? Que signifiait-elle? Où l'appréhender? Je bois une seconde gorgée où je ne trouve rien de plus que dans la première, une troisième qui m'apporte un peu moins que la seconde. Il est temps que je m'arrête, la vertu du breuvage semble diminuer. Il est clair que la vérité que je cherche n'est pas en lui, mais en moi.

MARCEL PROUST

---

7.   Marcel Proust, *Du côté de chez Swann*, from *À la recherche du temps perdu*, volume I, first part, « Combray », coll. GF, © Flammarion (Paris), 1987 [1913]), pp. 142. Reprinted by permission.

8.   *la valve rainurée:* the fluted shell

9.   *une coquille de Saint-Jacques:* a scallop

COMMON IDIOMATIC EXPRESSIONS

22.1. *TOUT*—GRAMMATICAL FUNCTIONS AND MEANINGS

Tout can function as an adjective, an adverb, and a pronoun.

As an adjective, *tout* usually precedes the noun it modifies. It may be followed by the definite article and then the noun, or it may be followed by the noun without any article at all. Its meaning changes according to whether there is a definite article following it or not:

tout	*toute*	each, every
tous	*toutes*	all, every
tout livre		each book, every book
toute maison		each house, every house
à tout âge		at any age
Tout citoyen a le droit de vote.		Each/every citizen has the right to vote.

tout le[1]	*toute la*	all, the whole
tous les	*toutes les*	all, all of the
tout le livre		the whole book
toute la maison		the whole house
toute ma vie		all my life
toute sa famille		all his/her family
tous les jours		every day (all the days)

---

1. The possessive pronoun can take the place of the definite article, as in *de tout mon cœur,* with all my heart

tous leurs livres	all their books
toutes les maisons	all the houses
Ils ont tous dit . . .	they all said (*tous* as an adj. that agrees with *ils*)

As an adverb, *tout* can modify an adjective, an adverb, or a preposition, meaning *all, very, completely*:

tout seul	all alone
tout petit	very little
Elle a parlé tout doucement.	She spoke very gently.
Elle était toute pensive.	She was very pensive.
Elle regardait tout autour d'elle.	She looked all around her.

Tout can be used as an indefinite pronoun:

Tout va bien aujourd'hui.	Everything is going well today.
Elle avait tout souffert et tout perdu.	She had suffered everything and lost everything.
Qui va payer l'université pour tous?	Who will pay the university for everyone?
Ils ont tout dit . . .	they said everything (*tout* as direct object pronoun)

22.2. IDIOMS WITH *TOUT*

The word *tout* is frequently paired up with one or two other words to form idiomatic expressions whose component parts cannot be reduced to literal translations in English. *Tout* is probably the word most often used in such idiomatic expressions in French. When you encounter *tout* in a sentence and it does not seem to make sense if you translate it in any of the previously mentioned ways, assume that it is part of an idiomatic expression.

Each word in the dictionary, including *tout*, is followed by a list of definitions, which in turn is followed by a paragraph of phrases or sentences demonstrating the idiomatic uses of the word. These sentences are arranged so that the idiomatic usages (but not necessarily the entire sentences) are in alphabetical order. When *tout* does not seem to make sense when translated as previously, you will need to track down its meaning in the paragraph of idiomatic phrases that follows the definition in the dictionary. However, because *tout* is one of the words most frequently found in idiomatic phrases, it will have an exceptionally long entry of idiomatic entries in the dictionary. It will be quicker if you look up the word that accompanies *tout,* and then search the paragraph that follows *its* definitions for a sentence that uses that word plus *tout.*

The following are some common idioms using *tout:*

tout à coup	all of a sudden
tout d'un coup	all of a sudden
tout à fait	quite, absolutely, completely
tout à l'heure	just a moment ago
tout d'abord	first of all
tout de suite	immediately, right away
tout le monde	everyone
tout de même	just the same
pas du tout	not at all
à tout jamais	forever
tout droit	straight ahead
de toute façon	in any case
à tout moment	at any moment
tout aussi	just as
tout en (followed by present participle):	while, all the while

Translation Exercise A

1. Ce tout petit changement a fait une énorme différence.
2. Elle consacre tout son temps à ses études.
3. En tout cas, je ne suis pas toujours chez moi.
4. Les prévenus ont tous plaidé non coupable.
5. Il avait toute confiance en ses recherches.
6. Il a vu le documentaire « Tout près des étoiles » du réalisateur Nils Tavernier, sur la vie des danseurs de l'Opéra de Paris.
7. Elle n'a pas gagné le prix qu'elle voulait, mais elle en a gagné un autre tout aussi important.
8. En principe je suis d'accord, mais je pense qu'il y a tout de même des détails à régler.
9. Ces mesures ont étonné tout le monde.
10. Pourquoi lui donner une telle importance tout à coup?
11. C'est un chef capable de diriger un parti politique d'une main de fer tout en utilisant un gant de velours.
12. De toute façon, il ne fait plus partie de la faculté.
13. Tout adulte devrait être capable de conduire.
14. Avant d'écrire votre réponse, veuillez tout d'abord vous connecter à l'internet.

22.3. *AUSSI; AUSSI BIEN QUE*

The usual meaning of *aussi* is *also*. In addition, we have seen *aussi* used as a comparative with *que: aussi grand que* = as tall as (see chapter 3, section 3.3.1).

Il est aussi grand que son père.	He is as tall has his father.
Il n'est pas aussi grand que son père.	He is not as tall as his father.

When *aussi* is used in the phrase *aussi bien . . . que*, it means *as well as*, or *both . . . and*. A similar phrase, *ainsi que*, means *as well as*, even though *ainsi* on its own means *thus*:

Je peux le faire aussi bien que toi.	I can do it as well as you.
Cet oiseau vole aussi bien qu'il marche sur terre.	This bird both flies and walks on the ground.
Ils sont aussi bien médecins que politiciens.	They are doctors as well as politicians.
J'ai écrit les noms des étudiants ainsi que ceux de leurs partenaires.	I wrote down the names of the students as well as those of their partners.

However, when *aussi* begins a sentence or phrase and is followed by an inverted subject-verb order, *aussi* is translated as *therefore*:

Nous avons aussi vu ce film.	We saw this film also.
Aussi avons-nous vu ce film.	Therefore we saw this film.

22.4. COMBINATIVE CONJUNCTIONS *ET . . . ET; OU . . . OU; SOIT . . . SOIT; NI . . . NI*

French does not have words for *both, either,* or *neither.* To indicate *both . . . and,* two consecutive phrases will both begin with *et:* the first *et* is translated as *both,* and the second *et* is translated as *and.* To indicate *either . . . or,* two consecutive phrases will both begin with *ou:* the first *ou* is translated as *either,* and the second *ou* is translated as *or.* A variation for *either . . . or* uses the third person singular of the subjunctive present of *être:* two consecutive phrases will begin with *soit.* The first *soit* is translated as *either* and the second *soit* is translated as *or.* Finally, *neither . . . nor* is a negative expression that, like all other forms of the negative, has two parts: the *ne* that precedes the verb, and, in this case, the *ni . . . ni* that follows the verb. The *ne* is not translated, and the first *ni* is translated as *neither* and the second *ni* is translated as *nor.*

Le matin il lit et des romans et des journaux.
In the morning he reads both some novels and some newspapers.

Le matin il lit ou des romans ou des journaux.
In the morning he reads either some novels or some newspapers.

Le matin il lit soit des romans soit des journaux.
In the morning he reads either novels or newspapers.

Le matin il ne lit ni romans ni journaux.
In the morning he reads neither novels nor newspapers.

22.5. IDIOMS WITH *METTRE/MIS*

Mettre, like *tout,* is commonly found in idiomatic forms that cannot be reduced to the literal translation of their components. When used idiomatically, *mettre* is usually in its infinitive or past participle form. Again, when *mettre* or *mis* don't seem to make sense when translated literally, consider the possibility that they are being used idiomatically sooner rather than later, look up the companion word, and search the paragraph following the definitions for an idiomatic phrase using some form of *mettre.* The following are some common idioms using *mettre* or *mis:*

mettre en œuvre	to carry out, to implement, to deploy
mettre en marche	to start up
mettre de côté	to save/to put aside
mettre en cause	to suspect, to accuse
mise au point	perfecting, developing, clarifying
mise en liberté	release
mise en scène	a theatrical production or direction

22.6. THE SEVERAL MEANINGS OF *MÊME*

The word *même* can be an adjective or an adverb. As an adjective, it can be either a preceding adjective or a following adjective. Its meaning differs in each case.

As a preceding adjective, *même* means *same:*

la même chose	the same thing
le même livre	the same book

As a following adjective, *même* means *–self,* or *very:*

Il l'a fait lui-même.	He did it himself.
En ce moment même.	At this very moment.
C'est dans la nature même de l'homme d'être violent.	It is in mankind's very nature to be violent.

As an adverb, *même* means *even*:

Elle a même envoyé une carte.	She even sent a card.
Tout le monde y a cru, même Albert.	Everyone believed it, even Albert.

Quand même means *just the same, nevertheless*:

Il l'a fait quand même.	He did it nevertheless/all the same.

22.7. THE SEVERAL MEANINGS OF *SI*

Si is often used to mean *if*. In this usage, if *si* is followed by a pronoun beginning with a vowel, it is shortened to *s'*:

Si cela vous convient on fera le tour de la ville cet après-midi.
If it suits you we'll take a tour of the city this afternoon.

S'il sort comme ça, il aura froid.
If he goes out like that, he will be cold.

Passez-moi le sel s'il vous plaît. Or Passe-moi le sel s'il te plaît.
Please pass me the salt. (Literally: pass me the salt if it pleases you.)

When used as an adverb to modify an adjective or another adverb, *si* means *so*:

Elle marche si vite!	She walks so quickly.

Il était si fatigué qu'il s'est couché tout l'après-midi.
He was so tired that he lay down all afternoon.

The word *si* can mean *yes*, when used as an affirmative answer to a negative question or statement, generally in spoken or quoted speech. This usage is found in France but not in Canada:

Tu n'arrives jamais à l'heure. Si, j'arrive presque toujours à l'heure!
You never arrive on time. Yes, I almost always arrive on time!

22.8. THE SEVERAL MEANINGS OF *ENCORE*

Encore can mean *more, again, still, (not) yet, even, only.*

Je veux encore du café, s'il vous plaît.	I want some more coffee, please.
Faites-le encore.	Do it again.
Il n'est pas encore venu.	He hasn't yet come.
Je l'attendais encore.	I was still waiting for him.
encore moins	even less
hier encore	only yesterday

Translation Exercise B

1. Elle voudrait soit que nous allions au théâtre, soit que nous allions au cinéma.
2. Ils sont aussi bien acteurs que musiciens.
3. Tout le monde aime parler au téléphone, aussi avons-nous tous des portables (cellulaires[2]).
4. Le metteur en scène offre une vision vivante du chef d'œuvre de Bizet.
5. Mis en cause par les familles des victimes, il a demandé à être entendu.
6. Ces lois expriment, au plus haut niveau, la volonté politique de mettre en œuvre une meilleure protection de l'enfance.
7. Il avait la même idée que moi.
8. Il pleuvait, mais je suis quand même allé chez lui.
9. Même si les recherches ne sont pas achevées, il nous reste à travailler l'analyse politique.
10. La nostalgie n'est ni le seul ni même le principal thème de ce film.
11. Le danger est si peu connu et les risques sont si considérables, qu'il nous faut faire des recherches.
12. Donnez-moi mon cahier, s'il vous plaît.
13. Je n'ai pas encore fait le tour de la ville.
14. Je veux encore entendre sa belle voix.
15. L'automne le rend plus triste encore.

---

2. *Portables cellulaires:* cell phones: *Portable* is used in France, while *cellulaire* is more common in Quebec. Cf. the use of *mobile* in the U.K. versus *cell phone* in the U.S.

22.9. TRANSLATION PASSAGE

POUR UNE ANTHROPOLOGIE RÉFLEXIVE[3]

. . . j'ai essayé aussi de surmonter les insuffisances d'une analyse ou purement économique ou purement linguistique du langage, de détruire l'opposition ordinaire entre le matérialisme et le culturalisme. En effet, pour résumer une démonstration longue et difficile en une phrase, on peut dire que ces deux positions ont en commun d'oublier que les relations linguistiques sont toujours des rapports de force symbolique à travers lesquels les rapports de force entre les locuteurs et leurs groupes respectifs s'actualisent sous une forme transfigurée. En conséquence, il est impossible d'interpréter un acte de communication dans les limites d'une analyse *purement* linguistique. Même l'échange linguistique le plus simple met en jeu un réseau complexe et ramifié de relations de force historiques entre le locuteur, doté d'une autorité sociale spécifique, et son interlocuteur ou son public, qui reconnaît son autorité à différents degrés, ainsi qu'entre les groupes respectifs auxquels ils appartiennent. Ce que je cherche à démontrer, c'est qu'une partie très importante de ce qui se produit dans la communication verbale, jusqu'au contenu même du message, reste inintelligible aussi longtemps qu'on ne prend pas en compte la totalité de la structure des rapports de force qui est présente, quoique[4] à l'état invisible, dans l'échange.

PIERRE BOURDIEU

22.10. TRANSLATION PASSAGE

LES BESOINS DE L'ÂME[5]

L'égalité est un besoin vital de l'âme humaine. Elle consiste dans la reconnaissance publique, générale, effective, exprimée réellement par les institutions et

---

3. Pierre Bourdieu avec Loïc J. D. Wacquant, *Réponses: Pour une anthropologie réflexive*, coll. *Libre Examen*, © Éditions du Seuil (Paris), 1992, p.118. Reprinted by permission.
4. *quoique*: although
5. Simone Weil, « L'égalité » et « L'honneur», *Les Besoins de l'âme*, extrait de *L'Enracinement*, © Éditions Gallimard (Paris), 1949, pp. 21–2, 25. Reprinted by permission.

les mœurs, que la même quantité de respect et d'égards est due à tout être humain, parce que le respect est dû à l'être humain comme tel et n'a pas de degrés.

Par suite, les différences inévitables parmi les hommes ne doivent jamais porter la signification d'une différence dans le degré de respect. Pour qu'elles ne soient pas ressenties comme ayant cette signification, il faut un certain équilibre entre l'égalité et l'inégalité.

Une certaine combinaison de l'égalité et de l'inégalité est constituée par l'égalité des possibilités. Si n'importe qui[6] peut arriver au rang social correspondant à la fonction qu'il est capable de remplir, et si l'éducation est assez répandue pour que nul ne soit privé d'aucune capacité du seul fait de sa naissance, l'espérance est la même pour tous les enfants. Ainsi chaque homme est égal en espérance à chaque autre, pour son propre compte[7] quand il est jeune, pour le compte de ses enfants plus tard. . . .

L'honneur est un besoin vital de l'âme humaine. Le respect dû à chaque être humain comme tel, même s'il est effectivement accordé, ne suffit pas à satisfaire ce besoin; car il est identique pour tous et immuable; au lieu que l'honneur a rapport à un être humain considéré, non pas simplement comme tel, mais dans son entourage social. Ce besoin est pleinement satisfait, si chacune des collectivités dont un être humain est membre lui offre une part à une tradition de grandeur enfermée dans son passé et publiquement reconnue au-dehors.

. . . Toute oppression crée une famine à l'égard du besoin d'honneur, car les traditions de grandeur possédées par les opprimés ne sont pas reconnues, faute de prestige social.

SIMONE WEIL

---

6. *n'importe qui*: anyone (it matters not who)
7. *pour son propre compte:* on his own account

CONFIGURATIONS OF THE INFINITIVE

23.1. VERBS FOLLOWED BY THE INFINITIVE

Some verbs are followed directly by the infinitive; others require the preposition *à* or *de* before the infinitive. When *à* or *de* follows a verb and precedes an infinitive, it is not translated.

Some verbs followed by the infinitive directly are

aller	*Nous allons chanter ce soir.*	We are going to sing this evening.
aimer	*J'aime manger du gâteau.*	I like to eat cake.
venir	*Venez voir mon petit chien.*	Come see my little dog.
sembler	*Elle semble être heureuse.*	She seems to be happy.

Some verbs requiring the preposition *à* before an infinitive are

aider	*Aidez-moi à lever la table.*	Help me to lift the table.
commencer	*Ils commencent à faire leur travail.*	They begin to do their work.
apprendre	*Elle a appris à lire en français.*	She learned to read in French.
continuer	*Il a continué à parler à haute voix.*	He continued to speak loudly.

Some verbs requiring the preposition *de* before an infinitive are

oublier	*J'ai oublié de faire mes devoirs.*	I forgot to do my homework.
demander	*Il vous demande de venir avec nous.*	He is asking you to come with us.
cesser	*Elle a cessé de chanter.*	She stopped singing.
rêver	*Je rêve de le voir encore.*	I dream of seeing him again.

23.2. THE INFINITIVE AFTER PREPOSITIONS

The infinitive is used after the prepositions *sans, pour,* and *avant de.* After *sans* and *avant de,* the infinitive is translated into English with the present participle.

Il est parti sans manger.	He left without eating.
Il faut travailler pour vivre.	It is necessary to work in order to live.
Nous lisons sans comprendre tous les mots.	We are reading without understanding all the words.
Finissez la lettre avant de partir.	Finish the letter before leaving.

23.3. THE INFINITIVE AFTER THE PREPOSITION *APRÈS*

With the preposition *après,* the perfect infinitive (i.e., the auxiliary in the infinitive form, accompanied by the past participle) is used, and the action is considered as having been completed. Whether the auxiliary in the infinitive form is *avoir* or *être,* the perfect infinitive is translated as *after having* + the past participle of the verb.

Après avoir fini notre travail, nous sommes allés au cinéma.
After having finished our work, we went to the movies.

Après avoir mangé, il est parti.
After having eaten, he left.

Après être rentrée chez elle, elle a mis ses achats sur la table.
After having returned home, she put her purchases on the table.

Après s'être arrêtée quelque temps, elle s'est avancée à l'autre bout de la rue.
After having stopped for some time, she continued to the other end of the street.

23.4. THE INFINITIVE AFTER ADJECTIVES

Some adjectives require the preposition *à* and most adjectives require the preposition *de* when followed by an infinitive. These prepositions are not translated.

Elle est prête à sortir.	She is ready to leave.
Ce livre est difficile à comprendre.	This book is difficult to understand.
Cette pomme est bonne à manger.	This apple is good to eat.

Nous sommes heureux de vous aider.	We are happy to help you.
Il sera content de vous voir.	He will be happy to see you.
Il n'est pas capable de le faire.	He is not able to do it.

23.5. THE INFINITIVE AFTER NOUNS

Most nouns require the preposition *de* before they can be followed by an infinitive, and some require the preposition *à*. When a noun is followed by *à* or *de* plus a preposition, the *à* or *de* is not translated:

Il n'a pas le courage de le dire.	He doesn't have the courage to say it.
J'ai envie de sortir ce soir.	I feel like going out this evening.
Elle a peur de chanter en public.	She is afraid of singing in public.
Sa capacité à écrire est très grande.	His capacity to write is huge.

Translation Exercise A

Translate with reference to sections 23.1–23.5.

1. Il préfère manger dans ce restaurant.
2. Voilà un appartement à louer.
3. Elle laissa tomber son mouchoir.
4. Après avoir couru pendant quelque temps, il s'arrêta.
5. Je suis désolé d'apprendre ces nouvelles.
6. Avant de sortir, il a mis ses bottes d'hiver.
7. J'ai décidé de prendre le train.
8. Il est parti sans faire aucun bruit.
9. Il hésite à critiquer l'auteur.
10. Après être allée à la bibliothèque, elle est allée prendre un café avec son ami.
11. Il est dangereux de se promener dans ce quartier le soir.
12. Après s'être habillé, il est sorti de la maison.
13. Les conflits politiques sont difficiles à résoudre.
14. Qu'est-ce qu'elle a fait après avoir fini son travail?
15. Je suis impatiente de faire la connaissance de son frère.

23.6. TRANSLATION PASSAGE

« NOTES PROVISOIRES SUR LA POSTCOLONIE »[1]

L'argument de base de cette étude est qu'en postcolonie, le « commandement »[2] entend s'instituer sur le mode d'un *fétiche*. Les signes, les langages et les récits qu'il produit ne sont pas seulement destinés à devenir des objets de représentation. Ils prétendent être investis d'un surplus de sens qu'il n'est pas permis de discuter, et dont on est interdit de se démarquer. Si tel est le cas, alors on comprend l'intérêt qu'il y a à se pencher sur les résultats de telles opérations: les ordres du monde qu'elles finissent par produire; les types d'institutions, de savoirs, de normes et de pratiques qu'elles sécrètent; la façon dont ces institutions, savoirs, normes et pratiques enserrent le quotidien et le structurent, et ce qu'ils donnent à voir et à penser au sujet des rapports entre domination et insubordination. . . .

Pour le reste, comment caractériser la relation postcoloniale sinon comme un rapport de promiscuité: une tension conviviale entre le commandement et ses « cibles ».[3] C'est précisément cette logique de la familiarité et de la domesticité qui a, pour conséquence inattendue, pas forcément la résistance, l'accommodation, le « désengagement », le refus d'être capturé ou l'antagonisme entre les faits et gestes publics et les autres « sous maquis »,[4] mais la « zombification » mutuelle des dominants et de ceux qu'ils sont supposés dominer. C'est elle qui les conduit à se « déforcer » réciproquement et à se bloquer dans la connivence, c'est-à-dire dans l'*impouvoir*.

Les exemples rapportés dans cette note laissent, en effet, suggérer que, plutôt qu'un seul, la postcolonie est faite d'une pluralité d'« espaces publics », chacune dotée d'une logique propre qui n'empêche pas que, sur des sites spécifiques, ils

---

1. Achille Mbembe, « Notes provisoires sur la postcolonie », *Politique Africaine,* Volume 60, pp. 76–109, © Éditions Karthala, Dec. 1995. Reprinted by permission. Born in Cameroon in 1957, Mbembe is a contemporary African philosopher, political scientist, journalist and public intellectual of international renown.
2. *commandement:* authoritarian structure of command. Refers to the structures of power and coercion, the instruments and agents that put them to work, and the relationship between those who give orders and those who are supposed to obey them without any discussion (freely adapted from Mbembe's footnote in this essay on this term).
3. Literally, *target* or *victim;* used here by Mbembe in a manner borrowed from Foucault to mean "*les gens qui habitent [la postcolonie,]*" i.e., the people who live in the postcolony and are subject to the power of those who govern them.
4. *sous maquis:* underground

s'enchevêtrent et obligent le « postcolonisé » à « zigzaguer », à « marchander ». Le « postcolonisé » dispose, par ailleurs, d'une formidable capacité à mobiliser, non pas une seule « identité », mais plusieurs, toutes fluides, et qu'il faut, à ce titre, « négocier » constamment.

. . . Du coup, il apparaît que l'on aurait bien tort de continuer d'interpréter la relation postcoloniale en termes de « résistance » ou de « domination » absolue, ou en fonction des dichotomies et des catégories binaires généralement de mise dans la critique classique des mouvements d'indiscipline et d'insubordination (contre-discours, contre-société, contrehégémonie, seconde société . . .).

ACHILLE MBEMBE

24

SOME VERB FAMILIES

AS WE SAW in chapter 10, a preliminary division of French verbs into three families simplifies the fact that a wide variety of verbs don't fully conform to any single pattern throughout all the different tense conjugations. Some verbs can be grouped in families, such as the *–oir* family, even though there remain variations among the family members as to how they are conjugated in each tense. In other families of verbs, like the *venir* and *tenir* family and all the other families listed after it below, all the members of a family are conjugated in exactly the same way in all tenses: once you know how one verb in each family is conjugated, you know how all the verbs in that family are conjugated. Here some of the most common of these diverse families of verbs are given, in the following forms: the present tense (from which the *imparfait* can be deduced), the present participle, the past participle (used in the *passé composé* and all other compound tenses), the future tense (from which the conditional tense can be deduced), and the *passé simple*. It is assumed that by now you know how these tenses are to be translated. (If not, be sure to learn them now.) The subjunctive forms of these verbs are given in chapter 19. For the many other verbs not presented here that don't conform to a single verb model, a solid knowledge of tense endings together with a good irregular verb index should reveal their forms and meanings.

24.1. -*OIR* VERBS

Often grouped as a family, the -*oir* verbs have important similarities (past participles ending in -*u*)) as well as variations among them.

VOIR—TO SEE

PRESENT TENSE	PRESENT PARTICIPLE	PAST PARTICIPLE	FUTURE TENSE	PASSÉ SIMPLE
je vois	*voyant*	*vu*	*je verrai*	*je vis*
tu vois			*tu verras*	*tu vis*
il/elle/on voit			*il/elle/on verra*	*it/elle/on vit*
nous voyons			*nous verrons*	*nous vîmes*
vous voyez			*vous verrez*	*vous vîtes*
ils/elles voient			*ils verront*	*ils virent*

VOULOIR—TO WANT

PRESENT TENSE	PRESENT PARTICIPLE	PAST PARTICIPLE	FUTURE TENSE	PASSÉ SIMPLE
je veux	*voulant*	*voulu*	*je voudrai*	*je voulus*
tu veux			*tu voudras*	*tu voulus*
il/elle/on veut			*il/elle/on voudra*	*il/elle/on voulut*
nous voulons			*nous voudrons*	*nous voulûmes*
vous voulez			*vous voudrez*	*vous voulûtes*
ils/elles veulent			*ils/elles voudront*	*ils/elles voulurent*

POUVOIR—TO BE ABLE

PRESENT TENSE	PRESENT PARTICIPLE	PAST PARTICIPLE	FUTURE TENSE	PASSÉ SIMPLE
*je peux/ je puis**	*pouvant*	*pu*	*je pourrai*	*je pus*
tu peux			*tu pourras*	*tu pus*
il/elle/on peut			*il/elle/on pourra*	*il/elle/on put*
nous pouvons			*nous pourrons*	*nous pûmes*
vous pouvez			*vous pourrez*	*vous pûtes*
ils/elles peuvent			*ils/elles pourront*	*ils/elles purent*

*See chapter 10, section 10.2, footnote 1.

SAVOIR—TO KNOW

PRESENT TENSE	PRESENT PARTICIPLE	PAST PARTICIPLE	FUTURE TENSE	PASSÉ SIMPLE
je sais	sachant	su	je saurai	je sus
tu sais			tu sauras	tu sus
il/elle/on sait			il/elle/on saura	il/elle/on sut
nous savons			nous saurons	nous sûmes
vous savez			vous saurez	vous sûtes
ils/elles savent			ils/elles sauront	ils/elles surent

DEVOIR—TO HAVE TO / TO OWE

PRESENT TENSE	PRESENT PARTICIPLE	PAST PARTICIPLE	FUTURE TENSE	PASSÉ SIMPLE
je dois	devant	dû	je devrai	je dus
tu dois			tu devras	tu dus
il/elle/on doit			il/elle/on devra	il/elle/on dut
nous devons			nous devrons	nous dûmes
vous devez			vous devrez	vous dûtes
ils/elles doivent			ils/elles devront	ils/elles durent

RECEVOIR—TO RECEIVE

PRESENT TENSE	PRESENT PARTICIPLE	PAST PARTICIPLE	FUTURE TENSE	PASSÉ SIMPLE
je reçois	recevant	reçu	je recevrai	je reçus
tu reçois			tu recevras	tu reçus
il/elle/on reçoit			il/elle/on recevra	il/elle/on reçut
nous recevons			nous recevrons	nous reçûmes
vous recevez			vous recevrez	vous reçûtes
ils/elles reçoivent			ils/elles recevront	ils/elles reçurent

FALLOIR*—TO BE NECESSARY

PRESENT TENSE	PAST PARTICIPLE	FUTURE TENSE	PASSÉ SIMPLE
il faut	fallu	il faudra	il fallut

*Impersonal verb used only in the third person (impersonal) singular.

VALOIR—TO BE WORTH

PRESENT TENSE	PRESENT PARTICIPLE	PAST PARTICIPLE	FUTURE TENSE	PASSÉ SIMPLE
je vaux	*valant*	*valu*	*je vaudrai*	*je valus*
tu vaux			*tu vaudras*	*tu valus*
il/elle/on vaut			*il/elle/on vaudra*	*il/elle/on valut*
nous valons			*nous vaudrons*	*nous valûmes*
vous valez			*vous vaudrez*	*vous valûtes*
ils valent			*ils vaudront*	*ils valurent*

24.2. FAMILIES OF VERBS WHOSE MEMBERS ARE ALL CONJUGATED IN THE SAME WAY

24.2.1. VERBS MADE UP OF *VENIR* OR *TENIR*

As noted earlier, *venir* (to come) and *tenir* (to hold) are twins and form the basis for an entire family of verbs, each of which is conjugated exactly like all the others. Be sure to memorize both verbs in all tenses, so that you will be able to recognize the conjugated forms of *venir* or *tenir* that may be embedded within a verb composed of a prefix plus *venir* or *tenir*:

VENIR—TO COME

PRESENT TENSE	PRESENT PARTICIPLE	PAST PARTICIPLE	FUTURE TENSE	PASSÉ SIMPLE
je viens	*venant*	*venu*	*je viendrai*	*je vins*
tu viens			*tu viendras*	*tu vins*
il/elle/on vient			*il/elle/on viendra*	*il/elle/on vint*
nous venons			*nous viendrons*	*nous vînmes*
vous venez			*vous viendrez*	*vous vîntes*
ils/elles viennent			*ils/elles viendront*	*ils/elles vinrent*

TENIR—TO COME

je tiens	*tenant*	*tenu*	*je tiendrai*	*je tins*
tu tiens			*tu tiendras*	*tu tins*
il/elle/on tient			*il/elle/on tiendra*	*il/elle/on tint*

nous tenons	*nous tiendrons*	*nous tînmes*
vous tenez	*vous tiendrez*	*vous tîntes*
ils/elles tiennent	*ils/elles tiendront*	*ils/elles tinrent*

All the following verbs are conjugated exactly like *venir*:

convenir	to suit, to agree	*retenir*	to retain
devenir	to become	*obtenir*	to obtain
parvenir	to attain	*contenir*	to contain
prévenir	to inform, to warn	*maintenir*	to maintain
provenir	to come from	*entretenir*	to support
revenir	to return		
se souvenir de	to remember		

24.2.2. VERBS FOLLOWING THE PATTERN OF *VENDRE* (TO SELL)

The following verbs . . .

attendre	to wait for
défendre	to forbid, defend
descendre	to go down
entendre	to hear
perdre	to lose
rendre	to give back, to return
répondre	to answer

. . . are all conjugated according to the pattern of *vendre*:

PRESENT TENSE	PRESENT PARTICIPLE	PAST PARTICIPLE	FUTURE TENSE	PASSÉ SIMPLE
je vends	*vendant*	*vendu*	*je vendrai*	*je vendis*
tu vends			*tu vendras*	*tu vendis*
il/elle/on vend			*il/elle/on vendra*	*il/elle/on vendit*
nous vendons			*nous vendrons*	*nous vendîmes*
vous vendez			*vous vendrez*	*vous vendîtes*
ils/elles vendent			*ils/elles vendront*	*ils/elles vendirent*

24.2.3. VERBS FOLLOWING THE PATTERN OF *OUVRIR* (TO OPEN)

The following verbs . . .

couvrir	to cover
découvrir	to discover
offrir	to offer
souffrir	to suffer

. . . are all conjugated according to the pattern of *ouvrir*:

PRESENT TENSE	PRESENT PARTICIPLE	PAST PARTICIPLE	FUTURE TENSE	PASSÉ SIMPLE
j'ouvre	*ouvrant*	*ouvert*	*j'ouvrirai*	*j'ouvris*
tu ouvres			*tu ouvriras*	*tu ouvris*
il/elle/on ouvre			*il/elle/on ouvrira*	*il/elle/on ouvrit*
nous ouvrons			*nous ouvrirons*	*nous ouvrîmes*
vous ouvrez			*vous ouvrirez*	*vous ouvrîtes*
ils/elles ouvrent			*ils/elles ouvriront*	*ils/elles ouvrirent*

24.2.4. VERBS FOLLOWING THE PATTERN OF *PARTIR* (TO DEPART)

The following verbs . . .

dormir	to sleep
mentir	to lie
servir	to serve
sortir	to go out
sentir	to feel, to smell

. . . are all conjugated according to the pattern of *partir*:

PRESENT TENSE	PRESENT PARTICIPLE	PAST PARTICIPLE	FUTURE TENSE	PASSÉ SIMPLE
je pars	*partant*	*parti*	*je partirai*	*je partis*
tu pars			*tu partiras*	*tu partis*
il/elle/on part			*il/elle/on partira*	*il/elle/on partit*
nous partons			*nous partirons*	*nous partîmes*
vous partez			*vous partirez*	*vous partîtes*
ils/elles partent			*ils/elles partiront*	*ils/elles partirent*

24.2.5. VERBS FOLLOWING THE PATTERN OF *CUIRE* (TO COOK)

The following verbs . . .

conduire	to drive
construire	to construct, to build
déduire	to deduce
enduire	to coat
induire	to induce
instruire	to instruct
introduire	to introduce
produire	to produce
réduire	to reduce
traduire	to translate

. . . are all conjugated according to the pattern of *cuire*:

PRESENT TENSE	PRESENT PARTICIPLE	PAST PARTICIPLE	FUTURE TENSE	PASSÉ SIMPLE
je cuis	*cuisant*	*cuit*	*je cuirai*	*je cuisis*
tu cuis			*tu cuiras*	*tu cuisis*
il/elle/on cuit			*il/elle/on cuira*	*il/elle/on cuisit*
nous cuisons			*nous cuirons*	*nous cuisîmes*
vous cuisez			*vous cuirez*	*vous cuisîtes*
ils/elles cuisent			*ils/elles cuiront*	*ils/elles cuisirent*

24.2.6. VERBS FOLLOWING THE PATTERN OF *JOINDRE* (TO JOIN)

The following verbs . . .

atteindre	to attain, to reach
éteindre	to extinguish
craindre	to fear
plaindre	to pity
restreindre	to restrict
se plaindre	to complain

. . . are all conjugated according to the pattern of *joindre*:

PRESENT TENSE	PRESENT PARTICIPLE	PAST PARTICIPLE	FUTURE TENSE	PASSÉ SIMPLE
je joins	*joignant*	*joint*	*je joindrai*	*je joignis*
tu joins			*tu joindras*	*tu joignis*
il/elle/on joint			*il/elle/on joindra*	*il/elle/on joignit*
nous joignons			*nous joindrons*	*nous joignîmes*
vous joignez			*vous joindrez*	*vous joignîtes*
ils/elles joignent			*ils/elles joindront*	*ils/elles joignirent*

24.2.7. VERBS FOLLOWING THE PATTERN OF *CONNAÎTRE* (TO KNOW)

The following verbs . . .

paraître	to seem
reconnaître	to recognize

. . . are all conjugated according to the pattern of *connaître*:

PRESENT TENSE	PRESENT PARTICIPLE	PAST PARTICIPLE	FUTURE TENSE	PASSÉ SIMPLE
je connais	*connaissant*	*connu*	*je connaîtrai*	*je connus*
tu connais			*tu connaîtras*	*tu connus*
il/elle/on connaît			*il/elle/on connaîtra*	*il/elle/on connut*
nous connaissons			*nous connaîtrons*	*nous connûmes*
vous connaissez			*vous connaîtrez*	*vous connûtes*
ils/elles connaissent			*ils/elles connaîtront*	*ils/elles connurent*

FURTHER TRANSLATION PASSAGES

25.1. VICTOR HUGO

LES MISÉRABLES [1]

Jean Valjean était d'une pauvre famille de paysans de la Brie. Dans son enfance, il n'avait pas appris à lire. Quand il eut l'âge d'homme, il était émondeur[2] à Faverolles.... Il avait perdu en très-bas âge son père et sa mère. Sa mère était morte d'une fièvre de lait[3] mal soignée. Son père, émondeur comme lui, s'était tué en tombant d'un arbre. Il n'était resté[4] à Jean Valjean qu'une sœur plus âgée que lui, veuve, avec sept enfants, filles et garçons. Cette sœur avait élevé Jean Valjean, et tant qu[5]'elle eut son mari elle logea et nourrit son jeune frère. Le mari mourut. L'aîné des sept enfants avait huit ans, le dernier un an. Jean Valjean venait[6] d'atteindre, lui, sa vingt-cinquième année. Il remplaça le père, et soutint à son tour sa sœur qui l'avait élevé. Cela se fit simplement, comme un devoir, même avec quelque chose de bourru de la part de Jean Valjean. Sa jeunesse se dépensait ainsi dans un travail rude et mal payé. On ne lui avait jamais connu de « bonne amie »[7] dans le pays. Il n'avait pas eu le temps d'être amoureux....

---

1. Victor Hugo, « Jean Valjean », *Les Misérables,* First part: *Fantime,* Second Book, ch. VI, © Pagnerre (Paris), 1862, pp.199–203.
2. *Émondeur:* tree-pruner, tree-trimmer
3. *une fièvre de lait:* literally, milk fever, i.e., an infection associated with breast-feeding: mastitis
4. For this use of *rester*, see chapter 11, section 11.5.3.
5. *tant que:* as long as
6. *venait:* had just. See chapter 20, section 20.2.1.
7. *bonne amie:* sweetheart, girlfriend

Il gagnait dans la saison de l'émondage dix-huit sous par jour, puis il se louait comme moissonneur, comme manœuvre, comme garçon de ferme-bouvier, comme homme de peine.[8] Il faisait ce qu'il pouvait. Sa sœur travaillait de son côté, mais que faire avec sept petits enfants? C'était un triste groupe que la misère enveloppa et étreignit peu à peu. Il arriva qu'un hiver fut rude. Jean n'eut pas d'ouvrage. La famille n'eut pas de pain. Pas de pain. À la lettre. Sept enfants.

Un dimanche soir, Maubert Isabeau, boulanger sur la place de l'Église, à Faverolles, se disposait à se coucher, lorsqu'il entendit un coup violent dans la devanture grillée et vitrée de sa boutique. Il arriva à temps pour voir un bras passé à travers un trou fait d'un coup de poing dans la grille et dans la vitre. Le bras saisit un pain et l'emporta. Isabeau sortit en hâte; le voleur s'enfuyait à toutes jambes;[9] Isabeau courut après lui et l'arrêta. Le voleur avait jeté le pain, mais il avait encore le bras ensanglanté. C'était Jean Valjean.

Ceci se passait en 1795. Jean Valjean fut traduit devant les tribunaux du temps « pour vol avec effraction la nuit dans une maison habitée ». Il avait un fusil dont il se servait mieux que tireur au monde, il était quelque peu braconnier; ce qui lui nuisit. Il y a contre les braconniers un préjugé légitime. Le braconnier, de même que le contrebandier, côtoie de fort près le brigand. Pourtant, disons-le en passant, il y a encore un abîme entre ces races d'hommes et le hideux assassin des villes. Le braconnier vit dans la forêt; le contrebandier vit dans la montagne ou sur la mer. Les villes font des hommes féroces, parce qu'elles font des hommes corrompus. La montagne, la mer, la forêt, font des hommes sauvages;[10] elles développent le côté farouche, mais souvent sans détruire le côté humain.

Jean Valjean fut déclaré coupable. Les termes du Code étaient formels.[11] Il y a dans notre civilisation des heures redoutables; ce sont les moments où la pénalité prononce un naufrage. Quelle minute funèbre que celle où la société s'éloigne[12] et consomme[13] l'irréparable abandon d'un être pensant! Jean Valjean fut condamné à cinq ans de galères.

---

8. *homme de peine:* casual labourer
9. *à toutes jambes:* as fast as he could
10. *sauvages:* wild
11. *formels:* definite
12. *s'éloigne:* stands aloof (stands apart)
13. *consomme:* consummates

25.2. GUSTAVE FLAUBERT

MADAME BOVARY[14]

D'abord, ce fut comme un étourdissement; elle voyait les arbres, les chemins, les fossés, Rodolphe, et elle sentait encore l'étreinte de ses bras, tandis que le feuillage frémissait et que les joncs sifflaient.

Mais, en s'apercevant dans la glace,[15] elle s'étonna de son visage. Jamais elle n'avait eu les yeux si grands, si noirs, ni d'une telle profondeur. Quelque chose de subtil épandu sur sa personne la transfigurait.

Elle se répétait : « J'ai un amant ! un amant ! » se délectant à cette idée comme à celle d'une autre puberté qui lui serait survenue. Elle allait donc posséder enfin ces joies de l'amour, cette fièvre du bonheur dont elle avait désespéré. Elle entrait dans quelque chose de merveilleux où tout serait passion, extase, délire; une immensité bleuâtre l'entourait, les sommets du sentiment étincelaient sous sa pensée, et l'existence ordinaire n'apparaissait qu'au loin, tout en bas, dans l'ombre, entre les intervalles de ces hauteurs.

Alors elle se rappela les héroïnes des livres qu'elle avait lus, et la légion lyrique de ces femmes adultères se mit à[16] chanter dans sa mémoire avec des voix de sœurs qui la charmaient. Elle devenait elle-même comme une partie véritable de ces imaginations et réalisait la longue rêverie de sa jeunesse, en se considérant dans ce type d'amoureuse qu'elle avait tant envié. D'ailleurs, Emma éprouvait une satisfaction de vengeance. N'avait-elle pas assez souffert! Mais elle triomphait maintenant, et l'amour, si longtemps contenu, jaillissait tout entier avec des bouillonnements joyeux. Elle le savourait sans remords, sans inquiétude, sans trouble.

---

14. Gustave Flaubert, *Madame Bovary: Mœurs de province*, © Éditions Imprimerie Nationale (Paris), 1994 [1857], pp. 290–91.

15. *glace*: mirror

16. *se mit à*: began, from *se mettre à*

25.3. GABRIELLE ROY

BONHEUR D'OCCASION[17]

. . . .

Rose-Anna, s'étant arrêtée pour souffler un peu, laissa filer son regard autour d'elle. Une haute clôture se dressait à sa gauche sur un terrain vague.[18] Entre les tiges de fer, au loin, toute la ville basse se précisait: d'innombrables clochers s'élançaient vers le ciel; des rubans de fumée prolongeaient les cônes gris des cheminées d'usines; des enseignes suspendues coupaient l'horizon en morceaux de noir et de bleu; et, se disputant l'espace dans cette ville de prière et de travail, les toits descendaient par étages, et se faisaient de plus en plus resserrés jusqu'à ce que leur monotone assemblage cessât brusquement à la bordure du fleuve. Une légère brume, vers le milieu des eaux moirées, brouillait le lointain.

Rose-Anna contempla le spectacle à travers sa fatigue pendant qu'elle reprenait haleine; elle n'eut même pas l'idée de chercher au loin l'emplacement de sa maison. Mais, d'un coup d'œil,[19] elle mesura ce qui restait à gravir avant d'arriver à l'hôpital des enfants qu'on lui avait dit situé tout au haut de l'avenue des Cèdres.

Daniel y avait été transporté peu de temps après le voyage à Saint-Denis.

Un soir, en le dévêtant, Rose-Anna avait découvert de grandes taches violettes sur ses membres. Le lendemain, elle l'installa dans son petit traîneau et le conduisit à un jeune médecin de la rue du Couvent, chez qui elle avait fait des ménages autrefois. Le reste s'était accompli si vite qu'elle se le rappelait mal. Le docteur avait tout de suite emmené le petit à l'hôpital. Rose-Anna ne se souvenait que d'un détail précis: l'enfant n'avait point pleuré, point protesté. Se confiant dans l'excès de sa débilité à cet inconnu qui l'emportait, qui était fort et qui paraissait bon, il avait agité sagement au hasard sa main qui était déjà décharnée.

---

17. Gabrielle Roy, *Bonheur d'occasion* (Montreal: Éditions du Boréal, 2009 [1945]), © Fonds Gabrielle Roy. Reprinted by permission. Translated into English as *The Tin Flute* (although *Bonheur d'occasion* would be more literally translated as *Second-hand Happiness*), this book was considered an inaugural voice of Quebec's "Quiet Revolution" in the 1960's, which transformed the province and particularly Montreal from a traditional, clerical society into a cosmopolitan, more secular one with its own cultural, linguistic (francophone), and political identity. Roy won the French Prix Femina and the Canadian Governor General's Award in 1947 for this book.

18. *un terrain vague:* a vacant lot

19. *d'un coup d'œil:* at a glance

25.4. JEAN-PAUL SARTRE

L'EXISTENTIALISME EST UN HUMANISME[20]

Dostoïevsky avait écrit: « Si Dieu n'existait pas, tout serait permis. » C'est là le point de départ de l'existentialisme. En effet,[21] tout est permis si Dieu n'existe pas, et par conséquent l'homme est délaissé, parce qu'il ne trouve ni en lui, ni hors de lui une possibilité de s'accrocher. Il ne trouve d'abord pas d'excuses. Si, en effet, l'existence précède l'essence,[22] on ne pourra jamais expliquer par référence à une nature humaine donnée et figée; autrement dit, il n'y a pas de déterminisme, l'homme est libre, l'homme est liberté. Si, d'autre part, Dieu n'existe pas, nous ne trouvons pas en face de nous des valeurs ou des ordres qui légitimeront notre conduite. Ainsi, nous n'avons ni derrière nous, ni devant nous, dans le domaine numineux des valeurs, des justifications ou des excuses. Nous sommes seuls, sans excuses. C'est ce que j'exprimerai en disant que l'homme est condamné à être libre. Condamné, parce qu'il ne s'est pas créé lui-même, et par ailleurs cependant libre, parce qu'une fois[23] jeté dans le monde, il est responsable de tout ce qu'il fait. L'existentialiste ne croit pas à la puissance de la passion. Il ne pensera jamais qu'une belle passion est un torrent dévastateur qui conduit fatalement l'homme à certains actes, et qui, par conséquent, est une excuse. Il pense que l'homme est responsable de sa passion. L'existentialiste ne pensera pas non plus que l'homme peut trouver un secours dans un signe donné, sur terre, qui l'orientera; car il pense que l'homme déchiffre lui-même le signe comme il lui plaît. Il pense donc que l'homme, sans aucun appui et sans aucun secours, est condamné à chaque instant à inventer l'homme.

---

20. Jean Paul Sartre, *L'Existentialisme est un humanisme*, © Éditions Gallimard (Paris), 1996, pp. 39–40. Reprinted by permission. Text of a lecture given in Paris by Sartre in 1945.
21. Indeed
22. *existence précède l'essence:* existence precedes essence, a major tenet of existentialism that claims that what humans make of themselves through their acts is more fundamental than human nature per se.
23. *une fois:* once (literally: one time)

25.5. SIMONE DE BEAUVOIR

LE DEUXIÈME SEXE[24]

On ne naît pas femme: on le devient. Aucun destin biologique, psychique, économique ne définit la figure que revêt[25] au sein de la société la femelle humaine; c'est l'ensemble de la civilisation qui élabore ce produit intermédiare entre le mâle et le castrat qu'on qualifie de féminin. Seule la médiation d'autrui peut constituer un individu comme un *Autre*. En tant qu'il existe pour soi l'enfant ne saurait se saisir comme sexuellement différencié. Chez les filles et les garçons, le corps est d'abord le rayonnement d'une subjectivité, l'instrument qui effectue la compréhension du monde: c'est à travers les yeux, les mains, non par les parties sexuelles qu'ils appréhendent l'univers. . . .

Le monde n'est d'abord présent au nouveau-né que sous la figure de sensations immanentes; il est encore noyé[26] au sein du Tout comme au temps où il habitait les ténèbres d'un ventre. . . . D'une manière immédiate le nourrisson vit le drame originel de tout existant qui est le drame de son rapport à l'Autre. C'est dans l'angoisse que l'homme éprouve son délaissement. Fuyant sa liberté, sa subjectivité, il voudrait se perdre au sein du Tout: c'est là l'origine de ses rêveries cosmiques et panthéistiques, de son désir d'oubli, de sommmeil, d'extase, de mort.

25.6. ALBERT CAMUS

LE MYTHE DE SISYPHE[27]

Toute la joie silencieuse de Sisyphe est là. Son destin lui appartient. Son rocher est sa chose. De même,[28] l'homme absurde, quand il contemple son tourment, fait taire toutes les idoles. Dans l'univers soudain rendu à son silence, les mille

---

24. Simone de Beauvoir, « Enfance », *Le Deuxième Sexe*, Volume II, © Éditions Gallimard (Paris), 1976 (1949), pp. 15–16. Reprinted by permission.
25. *revêt:* from *revêtir,* to assume, to take the form of
26. *noyé:* immersed
27. Albert Camus, *Le Mythe de Sisyphe,* in *Œuvres complètes d'Albert Camus,* © Éditions Gallimard et Club de l'Honnête Homme (Paris), 1983, p. 238. Reprinted by permission.
28. *de même:* in the same way

petites voix émerveillées de la terre s'élèvent. Appels inconscients et secrets, invitations de tous les visages, ils sont l'envers nécessaire et le prix de la victoire. Il n'y a pas de soleil sans ombre, et il faut connaître la nuit. L'homme absurde dit oui et son effort n'aura plus de cesse. S'il y a un destin personnel, il n'y a point de destinée supérieure ou du moins il n'en est qu'une dont il juge qu'elle est fatale et méprisable. Pour le reste, il se sait le maître de ses jours. À cet instant subtil où l'homme se retourne sur sa vie, Sisyphe, revenant vers son rocher, contemple cette suite d'actions sans lien qui devient son destin, créé par lui, uni sous le regard de sa mémoire et bientôt scellé par sa mort. Ainsi, persuadé de l'origine tout humaine de tout ce qui est humain, aveugle qui désire voir et qui sait que la nuit n'a pas de fin, il est toujours en marche.[29] Le rocher roule encore.

Je laisse Sisyphe au bas de la montagne! On retrouve toujours son fardeau. Mais Sisyphe enseigne la fidélité supérieure qui nie les dieux et soulève les rochers. Lui aussi juge que tout est bien. Cet univers désormais sans maître ne lui paraît ni stérile ni futile. Chacun des grains de cette pierre, chaque éclat minéral de cette montagne pleine de nuit, à lui seul, forme un monde. La lutte elle-même vers les sommets suffit à remplir un cœur d'homme. Il faut imaginer Sisyphe heureux.

25.7. PAUL RICŒUR

LE CONFLIT DES INTERPRÉTATIONS[30]

Ce thème me contraint à relever un défi radical et à dire jusqu'où je suis capable d'assumer pour ma propre pensée la critique de la religion issue d'un athéisme tel que celui de Nietzsche et de Freud, et jusqu'à quel point je me considère comme chrétien au-delà de cette mise à l'épreuve. Si le titre « Signification religieuse de l'athéisme » n'est pas vain, il implique que l'athéisme n'épuise pas sa signification dans la négation et la destuction de la religion, mais qu'il libère l'horizon

---

29. *en marche:* on the go
30. Paul Ricœur, « Religion, athéisme, foi », *Le Conflit des interprétations: Essais d'herméneutique* coll. L'Ordre Philosophique, © Éditions du Seuil (Paris), 1969, pp. 431–32. Reprinted by permission.

pour quelque chose d'autre, pour une foi susceptible d'être appelée, au prix de précisions ultérieures, une foi post-religieuse, une foi pour un âge post-religieux. Telle est l'hypothèse que je me propose de mettre à l'épreuve et éventuellement de défendre.

Le titre plus personnel que je propose exprime assez bien ma propre intention : « Religion, athéisme et foi. » Le mot « athéisme » a été placé en position intermédiaire, à la fois comme une coupure et comme un lien entre la religion et la foi ; il regarde en arrière vers ce qu'il nie, et en avant vers ce qu'il ouvre. Je n'ignore pas les difficultés de cette entreprise ; elle est à la fois trop facile et trop difficile. Trop facile, si l'on tient la distinction entre religion et foi pour acquise, ou si l'on se permet d'utiliser l'athéisme comme un instrument indiscret d'apologétique pour « sauver la foi » ; ou pire, si on en use comme d'un procédé habile et hypocrite destiné à reprendre d'une main ce qu'il a fallu céder de l'autre : cette opposition elle-même doit être élaborée de manière responsable ; ce n'est pas un donné : c'est une tâche difficile offerte à la pensée. Je préfère courir le risque inverse, celui de manquer le but en ouvrant un chemin qui se perd en route. En un sens c'est ce qui arrivera dans ces deux études qui commencent quelque chose mais n'achèvent rien, qui pointent vers quelque chose mais ne montrent point et à plus forte raison ne donnent point ce qu'elles désignent de loin et en ce sens, l'entreprise est trop difficile. Mais je pense que telle est la position inéluctable du philosophe lorsqu'il est confronté, en tant que tel, à la dialectique entre religion, athéisme, et foi.

25.8. ÉDOUARD GLISSANT

PHILOSOPHIE DE LA RELATION[31]

La conscience de la diversité du monde, non pas de sa disparité mais de la solidarité de ses différences entre elles, immédiatement nous exhorte à une autre vive passion, celle de la considération du temps, qui certes va son orbe mais qui procède aussi de toute différence à toutes les autres, et dont nous osons désor-

---

31. Édouard Glissant, *Philosophie de la relation : Poésie en étendue*, © Éditions Gallimard (Paris), 2009, pp. 31–32. Reprinted by permission. Glissant (1928–2011), writer and poet, was one of the most influential figures in contemporary Caribbean thought ; a critic of the *Négritude* movement and a proponent of *créolisation* and *le Tout-Monde*, his nontotalizing vision of the vitality arising out of the hybridity of different cultures despite the violence that often first brought them together.

mais fréquenter la pensée comme la poussée d'un relatif (il y a des temps concassés) au travers d'un absolu (il y a un fleuve du temps), alliés dans des instances variables.

Les différences dans le monde (les différents) s'offrent à nous dans leurs temps distendus, qui sont pourtant (aujourd'hui, par tout ce temps de la Relation dans la totalité) contemporains les uns des autres. Les temps du campement inuit et du village breton et de cette désolation du Darfour et de la forêt perdue sont maintenant concourants, réellement, de celui de la Banque de Wall Street à New York, États-Unis, et non pas seulement contigus, à même des parallèles de temps. Le temps de l'archipel est le temps des continents, voyez-y merveille.

Des peuples qu'on a voulu couper de leurs histoires, reconstituent par pans discontinus leurs mémoires collectives, et ils sautent de roche en roche sur les rivières du temps, ils créent leurs temps et les dépensent infiniment, et cependant, ils partagent avec les autres peuples, peut-être même avec ceux-là qui avaient voulu raturer ainsi leurs mémoires collectives, la trame de ce temps découvert, tout actuel, à vif, imprévu et vertigineux, du Tout-monde. Temps des mémoires humaines et temps des affûts cosmiques. Pour celui qui aujourd'hui se lève, d'où que ce soit au monde et pour quelque raison qu'il dise, tout horizon est originel, ouvrant une autre région dans une autre totalité.

25.9. ROGER-POL DROIT

MICHEL FOUCAULT: ENTRETIENS[32]

Au milieu des années 1950, j'ai publié quelques travaux sur la psychologie et la maladie mentale. Un éditeur m'a demandé d'écrire une histoire de la psychiatrie. J'ai pensée à écrire une histoire qui n'apparaissait jamais, celle des fous euxmêmes. Qu'est-ce que c'est, être fou? Qui en décide? Depuis quand? Au nom de quoi? . . .

J'avais aussi fait des études de psychopathologie. Cette prétendue discipline n'apprenait pas grand-chose. Alors naissait cette question: comment si peu

---

32. Roger-Pol Droit, « Je suis un artificier », *Michel Foucault: Entretiens*, © Éditions Odile Jacob (Paris), 2004, pp. 93–95. Reprinted by permission.

de savoir peut-il entraîner tant de pouvoir? Il y avait de quoi être stupéfait. Je l'étais d'autant plus que j'ai fait des stages dans les hôpitaux, deux ans à Sainte-Anne. N'étant pas médecin, je n'avais aucun droit, mais étant étudiant et non pas malade, je pouvais me promener. Ainsi, sans jamais avoir à exercer le pouvoir lié au savoir psychiatrique, je pouvais tout de même l'observer à chaque instant. J'étais à la surface de contact entre les malades, avec lesquels je discutais sous prétexte de faire des tests psychologiques, et le corps médical, qui passait régulièrement, et prenait des décisions. Cette position, qui était due au hasard, m'a fait voir cette surface de contact entre le fou et le pouvoir qui s'exerce sur lui, et j'ai essayé ensuite d'en restituer la formation historique. . . .

Dans ma vie personnelle, il se trouve que je me suis senti, dès l'éveil de ma sexualité, exclu, pas vraiment rejeté, mais appartenant à la part d'ombre de la société. C'est tout de même un problème impressionnant quand on le découvre pour soi-même. Très vite, ça s'est transformé en une espèce de menace psychiatrique: si tu n'es pas comme tout le monde, c'est que tu es anormal, si tu es anormal, c'est que tu es malade. Ces trois catégories: n'être pas comme tout le monde, n'être pas normal et être malade, sont tout de même très différentes et se sont trouvées assimilées les unes aux autres.

25.10. JULIA KRISTEVA

POUVOIRS DE L'HORREUR[33]

Insistons encore sur le mouvement tragique d'*Œdipe roi:* ne résume-t-il pas la variante mythique de l'abjection? Entrant dans une cité impure—dans un *miasma*—Œdipe se fait lui-même *agos*, souillure, pour la purifier et devenir *katharmos.*[34] Purificateur, il l'est donc du fait même d'être *agos*. Son abjection tient à[35] cette ambiguïté permanente des rôles qu'il assume à son insu,[36] alors qu[37]'il croit savoir. Et c'est précisément cette dynamique des renversements, qui fait de lui et

---

33. Julia Kristeva, « De la saleté à la souillure », *Pouvoirs de l'horreur, Essai sur l'abjection,* Coll. *Tel Quel,* © Éditions du Seuil (Paris) 1980 (coll. *Points Essais,* 1983), pp. 100–101. Reprinted by permission.
34. *katharmos:* (Greek), purifier
35. *tient à:* is due to. See chapter 20, section 20.2.2
36. *à son insu:* without knowing it
37. *alors que:* even when, even though

un être d'abjection et un *pharmakos,* un bouc émissaire qui, expulsé, permet de libérer la ville de la souillure. Le ressort[38] de la tragédie est dans cette ambiguïté: l'interdit et l'idéal se conjoignent en un seul personnage pour signifier que l'être parlant n'a pas d'espace propre mais se tient, sur un seuil fragile, comme par un impossible démarquage. Si telle est la logique du *pharmakos katharmos* qu'est Œdipe, force est[39] de constater que la pièce de Sophocle tire sa puissance non seulement de cette mathesis[40] de l'ambiguïté, mais des valeurs toutes sémantiques qu'elle donne aux termes opposés. Quelles « valeurs »?

Thèbes est un *miasma* à cause de la stérilité, de la maladie, de la mort. Œdipe est *agos* du fait d'avoir, par le meurtre du père et l'inceste avec la mère, perturbé et interrompu la chaîne de la reproduction. La souillure est l'arrêt de la vie: (comme) une sexualité sans reproduction (les fils nés de l'inceste d'Œdipe périront, les filles ne survivront que dans une autre logique, celle du contrat ou de l'existence symbolique, comme on le verra dans *Œdipe à Colone*). Une certaine sexualité, qui n'a pas dans la tragédie grecque la signification qu'elle a pour les modernes, qui ne se pare même pas de plaisir mais de *souveraineté* et de *connaissance,* équivaut à la maladie et à la mort. La souillure s'y confond: elle consiste, pratiquement[41], à toucher à[42] la mère. La souillure, c'est l'inceste comme transgression des limites du propre.

25.11. NICOLAS BOURRIAUD

RADICANT: POUR UNE ESTHÉTIQUE DE LA GLOBALISATION[43]

Mais comment défendre en même temps l'existence des singularités culturelles, et s'opposer à l'idée de juger les œuvres au nom de ces singularités, c'est-à-dire refuser de se tenir dans le droit fil de leurs traditions? C'est cette aporie qui fonde le discours postmoderne, et qui en constitue la fragilité ontologique. En d'autres termes, la postmodernité consiste à *ne pas répondre* à la question. Car pour formuler une réponse, il faudrait choisir entre deux options opposées:

---

38. *le ressort:* the driving force
39. *force est:* it is necessary
40. *mathesis:* mathesis, mental discipline
41. *pratiquement:* in effect
42. *toucher à:* to come too close to
43. Nicolas Bourriaud, *Radicant: Pour une esthétique de la globalisation,* © Denoël (Paris), 2009, pp. 44–45. Reprinted by permission. Art curator, writer and critic, Bourriaud co-founded the Palais de Tokyo in Paris and curated, among other exhibitions, the Fourth Tate Triennial in London, entitled Altermodern.

un acquiescement tacite à la tradition, si l'on pense que chaque culture sécrète[44] ses propres critères de jugement et doit se voir estimée en fonction de ces critères, ou bien le pari de l'émergence d'une forme de pensée susceptible d'opérer des interconnexions entre des cultures disparates, sans que soit niée leur singularité. Le discours postmoderne, qui oscille entre la déconstruction critique du modernisme et l'atomisation multiculturaliste, favorise implicitement un infini *statu quo*. De ce point de vue, il représente une force répressive, en contribuant à maintenir les cultures mondiales dans un état de pseudo-authenticité, en entreposant les signes vivants dans un parc naturel des traditions et des modes de pensée où ils se tiennent disponibles pour toute entreprise de marchandisation. Qu'est-ce qui, alors, perturberait cette réification idéale? Quel est cet objet soigneusement refoulé dont l'on perçoit les contours, en creux, dans ce dispositif idéologique? Un mot à ne jamais prononcer: une modernité. Autrement dit, un projet collectif qui ne se rapporte à nulle origine, mais dont la direction transcenderait les codes culturels existants, et en emporterait les signes dans un mouvement nomade.

Ce que j'appelle *altermodernité* désigne ainsi un plan de construction qui permettrait de nouveaux aiguillages[45] interculturels, la construction d'un espace de négociations allant au-delà du multiculturalisme postmoderne, qui s'attache à l'origine des discours et des formes plutôt qu'à leur dynamique. À cette question de la provenance, il s'agit de substituer celle de la destination. « Où aller? » Telle est la question moderne par excellence.

25.12. MICHEL TREMBLAY

LE CAHIER BLEU[46]

....

La chute du Boudoir a été spectaculaire, la débâcle affolante.

Nous nous y attendions, bien sûr, nous savions que l'Expo 67 terminée, la ville vidée de ses touristes, le grand party[47] du siècle porté à ses derniers excès, le

---

44. *sécrète:* from *sécréter*, to secrete, to generate
45. *aiguillages:* interchanges
46. Michel Tremblay, *Le Cahier bleu,* © Leméac Éditeur/Actes Sud (Montreal), 2005 pp. 19–20. Reprinted by permission. Michel Tremblay, Québécois writer and playwright, is among those whose works spearheaded the changes of Quebec's "Quiet Revolution" in the 1960's. Winner of the Chevalier de l'Ordre National du Québec, the Chevalier de l'Ordre des Arts et des Lettres de France, and the Canadian Governor General's Award for the Performing Arts.
47. *party:* party. An example of the mixing in of bits of English that is a characteristic of Québécois French.

bar de Fine Dumas ne pourrait pas survivre: trop chic pour le quartier, trop cher pour ses habitants, trop prétentieux pour ce qu'offre d'habitude la *Main*,[48] ce paradis des pauvres et des âmes perdues élevé pendant un moment, grâce à la seule présence du Boudoir et peut-être pour son plus grand malheur, au statut de must absolu[49] et de rendez-vous des nantis[50] du monde entier. L'Expo fut pour nous une merveilleuse parenthèse dont nous avons tous profité, c'est vrai, une manne dorée tombée du ciel, l'occasion, comme le disait si bien la patronne elle-même, de nous « mettre riches », du moins pour un temps, et une permission de six mois de vivre à ciel ouvert sans peur des autorités qui, pour une fois, semblait-il, nous protégeaient au lieu de nous persécuter. Six mois trop vite passés dans un invraisemblable tourbillon de fêtes sans fin, de beuveries[51] indescriptibles et de pluies de dollars qui semblaient ne jamais vouloir s'arrêter.

Mais quand l'heure a sonné, quand est venu le temps de réaliser que la fête était bel et bien terminée et que le Boudoir devenait du jour au lendemain obsolète, nous avons tous subi un choc. Nous en avions pourtant parlé pendant tout le mois de septembre parce que la ville était de plus en plus désertée par les étrangers et que le Boudoir se vidait à vue d'œil.[52] Même les week-ends étaient déprimants vers la fermeture de l'Expo. L'argent se faisait plus rare, le fun[53] aussi. Nous en parlions, oui, mais c'était comme si nous refusions de comprendre ce que nous disions ou d'entrevoir les véritables conséquences de la fermeture du Boudoir pour chacun d'entre nous, les ramifications dans la vie de la *Main*. . . .

25.13. PATRICK CHAMOISEAU

TEXACO[54]
....

Le papa de mon papa était empoisonneur. Ce n'était pas un métier mais un combat contre l'esclavage sur les habitations. Je ne vais pas te refaire l'Histoire, mais

---

48. *La Main* (also known in English as The Main): affectionate nickname of the Blvd. St. Laurent, which for years effectively divided the predominantly anglophone west side from the predominantly francophone east side of Montreal.
49. *must absolu:* an "absolute must." see note 47 above.
50. *nantis:* well-to-do
51. *beuveries:* drinking binges
52. *à vu d'œil:* before our eyes
53. *le fun:* more mixing in of bits of English
54. Patrick Chamoiseau, *Texaco,* © Editions Gallimard (Paris), 1992, pp. 49–50. Reprinted by permission. Chamoiseau, writer from Martinique and theoretician of *créolité,* won the Prix Goncourt in 1992 for this book.

le vieux nègre de la Doum[55] révèle, dessous l'Histoire, des histoires dont aucun livre ne parle, et qui pour nous comprendre sont le plus essentielles. Donc, parmi ceux qui rouclaient[56] pour planter au béké[57] ses cannes ou son café, régnaient des hommes de force. Ceux-là savaient des choses que l'on ne doit pas savoir. Et ils faisaient vraiment ce que l'on ne peut pas faire. Ils avaient mémoire des merveilles oubliées: Pays d'Avant, le Grand Pays, la parole du grand pays, les dieux du grand pays … sans les différencier cela les soumettait à d'autres exigences. Ils charriaient à l'épaule une souffrance commune. Ils guérissaient les pians mais pas les douces langueurs qui renvoyaient le mort vers le pays d'avant. Comme ça, ils contrariaient l'injuste prospérité de ces habitations dans cette chaux de douleurs. Les hommes de force disaient *Pas d'enfants d'esclavage,* et les femmes n'offraient que des matrices crépusculaires aux soleils de la vie. Ils disaient *Pas de récoltes,* et les rates se mettaient à ronger les racines, les vents à dévaster, la sécheresse à flamber dans les cannes, la pluie à embourber jusqu'à hauteur des mornes. Ils disaient *Plus de forces-l'esclavage,* et les bœufs perdaient leur foie en une pourriture verte, les mulets[58] tout au même et les chevaux pareils. Le bétail décimé bloquait l'aléliron des moulins et privait de bagasse[59] la flamme des sept chaudières dans chaque sucrerie.

25.14. ABDOURAHMAN A. WABERI

PASSAGE DES LARMES[60]

J'ai étudié tout cela à Montréal. C'est cette ville qui m'a sauvé la vie sinon je serais parti à la dérive, au hasard, à Dieu vat. Frayant avec des gens louches, faisant n'importe quoi pour tromper une vie sans nerf. Montréal a donné un sens à mon destin et, plus prosaïquement, un doctorat en science de l'information. Montréal

---

55. *La Doum:* a wild area adjoining the neighborhood of the Texaco shanty-town
56. *rouclaient:* grumbled
57. *békés:* white men, descendants of the established planters
58. *mulets:* mules
59. *bagasse:* sugarcane fibers used as fuel
60. Abdourahman A. Waberi, *Passage des larmes,* © Éditions Jean-Claude Lattès (Paris), 2009, pp. 73–75. Reprinted by permission. Waberi, born in what is now known as Djibouti, won the Grand Prix Littéraire de l'Afrique noire in 1996.

avait un visage lorsque je l'ai rencontré pour la première fois. Un visage ovale, des yeux azur. Une peau de nacre. Un pull au col rondé. C'était Denise assise sur un banc, dans le jardin de la Cité Internationale, boulevard Jourdan, à Paris.

Je traînais mon mal-être depuis des semaines et des mois. À tout le monde, je lançais des appels comme des signaux de phare. Seule Denise m'a souri. Et ce fut le coup de foudre. Malgré son accent québécois, Denise est née à Paris en 1968. Elle est de neuf ans mon aînée. Son père, Isaac Rosenzweig, autrichien de Vienne, s'était engagé dans la Légion étrangère et avait été blessé en Afrique du Nord, en 1961. J'ignore s'il avait traîné ses guêtres dans mon pays d'origine qui s'appelait alors la Côte française des Somalis. Un an plus tard, il avait épousé une femme de braise, moitié normande, moitié panaméenne, native de Trouville: Elvira Triboulet. Lui était devenu serveur de café; elle, strip-teaseuse et comédienne. Avec leur fille, ils habitaient un petit hôtel sordide sur le boulevard Ornano, dans le XVIIIe arrondissement. La famille Rosenzweig émigra au Québec en pleine révolution de velours. Elle l'adopta, ne le quitta plus sauf pour des excursions hivernales à Paris. Voilà comment Denise en connaît chaque ruelle, chaque faubourg, chaque pan d'histoire.

Ce fut à Paris aussi, sur un autre banc de la Cité internationale, que Denise me parla pour la première fois d'un autre arpenteur de la Ville lumière. Un philosophe du siècle dernier. Walter Benjamin. Elle conservait religieusement sa photo signée Gisèle Freund dans son portefeuille entre les tickets de métro et les coupons à 4,30 francs du restaurant universitaire où nous prenions nos repas. C'est Denise qui m'a introduit dans les arcanes de la vie de ce Walter Benjamin. Par bonheur, je fus séduit, non pas sur-le-champ mais bien plus tard, par son esprit encyclopédique, sa méthode intuitive, sa conception de l'histoire qui n'a rien de théorique ou d'aride. Au contraire, elle est aussi sensible que les histoires colportées par grand-père Assod. J'ai adopté à mon tour l'ange de l'histoire dont voici la description telle que nous restitue le philosophe juif allemand. . . .

APPENDIX

PRONOUN CHART

SUBJECT PRONOUNS	REFLEXIVE PRONOUNS	DIRECT OBJECT PRONOUNS	INDIRECT OBJECT PRONOUNS	DISJUNCTIVE PRONOUNS
je	me (me, myself)	me (me)	me (to/for me)	moi (me, for/to me)
tu	te (you, yourself)	te (you)	te (to/for you)	toi (etc.)
il, elle, on	se (him/her/itself)	le, la (him, her, it)	lui (to/for him/her)	lui, elle, soi
nous	nous (ourselves)	nous (us)	nous (to/for us)	nous
vous	vous (yourself, -ves)	vous (you)	vous (to/for you)	vous
ils, elles	se (themselves)	les (them)	leur (to/for them)	eux, elles

(INDICATIVE) VERB TENSE CHART I

-ER VERBS PARLER	*-IR VERBS* SORTIR	*-IR VERBS* FINIR	*-RE VERBS* VENDRE	REFLEXIVE VERBS SE LEVER
LE PRÉSENT DE L'INDICATIF/PRESENT TENSE				
I speak, I am speaking	I leave, I am leaving	I finish, I am finishing	I sell, I am selling	I get up, I am getting up
je parle	je sors	je finis	je vends	je me lève
tu parles	tu sors	tu finis	tu vends	tu te lèves
il/elle/on parle	il/elle/on sort	il/elle/on finit	il/elle/on vend	il/elle/on se lève
nous parlons	nous sortons	nous finissons	nous vendons	nous nous levons
vous parlez	vous sortez	vous finissez	vous vendez	vous vous levez
ils/elles parlent	ils/elles sortent	ils/elles finissent	ils/elles vendent	ils/elles se lèvent

L'IMPARFAIT/IMPERFECT

I was speaking, I spoke, I used to speak	*I was leaving, I left, I used to leave*	*I was finishing, I finished, I used to finish*	*I was selling, I sold, I used to sell*	*I was getting up, I got up, I used to get up*
je parlais	je sortais	je finissais	je vendais	je me levais
tu parlais	tu sortais	tu finissais	tu vendais	tu te levais
il/elle/on parlait	il/elle/on sortait	il/elle/on finissait	il/elle/on vendait	il/elle/on se levait
nous parlions	nous sortions	nous finissions	nous vendions	nous nous levions
vous parliez	vous sortiez	vous finissiez	vous vendiez	vous vous leviez
ils/elles parlaient	ils/elles sortaient	ils/elles finissaient	ils/elles vendaient	ils/elles se levaient

LE PASSÉ COMPOSÉ/COMPOUND PAST

I spoke, I have spoken	*I left, I have left*	*I finished, I have finished*	*I sold, I have sold*	*I got up, I have gotten up*
j'ai parlé	je suis sorti(e)	j'ai fini	j'ai vendu	je me suis levé(e)
tu as parlé	tu es sorti(e)	tu as fini	tu as vendu	tu t'es levé(e)
il/elle/on a parlé	il/elle/on est sorti(e)	il/elle/on a fini	il/elle/on a vendu	il/elle/on s'est levé(e)
nous avons parlé	nous sommes sorti(e)s	nous avons fini	nous avons vendu	nous nous sommes levé(e)s
vous avez parlé	vous êtes sorti(e)(s)	vous avez fini	vous avez vendu	vous vous êtes levé(e)(s)
ils/elles ont parlé	ils/elles sont sorti(e)s	ils/elles ont fini	ils/elles ont vendu	ils/elles se sont levé(e)s

LE FUTUR/FUTURE

I will speak	I will leave	I will finish	I will sell	I will get up
je parlerai	je sortirai	je finirai	je vendrai	je me lèverai
tu parleras	tu sortiras	tu finiras	tu vendras	tu te lèveras
il/elle/on parlera	il/elle/on sortira	il/elle/on finira	il/elle/on vendra	il/elle/on se lèvera
nous parlerons	nous sortirons	nous finirons	nous vendrons	nous nous lèverons
vous parlerez	vous sortirez	vous finirez	vous vendrez	vous vous lèverez
ils/elles parleront	ils/elles sortiront	ils/elles finiront	ils/elles vendront	ils/elles se lèveront

LE CONDITIONNEL/CONDITIONAL

I would speak	I would leave	I would finish	I would sell	I would get up
je parlerais	je sortirais	je finirais	je vendrais	je me lèverais
tu parlerais	tu sortirais	tu finirais	tu vendrais	tu te lèverais
il/elle/on parlerait	il/elle/on sortirait	il/elle/on finirait	il/elle/on vendrait	il/elle/on se lèverait
nous parlerions	nous sortirions	nous finirions	nous vendrions	nous nous lèverions
vous parleriez	vous sortiriez	vous finiriez	vous vendriez	vous vous lèveriez
ils/elles parleraient	ils/elles sortiraient	ils/elles finiraient	ils/elles vendraient	ils/elles se lèveraient

(INDICATIVE) IRREGULAR VERB CHART I

AVOIR	ÊTRE	ALLER	FAIRE	VENIR
*LE PRÉSENT DE L'INDICATIF/*PRESENT TENSE				
I have (irregular: only 1 translation)	I am (irregular: only 1 translation)	I go, I am going (two translations)	I do, I am doing, I make, I am making	I come, I am coming
j'ai	je suis	je vais	je fais	je viens
tu as	tu es	tu vas	tu fais	tu viens
il/elle/on a	il/elle/on est	il/elle/on va	il/elle/on fait	il/elle/on vient
nous avons	nous sommes	nous allons	nous faisons	nous venons
vous avez	vous êtes	vous allez	vous faites	vous venez
ils/elles ont	ils/elles sont	ils/elles vont	ils/elles font	ils/elles viennent

L'IMPARFAIT/IMPERFECT

I had	*I was going, I went, I used to go*	*I was*	*I was doing/making; I did/made; I used to do/make.*	*I was coming, I came, I used to come*
j'avais	j'allais	j'étais	je faisais	je venais
tu avais	tu allais	tu étais	tu faisais	tu venais
il/elle/on avait	il/elle/on allait	il/elle/on était	il/elle/on faisait	il/elle/on venait
nous avions	nous allions	nous étions	nous faisions	nous venions
vous aviez	vous alliez	vous étiez	vous faisiez	vous veniez
ils/elles avaient	ils/elles allaient	ils/elles étaient	ils/elles faisaient	ils/elles venaient

LE PASSÉ COMPOSÉ/COMPOUND PAST

I had, I have had	*I went, I have gone*	*I was, I have been*	*I did, I have done*	*I came, I have come*
j'ai eu	je suis allé(e)	j'ai été	j'ai fait	je suis venu(e)
tu as eu	tu es allé(e)	tu as été	tu as fait	tu es venu(e)
il/elle/on a eu	il/elle/on est allé(e)	il/elle/on a été	il/elle/on a fait	il/elle/on est venu(e)
nous avons eu	nous sommes allé(e)s	nous avons été	nous avons fait	nous sommes venu(e)s
vous avez eu	vous êtes allé(e)(s)	vous avez été	vous avez fait	vous êtes venu(e)(s)
ils/elles ont eu	ils/elles sont allé(e)s	ils/elles ont été	ils/elles ont fait	ils/elles sont venu(e)s

LE *FUTUR*/FUTURE

I will have	I will be	I will go	I will do, I will make	I will come
j'aurai	je serai	j'irai	je ferai	je viendrai
tu auras	tu seras	tu iras	tu feras	tu viendras
il/elle/on aura	il/elle/on sera	il/elle/on ira	il/elle/on fera	il/elle/on viendra
nous aurons	nous serons	nous irons	nous ferons	nous viendrons
vous aurez	vous serez	vous irez	vous ferez	vous viendrez
ils/elles auront	ils/elles seront	ils/elles iront	ils/elles feront	ils/elles viendront

LE *CONDITIONNEL*/CONDITIONAL

I would have	I would be	I would go	I would do, make	I would come
j'aurais	je serais	j'irais	je ferais	je viendrais
tu aurais	tu serais	tu irais	tu ferais	tu viendrais
il/elle/on aurait	il/elle/on serait	il/elle/on irait	il/elle/on ferait	il/elle/on viendrait
nous aurions	nous serions	nous irions	nous ferions	nous viendrions
vous auriez	vous seriez	vous iriez	vous feriez	vous viendriez
ils/elles auraient	ils/elles seraient	ils/elles iraient	ils/elles feraient	ils/elles viendraient

(INDICATIVE) VERB TENSE CHART II

PARLER	LIRE	SORTIR	PRENDRE	SE LEVER

LE PASSÉ SIMPLE/ SIMPLE PAST/PAST HISTORIC

PARLER	LIRE	SORTIR	PRENDRE	SE LEVER
I spoke,	*I read*	*I left*	*I took*	*I got up*
je parlai	je lus	je sortis	je pris	je me levai
tu parlas	tu lus	tu sortis	tu pris	tu te levas
il/elle/on parla	il/elle/on lut	il/elle/on sortit	il/elle/on prit	il/elle/on se leva
nous parlâmes	nous lûmes	nous sortîmes	nous prîmes	nous nous levâmes
vous parlâtes	vous lûtes	vous sortîtes	vous prîtes	vous vous levâtes
ils/elles parlèrent	ils/elles lurent	ils/elles sortirent	ils/elles prirent	ils/elles se levèrent

LE PLUS-QUE-PARFAIT/PLUPERFECT

PARLER	LIRE	SORTIR	PRENDRE	SE LEVER
I had spoken	*I had read*	*I had left*	*I had taken*	*I had gotten up*
j'avais parlé	j'avais lu	j'étais sorti(e)	j'avais pris	je m'étais levé(e)
tu avais parlé	tu avais lu	tu étais sorti(e)	tu avais pris	tu t'étais levé(e)
il/elle/on avait parlé	il/elle/on avait lu	il/elle/on était sorti(e)	il/elle/on avait pris	il/elle/on s'était levé(e)
nous avions parlé	nous avions lu	nous étions sorti(e)s	nous avions pris	nous nous étions levé(e)s
vous aviez parlé	vous aviez lu	vous étiez sorti(e)(s)	vous aviez pris	vous vous étiez levé(e)(s)
ils/elles avaient parlé	ils/elles avaient lu	ils/elles étaient sorti(e)s	ils/elles avaient pris	ils/elles s'étaient levé(e)s

LE FUTUR ANTÉRIEUR/FUTURE PERFECT

I will have spoken	*I will have read*	*I will have left*	*I will have taken*	*I will have gotten up*
j'aurai parlé	j'aurai lu	je serai sorti(e)	j'aurai pris	je me serai levé(e)
tu auras parlé	tu auras lu	tu seras sorti(e)	tu auras pris	tu te seras levé(e)
il/elle/on aura parlé	il/elle/on aura lu	il/elle/on sera sorti(e)	il/elle/on aura pris	il/elle/on se sera levé(e)
nous aurons parlé	nous aurons lu	nous serons sorti(e)s	nous aurons pris	nous nous serons levé(e)s
vous aurez parlé	vous aurez lu	vous serez sorti(e)(s)	vous aurez pris	vous vous serez levé(e)(s)
ils/elles auront parlé	ils/elles auront lu	ils/elles seront sorti(e)s	ils/elles auront pris	ils/elles se seront levé(e)s

LE CONDITIONNEL PASSÉ/CONDITIONAL PERFECT

I would have spoken	*I would have read*	*I would have left*	*I would have taken*	*I would have gotten up*
j'aurais parlé	j'aurais lu	je serais sorti(e)	j'aurais pris	je me serais levé(e)
tu aurais parlé	tu aurais lu	tu serais sorti(e)	tu aurais pris	tu te serais levé(e)
il/elle/on aurait parlé	il/elle/on aurait lu	il/elle/on serait sorti(e)	il/elle/on aurait pris	il/elle/on se serait levé(e)
nous aurions parlé	nous aurions lu	nous serions sorti(e)s	nous aurions pris	nous nous serions levé(e)s
vous auriez parlé	vous auriez lu	vous seriez sorti(e)(s)	vous auriez pris	vous vous seriez levé(e)(s)
ils/elles auraient parlé	ils/elles auraient lu	ils/elles seraient sorti(e)s	ils/elles auraient pris	ils/elles se seraient levé(e)s

LE PASSÉ ANTÉRIEUR

I had spoken	*I had read*	*I had left*	*I had taken*	*I had gotten up*
j'eus parlé	j'eus lu	je fus sorti(e)	j'eus pris	je me fus levé(e)
tu eus parlé	tu eus lu	tu fus sorti(e)	tu eus pris	tu te fus levé(e)
il/elle/on eut parlé	il/elle/on eut lu	il/elle/on fut sorti(e)	il/elle/on eut pris	il/elle/on se fut levé(e)
nous eûmes parlé	nous eûmes lu	nous fûmes sorti(e)s	nous eûmes pris	nous nous fûmes levé(e)s
vous eûtes parlé	vous eûtes lu	vous fûtes sorti(e)(s)	vous eûtes pris	vous vous fûtes levé(e)(s)
ils/elles eurent parlé	ils/elles eurent lu	ils/elles furent sorti(e)s	ils/elles eurent pris	ils/elles se furent levé(e)s

L'IMPÉRATIF/IMPERATIVE

Tu :	Parle (Speak!)	Sors! (Leave!)	Prends! (Take!)	Lève-toi! (Get up!)
Nous:	Parlons! (Let's speak!)	Sortons! (Let's leave!)	Prenons! (Let's take!)	Levons-nous! (Let's get up!)
Vous:	Parlez! (Speak!)	Sortez! (Leave!)	Prenez! (Take!)	Levez-vous! (Get up!)

(INDICATIVE) IRREGULAR VERB TENSE CHART II

AVOIR	ÊTRE	ALLER	FAIRE	VENIR

LE PASSÉ SIMPLE/SIMPLE PAST/PAST HISTORIC

AVOIR	ÊTRE	ALLER	FAIRE	VENIR
I had	I was	I went	I did/I made	I came
j'eus	je fus	j'allai	je fis	je vins
tu eus	tu fus	tu allas	tu fis	tu vins
il/elle/on eut	il/elle/on fut	il/elle/on alla	il/elle/on fit	il/elle/on vint
nous eûmes	nous fûmes	nous allâmes	nous fîmes	nous vînmes
vous eûtes	vous fûtes	vous allâtes	vous fîtes	vous vîntes
ils/elles eurent	ils/elles furent	ils/elles allèrent	ils/elles firent	ils/elles vinrent

LE PLUS-QUE-PARFAIT/PLUPERFECT

AVOIR	ÊTRE	ALLER	FAIRE	VENIR
I had had	I had been	I had gone	I had done/made	I had come
j'avais eu	j'avais été	j'étais allé(e)	j'avais fait	j'étais venu(e)
tu avais eu	tu avais été	tu étais allé(e)	tu avait fait	tu étais venu(e)
il/elle/on avait eu	il/elle/on avait été	il/elle/on était allé(e)	il/elle/on avait fait	il/elle/on était venu(e)
nous avions eu	nous avions été	nous étions allé(e)s	nous avions fait	nous étions venu(e)s
vous aviez eu	vous aviez été	vous étiez allé(e)(s)	vous aviez fait	vous étiez venu(e)(s)
ils/elles avaient eu	ils/elles avaient été	ils/elles étaient allé(e)s	ils/elles avaient fait	ils/elles étaient venu(e)s

LE FUTUR ANTÉRIEUR/FUTURE PERFECT

I will have had	I will have been	I will have gone	I will have done/made	I will have come
j'aurai eu	j'aurai été	je serai allé(e)	j'aurai fait	je serai venu(e)
tu auras eu	tu auras été	tu seras allé(e)	tu auras fait	tu seras venu(e)
il/elle/on aura eu	il/elle/on aura été	il/elle/on sera allé(e)	il/elle/on aura fait	il/elle/on sera venu(e)
nous aurons eu	nous aurons été	nous serons allé(e)s	nous aurons fait	nous serons venu(e)s
vous aurez eu	vous aurez été	vous serez allé(e)(s)	vous aurez fait	vous serez venu(e)(s)
ils/elles auront eu	ils/elles auront été	ils/elles seront allé(e)s	ils/elles auront fait	ils/elles seront venu(e)s

LE CONDITIONNEL PASSÉ/CONDITIONAL PERFECT

I would have had	I would have been	I would have gone	I would have done/made	I would have come
j'aurais eu	j'aurais été	je serais allé(e)	j'aurais fait	je serais venu(e)
tu aurais eu	tu aurais été	tu serais allé(e)	tu aurais fait	tu serais venu(e)
il/elle/on aurait eu	il/elle/on aurait été	il/elle/on serait allé(e)	il/elle/on aurait fait	il/elle/on serait venu(e)
nous aurions eu	nous aurions été	nous serions allé(e)s	nous aurions fait	nous serions venu(e)s
vous auriez eu	vous auriez été	vous seriez allé(e)(s)	vous auriez fait	vous seriez venu(e)(s)
ils/elles auraient eu	ils/elles auraient été	ils/elles seraient allé(e)s	ils/elles auraient fait	ils/elles seraient venu(e)s

LE PASSÉ ANTÉRIEUR

I had had	I had been	I had gone	I had done/made	I had come
j'eus eu	j'eus été	je fus allé(e)	j'eus fait	je fus venu(e)
tu eus eu	tu eus été	tu fus allé(e)	tu eus fait	tu fus venu(e)
il/elle/on eut eu	il/elle/on eut été	il/elle/on fut allé(e)	il/elle/on eut fait	il/elle/on fut venu(e)
nous eûmes eu	nous eûmes été	nous fûmes allé(e)s	nous eûmes fait	nous fûmes venu(e)s
vous eûtes eu	vous eûtes été	vous fûtes allé(e)(s)	vous eûtes fait	vous fûtes venu(e)(s)
ils/elles eurent eu	ils/elles eurent été	ils/elles furent allé(e)s	ils/elles eurent fait	ils/elles furent venu(e)s

L'IMPÉRATIF / IMPERATIVE

Tu:	Aie! (*Have!*)	Sois! (*Be!*)	Va! (*Go!*)	Fais! (*Do/make!*)
Nous:	Ayons! (*Let's have!*)	Soyons! (*Let's be!*)	Allons! (*Let's go!*)	Faisons! (*Let's do/make!*)
Vous:	Ayez! (*Have!*)	Soyez! (*Be!*)	Allez! (*Go!*)	Faites! (*Do/make!*)

INDEX